REDISCOVERING

AMERICA'S

SACRED GROUND

SUNY series, Religion and American Public Life

William Dean, editor

REDISCOVERING AMERICA'S SACRED GROUND

Public Religion and Pursuit of the Good in a Pluralistic America

Barbara A. McGraw

State University of New York Press

Published by
State University of New York Press, Albany

For information, address State University of New York Press,
90 State Street, Suite 700, Albany, NY 12207

Production by Michael Haggett
Marketing by Anne M. Valentine

Library of Congress Cataloging-in-Publication Data

McGraw, Barbara A.
  Rediscovering America's sacred ground : public religion and pursuit of the
  good in a pluralistic America / Barbara A. McGraw.
    p. cm.—(SUNY series, religion and American public life)
  Includes bibliographical references and index.
  ISBN 0–7914–5705–2 (alk. paper)—ISBN 0–7914–5706–0 (pbk. : alk. paper)
  1. Civil religion—United States. 2. United States—Religion. I. Title. II. Series.

BL2525 .M42 2003
322'.1'0973—dc21   2002042630

10 9 8 7 6 5 4 3 2 1

This book is dedicated to

Patrick McCollum,
my husband and champion

and to

my mother, Gloria McGraw,
who taught me the value of a reasoned debate

Contents

Part I
Looking Back to Rediscover
America's Sacred Ground

Part II
Rooting the Contemporary Debate in Sacred Ground

Acknowledgments

This book began as a kernel of an idea that I explored briefly in two papers for graduate courses in the University of Southern California, Department of Religious Studies' "Religion and Social Ethics" Doctoral Program. That idea then became the basis for my dissertation, completed in 1999. Needless to say, I am immensely grateful to my professors at USC, in particular Robert S. Ellwood, John P. Crossley, and William W. May for their wisdom during the program, and for their ongoing encouragement and support since then.

Because I wanted the published version of my manuscript to be accessible to a wide range of readers interested in the field of Religion in Public Life, it was necessary to do quite a bit of revising to bring the dissertation "down to earth." I believe this has been accomplished, and, if it has, it is due in large part to many valuable discussions about the ideas in the manuscript and in other readings among the students in my "Culture Wars" and "Religion and Politics" courses at Saint Mary's College of California. I am grateful to them for their enthusiasm for the subject-matter and their insightful comments, which helped me to clarify the ideas for this book.

Material from earlier versions of the manuscript has been presented in various sessions at American Academy of Religion Annual Conferences and Society for the Scientific Study of Religion Annual Conferences. I am immensely grateful for having had opportunities to exchange ideas with colleagues in those fora. In this regard, I also want to thank the Saint Mary's College of California Faculty Development Committee for providing the financing that made many of those opportunities possible.

I also am indebted to BasicBooks, the publisher of *The Culture of Disbelief: How American Law and Politics Trivialize Religious Devotion* by Stephen L. Carter, copyright © 1993, and Regnery Publishing, Inc., the publisher of *The Theme is Freedom: Religion, Politics, and the American Tradition* by M. Stanton Evans, copyright © 1994, all rights reserved, both of which have given special permission to reprint in this book material from those works.

Thanks also goes to the editorial staff at the State University of New York Press. In particular, I want to acknowledge Nancy Ellegate, Acquisitions Editor, whose wisdom and experience about the publishing process has been invaluable; Anne Valentine, Marketing Manager, whose enthusiasm for the process is very much appreciated; and Michael Haggett, Production Editor, who has gone the extra mile to make the presentation of the book especially attractive.

I am very pleased with the cover design for this book and, consequently, I want to acknowledge Amy Stirnkorb and Patrick McCollum, who worked together to arrive at the cover's inspired design. In this regard as well, thanks go to Patrick for permission to incorporate his rendering of the Statue of Liberty, copyright © 2002, all rights reserved, in the cover design and elsewhere in the book.

I also thank the helpful librarians at the University of California at Berkeley Doe Library and at the University of Southern California Hoose Library of Philosophy. In particular, I want to acknowledge Hoose's Ross Scimeca, philosophy librarian *extraordinaire*, who makes research fun.

Thank you to the anonymous readers contacted by the State University of New York Press to review my manuscript. Their commentary resulted in revisions that, in my view, vastly improved the manuscript. In particular, I especially want to acknowledge Phillip E. Hammond, who, after the manuscript had been accepted for publication, identified himself to me at an American Academy of Religion Annual Conference as being one of those readers. I am very grateful for our new friendship and his continued championing of my work and career.

And I cannot thank my colleague and good friend, Catherine Banbury, enough for painstakingly reading the final manuscript just before it was sent to the publisher, even though it is not a work in her field of study. Her comments improved the clarity of the writing immensely and I am forever grateful.

Most of all, I want thank my husband, Patrick McCollum, who has shared all the ups and downs of the entire writing process with me, and whose love is my anchor, and my mother, Gloria McGraw, who was the first to believe in me.

Prologue

I had long been interested and involved in debates about the
United States Constitution's First Amendment Religion Clauses,
and had been a strong advocate of the "separation of church and
state" doctrine, when I began to look more deeply into church/
states issues in the mid-1990s. As I did so, however, I became dis-
concerted by those who advocated lowering the "wall of separation" when they cited the American founding fathers in support of
their positions. I had understood the wall of separation between
church and state to derive directly from the ideologies that had inspired the American Revolutionaries in their quest for liberty, including religious liberty. And, despite the fact that I had thought of
myself then, as I do now, as "religious," I had understood that ideology to include the idea that religion is a threat to liberty in the
public arena and that "secular" society is the bulwark against it.
Yet, again and again, the founders were invoked in support of religion's participation in public life by those holding positions on
church/state issues that were wholly contrary to those I had been
taught and had held so strongly. I could not make sense of this. I
decided to go back and look for myself.

As others have done, I looked back to the works of John Locke
and recognized the Lockean fundamentals that shaped the conscience
of the American founders. And I looked back to the words of the
founders, themselves, to find out how those Lockean fundamentals

were put into practice by the American founders in original ways. But, in my effort to understand the discrepancies in the discourse of the past couple of decades in America in light of all of this, I found something more. I found that the ground of the American system was conceived by the founders as America's sacred foundation, reflected in a simple theology. I rediscovered "America's Sacred Ground."

Of course, many scholars and others have argued that a return to the founders' original intentions or to any other "grounding" claim is unwarranted. They hold that a society ought to change, drawing from many sources in resolving its problems, rather than being restricted to any particular absolutist foundational claim. And there is a whole literature discussing the relative merits of foundationalism and what is thought to be a more open-ended relativistic give-and-take approach. What I found, however, is that America's Sacred Ground provides a justification for itself. That justification is found in the realization that all of those participating in the debate assume the context for the debate created by America's Sacred Ground. That is, while some may disagree with the underlying basis of the founders' original intentions as I present them, that underlying basis—that is America's Sacred Ground itself—nevertheless is the starting point for argumentation about it. This is so even for those who have the view that a return to anyone's idea of the founders' original intentions, or other ground, is unfounded.

But this is getting somewhat ahead of myself. Instead of merely alluding to the substance of my thesis, let me say something about my method, style, and purpose and then turn to the body of the work.

Of course it is no surprise to find a variety of nuanced views in an important and well-covered field such as this one. And one could survey those views in depth. However, I have decided not to take that approach here. Rather, I have chosen to set out my thesis and the arguments to support it, and not to compare and contrast it with the numerous ideas of others and, consequently, risk producing an unwieldy work, inaccessible to those interested in the field who may not be familiar with all such views. Moreover, the exploration of an issue often can be accomplished well by choosing representatives of particular views who then serve as "dialogue partners" for one's own position. This is the method I have chosen here.

After introducing the issues in chapter 1, I explore the roots of America's Sacred Ground in the history of ideas leading to the American founding in Part I, specifically the roots in John Locke, whose ideas are then reflected and expanded in the views of the American founders. Then, in Part II, I explore the implications of America's Sacred Ground for American debates about public policy and moral values by contrasting America's Sacred Ground with representatives of three factions in the popular, political, and academic debate: (1) the secular left, which seeks to "neutralize" religion in public life; (2) the Christian right, which seeks to promote greater acceptance of the Judeo-Christian tradition in public life; and (3) those who argue for an accommodation of religion in public life—the "accommodationists."

This "dialogue partner" method reveals the ways in which America's Sacred Ground provides a perspective for the contemporary popular and political discourse about public religion and its role in shaping American values, which might not be as easily grasped without the presentation of such clear distinctions. At the same time, as the reader will see, this method makes sense of what have appeared in the contemporary debate to be inconsistencies in the views of the American founders, and it reveals significant aspects of their views that previously have been obscured by all sides.

In addition, because the debate about America's moral ground has been occurring in several overlapping discourses (all of which I hope to enter with this work), I decided that, rather than presenting my ideas about America's Sacred Ground only in the ivory towers of the academic world, I would present them so that they would be accessible to those participating in all of these discourses—in politics, in the media, in social institutions, or even at home, as well as in the academy. I especially wanted to make sure that this work would not be a ponderous tome that no one but the academically hearty would be interested in exploring. That is why this work is written for the educated reader with a previous interest in this important subject, while, at the same time, this work is relatively brief, does not explore the views of every author writing in the field, does not pursue every tangent that may be impacted by the ideas expressed here, and uses examples from popular media and political commentary to illustrate points.

Still, it is important that a work like this be academically sound so that it is credible to those participating in the debate as something more than an unfounded opinion. That is why Part I, in which we rediscover America's Sacred Ground, is rich with material from relevant primary sources. It is also why considerable space is given in Part II to the in-depth "dialogue" with the popular, political, and scholarly "partners" I have chosen, which illustrates precisely the ways in which the reframing of the debate in light of America's Sacred Ground contributes to the debate. I have also provided a selected bibliography in "Suggested Readings" at the end of this work for those who wish to pursue this important area in more depth.

Most important, I have attempted to open the boundaries between disciplines and discourse communities in order to reach those whose views are likely to shape public policy in this important field as America moves forward in this new century. I hope that this work can be a resource for those who participate in these most important conversations for the future of the United States— and the world.

Barbara A. McGraw
November 2002
Moraga, California

CHAPTER 1

Toward a Debate on Common Ground

> Liberty is to faction what air is to fire, an aliment
> without which it instantly expires. But it could not
> be a less folly to abolish liberty, which is essential to
> political life, because it nourishes faction than it
> would be to wish the annihilation of air, which is
> essential to animal life, because it imparts to fire its
> destructive agency. . . . To secure the public good
> and private rights against the danger of faction, and
> at the same time to preserve the spirit and the form
> of popular government, is then the great object to
> which our inquiries are directed.
> —James Madison, *Federalist Paper No. 10*

AT THE CROSSROADS OF THE TWENTY-FIRST CENTURY

Economic prosperity fostered a renewed optimism at the turn of
twenty-first century. Yet there remained an underlying turmoil and
confusion in America. Obviously, this was not due to disruptive
military battles, economic upheavals, or other things that are generally associated with great societal and political turmoil. Rather, the
turmoil and confusion was about matters that were believed by
many to be more fundamental. It involved battles over American
sociopolitical identity, more specifically, the American moral character on which that identity is built. Then, with the horrific events of

September 11th and their aftermath, the questions raised in that turmoil and confusion came powerfully to the fore: Who are we as a people and what do we stand for? What is the moral basis of our political system and law? Where do we go to find what certain politicians have referred to as America's "moral consciousness?" Can religion provide us with guidance? Or, are secular sources more neutral?

The "war of words" about such questions is what was referred to in the last decade as the American "culture war." This was a war in which various factions attempted to gain the necessary political and legal clout to determine, or at least influence, the answers to these questions by those who count—the Justices of the United States Supreme Court and those who make the laws of the land. Significantly, with few exceptions, this was not merely a vying for power by such factions. Generally, it was derived from a sincere, and in some cases urgently felt, need to assert what each believed are fundamental American moral values in the face of a perceived moral decline and an increasing pluralism at home, as well as the strain of demands placed on America from sources abroad as the economy continued to globalize.

Today, some claim that the culture war is over. Others argue that what was termed the "culture war" of the late twentieth century was in actuality nothing new—only a continuation of battles that had begun only a few decades after the American Revolution. Even if those views are true, however, what is important to recognize is that the questions raised in the debate still loom large, even larger than ever before.

As American economic concerns globalize and become part of an economy that is in the process of eclipsing national boundaries, and American security interests reach all across the globe, there is new urgency to the old questions about American moral identity. American moral ideals grounded in the concept of human rights have run headlong into very different cultural conceptions of the good society outside of the West. This clash of cultures has resulted in increased tensions at home about the moral dilemmas of the culture war of the 1980s and 1990s as they now become global concerns for America as it asserts its interests around the world. In the face of this, many Americans are trying to come together as we reassess ourselves in light of September 11th and related events—as we try to grasp what it is that joins all of the multifarious beauty of the diversity of our people and the plurality of our beliefs to something we call America. And as we Americans spread our influence politically, economically, and militarily around the world, it is even more clear that we must know who we are.

And so the battles about the foundations of American liberty and conceptions of the good that are won and lost at home will give shape to the American moral character that we take with us into the twenty-first century's evermore pluralistic, globally interdependent economic, and increasingly uncertain political environment. We are at the crossroads. What is the right direction?

ROOTS OF THE CONFLICT

In the last decades of the twentieth century, America's pluralistic society became increasingly more diverse, placing what many considered to be American traditions, settled customs, and core American beliefs under strain. Of course America has always experienced the strain of new cultural input as waves of immigrants have entered American life. Perhaps this was no more true than in the nineteenth century when America opened her borders to massive numbers of immigrants from many diverse nations.

Yet something different was occurring in late-twentieth-century America. Previously, the dominant ideology insisted on the assimilation of the new into the old, the traditional, American society. This was the American "melting pot"—melting, that is "Americanizing," recent immigrants into the American way of life, however defined by those in power and however successful such "Americanizing" actually was. In contrast, the late twentieth century saw the newly emerging dominant ideology moving toward "multiculturalism"—an embracing of all cultural expressions as equally valid. This, in turn, resulted in a resistance to the idea of the "melting away" of cultural differences, and instead the encouragement of a greater acceptance, and even celebration, of religious and cultural diversity.

Moreover, as dominant popular culture adopted multicultural-ism, there was strong prompting from media and others to embrace (in the public sphere at least) moral relativism as well—the idea that no moral claim has any greater validity or foundation than another—as an element of tolerance and in promotion of greater liberty. If all cultural expressions are equally valid including their moral implications, one simplified version of the argument goes, then there is no particularly valid foundational moral core to Amer-ica either. American cultural expressions in all their diversity, in-cluding their moral implications, whatever they are, are merely some among many. To think otherwise, is cultural imperialism, it was said.

On the other hand, some began to question the wisdom of as-similating everything and everyone brought to America or brought up in America into an amalgamation that is constantly changing as the new is mixed with the old. They argued that there must be a moral foundation that provides America with its sociopolitical identity. With no such identity, there is nothing on which America can make a moral claim about anything. Still, others claimed that it is the American way to take in new ideas and ways of thinking about society and assimilate the best of them as we move forward into our future. But this view really begged the question: How do we determine just what is "best" for America; what leads to a "good" society?

And so the debate on these issues became polarized, leaving many to ponder whether there is or can be any common ground on which to build a consensus. Yet nearly everyone perceived that the American political system and the laws that preserve liberty were at stake in the outcome of the debate. And because our ultimate un-derstanding of ourselves as Americans is at the core of the issue, it is no wonder that the debate became a very contentious one.

ORIGINAL INTENT AND THE RELIGION CLAUSES: AT THE CORE OF THE DEBATE

What made the discourse—particularly the popular political discourse—most combative in the late twentieth century was the reentry of religious voices into the debate. These voices had been marginalized midcentury as "secular" society took hold, bolstered by several United States Supreme Court decisions, in particular *Everson v. Board of Education* (1947), which made the "wall of separation" between church and state the law of the land.[1]

Most vocal among these religious voices in the 1980s was an assortment of groups that became known as the "Christian right," who claimed that the American political system evolved out of the Western "Judeo-Christian" religious and moral tradition, which they held serves as its "traditional" moral foundation. The Christian right found, however, that its contribution to the debate was not welcomed because it was perceived by the secular left (whose views held sway at the time) as promoting the conflation of religion with the state in contravention of the "wall of separation" views expressed in the *Everson* decision and other Supreme Court decisions. In order to "have a place at the table" in the conversation about America's moral character, the Christian right had to find a way to undercut the strongly held view of the secular left—the *Everson* court view—that the "wall of separation" between church and state was firmly grounded in the original intent of the American founders.

This required reinterpretation of the Constitutional provisions known as the "Religion Clauses" of the First Amendment: "Congress shall make no law respecting an establishment of religion, or prohibiting the free exercise thereof . . . ." Since the 1940s, the Religion Clauses generally have been interpreted by the United States Supreme Court as providing for two things: (1) the separation of church and state (the "Anti-Establishment Clause" or "Establishment Clause") and (2) freedom of religion (the "Free Exercise Clause"). It was the former clause that proved to be problematic for the Christian right, and other religious groups who held views similar to the Christian right and who sought to promote those views in American public life.

It was not surprising, then, that in 1984, Richard Neuhaus's treatise, *The Naked Public Square: Religion and Democracy in America*, touched a nerve when it questioned the validity of a secularized public discourse devoid of religion and morality.[2] The American founders never intended to neutralize the public square of religious influence, he argued. Yet strict separation of church and state requires the "public square" to be "naked" of any moral or religious symbols that serve as beacons for the "good." The result is that the "public square" never remains entirely "naked" and so it becomes filled with other things, as symbols of the good life, which threaten the goals at which the founders had aimed when they devised the American system.

In no small part because Neuhaus positioned himself as a moderate voice on the issue of religion in public life, the debate became even more vigorous with many works arguing for a greater place for religion in the debate about the moral foundations of America and the shape of freedom. Such works provided credible and well-researched evidence in this vein and, therefore, supported popular, political, and scholarly arguments. Legal and political analyses—popular, political, and scholarly—followed in an effort to shift, not only public opinion, but law, in particular, the views of the United States Supreme Court Justices. One representative work, John Eidsmore's *Christianity and the Constitution: The Faith of Our Founding Fathers*, argued that, contrary to the prevailing view reflected in *Everson*, history shows that the founders intended for there to be a relationship between Christianity, God, and the Constitution, which, the author contended, is grounded in biblical principles.[3]

The right was now armed with scholarly evidence and so was quick to point out in popular and political debates that history shows us that the founders were religious people, not the Enlightenment secular philosophers of the then prevailing secular myth of the American founding. Direct quotations from prominent founders called the left's "secularist" views into question. For example, in

1798, John Adams said: "Our Constitution was made only for a moral and religious people. It is wholly inadequate to the government of any other."[4] And George Washington proclaimed in his "First Inaugural Address" (1789):

> In tendering this homage to the Great Author of every public and private good, I assure myself that it expresses your sentiments not less than my own, nor those of my fellow-citizens at large less than either. No people can be bound to acknowledge and adore the invisible hand which conducts the affairs of men, more than the people of the United States.[5]

In the late 1980s and early 1990s, the religious right continued to promote greater recognition of the important role religion should play in public life, and began to make some inroads, sometimes relying on the First Amendment's Free Speech Clause, as well. This bolstered a further trend. Arguing for a greater role for religion in the "public square," but with some limits, those taking up this trend presented themselves as moderating influences in the debate.

Stephen L. Carter's *The Culture of Disbelief: How American Law and Politics Trivialize Religious Devotion*, published in 1993, was, and continues to be, a tremendously influential work in this vein.[6] Carter argued for greater respect for and deference to people of faith in law and politics— in effect, an "accommodation" of religion in America. Works such as Carter's were very appealing to those, probably a majority, who had become weary of the combative tone of the debate and were uncomfortable with either extreme on the left and right. They welcomed what they perceived to be a sort of middle ground.

The accommodationists draw from the arguments on the right about the great role religion has played in American public life from before the Revolution to the present. At the same time, they generally do not limit their focus to "Judeo-Christian" traditions. Rather, they perceive themselves as mediating the left/right extremes with greater tolerance for both. This is echoed in the popular political discourse of the news media as well, where the founders' references to religion are now acknowledged in spite of the secular left, but are presented as being more "careful" and "moderate" than the interpretations of the religious right.

This accommodationist trend proved to have appeal in important places. Certain Justices of the United States Supreme Court (in particular, Kennedy and Scalia) had been indicating a willingness to adopt an accommodationist approach to religion in American life. And public opinion began to shift in this new direction as well. Articles appeared in popular magazines that discussed the tremendous religiosity of Americans as compared with their counterparts in Europe, and cited surveys indicating, for example, that 90 percent of Americans claim a belief in God.

Influenced by the shift in popular opinion and works such as Carter's, in 1995 and 1997, respectively, President Clinton issued guidelines on "Religious Expression in the Public Schools" and "Religious Exercise and Religious Expression in the Federal Workplace." These were designed to promote a greater understanding of the latitude provided by the Religion Clauses and the Free Speech Clause for the practice and promotion of religious faiths in those contexts. In addition, in 1996 Congress passed, and President Clinton signed, a Welfare Reform Bill that included "charitable choice" provisions that made faith-based groups, along with nonreligious groups, eligible for federal funds. And, more recently, believing faith-based organizations to be more effective than government sponsored secular institutions in carrying out social programs, President Bush has been promoting "faith-based initiatives," which substantially extend "charitable choice," including the "Charity Aid, Recovery and Empowerment Act," known as the "CARE Act," which has been passed in the House, as well as grants to faith-based organizations awarded through the Department of Health and Human Services and the Department of Labor. In the words of Jim Towey, Director of the White House Office on Faith-Based and Community Initiatives, this is being done to further "the partnership between faith-based and community groups and the federal government in delivering social services to those in need."[7]

Along with this accommodating trend in government, there has been a greater acceptance of religion as a contributor to public discourse about morality in America on issues ranging from legal recognition of homosexual marriage, to private matters, such as those having to do with a husband's authoritative role in the home and the appropriateness of a woman with children working outside the home—"private" issues that often have public policy implications as well. And religious leaders are now frequent contributors on television issues programs, providing political opinions from their religious perspectives. Even politicians—from both the left and right—proclaim their religious affiliations as indicators of their having the character to lead.

But the secular left has decried this accommodationist trend, declaring the "wall of separation" between church and state to be in danger of tumbling with a pending opening of the floodgates, permitting unlimited religious influence on public policy decisions with the potential for religious domination. From the perspective of members of the secular left any encroachment by religion on secular society bodes poorly for the nation's future. Religion is a particularly dangerous entry in the public discourse, they contend. Its dogma promotes oppressive restrictions on liberty, they argue, and this is precisely what the founders sought to avoid when they drafted the Religion Clauses into the Bill of Rights. After all, Thomas Jefferson was the one who proclaimed that there should be a "wall of separation" between church and state, and he meant that the Establishment Clause was designed to protect the public sphere from the potentially oppressive views of the religious, they caution.

The secular left argues that the expansion of American freedoms mid-twentieth century was due in large part to the loosening of the hold of religion on society since *Everson*. And so the secular left contends that strict separation of church and state is necessary in order to accommodate America's ever-expanding pluralism, particularly religious pluralism. If we base the American political system on the right's religious views, through accommodation or otherwise, this will not occur, the left warns. In fact, it could lead to religious strife—something America has been fortunate enough to avoid, unlike many other nations of the world.

Thus, the secular left is the harbinger of the doom that it contends would result if religion were to become entangled with the coercive powers of government. Consequently, the secular left eschews arguments that support the view that America is fundamentally a religious nation founded on Judeo-Christian principles that inform the meaning of freedom and form the foundation for fundamental American moral values. Sounding the alarm, they warn that this "Christian nation view" surely will lead to religious oppression. As a result, they argue forcefully against rolling back what they hold are the protections afforded by the *Everson* Court's "wall of separation" interpretation of the Establishment Clause.

ENTERING THE FRAY

Such disputes involve much more than technical legal arguments about where to draw the line between church and state, however. Fundamentally, the entire debate is centered around the perceived conflict between liberty and morality—the pursuit of the good. On the one hand, the left reasons that if one is to be "free," then one must not be fettered by moral constraints not freely chosen. Therefore, the governments of the United States and the states must not impose moral foundational claims on the people. On the other hand, the right contends that there must be a moral order that will hold American society together—the Christian or "Judeo-Christian" moral tradition. Otherwise, American society will become evermore fragmented and chaotic as factions exercising liberty rights conflict with others, causing American society to falter and fail. To confuse matters more, all sides cite the American founders' views regarding the extents and limits of the role of religion in public life to support their very different views. As a consequence, there does not appear to be any real resolution of the important—even critical—questions raised by the clash of the extremes of the late-twentieth-century culture war debate. Each new encounter leaves us with more unanswered questions:

In a special edition of *Time* reporting on the September 11th attacks on the World Trade Center and the Pentagon, Nancy Gibbs wrote:

> The Twin Towers of the World Trade Center, planted at the base of Manhattan island with the Statue of Liberty as their sentry, and the Pentagon, a squat, concrete fort on the banks of the Potomac, are the sanctuaries of money and power that our enemies may imagine define us. But that assumes our faith rests on what we can buy and build, and that has never been America's true God.[8]

What does the author mean when she refers to "America's true God" and "our faith?" Does America have a faith? a God? If so, is this a faith and a God in the "religious" sense? Is this a faith and a God for all of the American people? Can that be possible in the face of American pluralism?

During the 2000 presidential campaign, a September issue of *Time* argued:

> "While no one doubts the sincerity of his beliefs, Lieberman seems to be dodging their implications on the campaign trail. He calls for 'a constitutional place for faith in our public life,' and yet he is against prayer in school and

defends church-state separation. So what, specifically does he mean? . . . And though many Orthodox Jews argue that abortion is immoral, Lieberman is pro-choice because, as he said in 1990, 'while I might personally argue against abortion, as a lawmaker I cannot impose my personal judgment on others.' "[9]

Was Senator Lieberman being inconsistent in his positions on these church-state issues, as the writer of the *Time* article seems to imply, or is there a basis on which Lieberman's views can be reconciled?

On an evening in October 1997, the topic on CNN's *Crossfire* was the "Promise Keepers." One of the guests was Patricia Ireland, the president of the National Organization of Women. She and Pat Buchanan were engaged in a contentious exchange. Pat Buchanan stated that he could understand that Patricia Ireland may not like the fact that the Promise Keepers wanted to return to a patriarchal family structure where women are subordinated to men. However, he questioned her as to what is wrong with the Promise Keepers advocating that: "Now, you might not like that . . . but what is wrong if they [the wives] like that and Promise Keepers like that?"

Patricia Ireland replied: "Well, let me just say that I do disagree with the patriarchal model of the family and the society, but . . . [i]f that's what they choose, that's their decision." She went on to say, however: "I would also urge you to remember that Bill McCartney [the founder of the Promise Keepers] has said 'wherever the truth is at risk, in schools, in legislatures, we will contend for it, we will win.' " She argued: "They are going to impose their views through public policy."

Pat Buchanan responded: "Patricia, you've been fighting to impose your views on public policy for forty years!" Patricia Ireland emphatically said: "I'm not hiding behind a facade of religiosity. . . . I'm not saying I'm a ministry." Buchanan shot back: "Well, Martin

Luther King imposed his philosophy on the country and he was a minister and it was civil rights. What is wrong with Bill McCartney saying 'these are my deeply held beliefs? They're rooted in the Bible and we hope to remake society along these lines [much the same way] as [Patricia Ireland] hopes to remake them along the lines of [feminism].' " He later pointedly said: "I mean, you are knocking the traditional marriage, the patriarchal marriage, love, honor and obey . . . that bugs you and you want to change that. What's the matter with these folks having their philosophy?"

Is there any difference between the work of the Promise Keepers and the National Organization of Women when they try to make their views law? Are all moral views equally valid in a values debate where any group can claim victory if it gets enough votes? If a group's views are religiously based, are they inherently suspect under the American system? How can that be when someone like Dr. Martin Luther King, Jr., has nearly been claimed as a secular saint by those who eschew religion in the public square?

On another night, in January 1998, one of the guests on ABC's *Politically Incorrect* was Marilyn Manson, a popular, but controversial male rock star who is known to perform lewd sex acts on stage during live performances, among other things offensive to many, but that delight others. During the course of the program he was asked what he is trying to accomplish with his act. He told the participants that his goal is to challenge people's values. Another guest responded that she had a lot of respect for him for doing what he believes in, although she also stated that she did not like what he was doing.

Why does the guest in the *Politically Incorrect* segment think that Marilyn Manson deserves her respect for views she finds repugnant? Is the free expression of all views on moral values something to be admired no matter the content? Is the expression of a strong point of view on morals in opposition to someone else's free expression contrary to the American goal to preserve liberty?

When Texas Governor George W. Bush was asked during a presidential candidate debate what political philosopher had influenced him most, he answered, "Jesus Christ—because he changed my heart." When asked what he meant by this, he said that if one had not experienced it, it would be difficult to explain.

Why did (then) Governor Bush think it was important for voters to know this about him? Does it tell us something about whether he would make an especially good or qualified president? Does it indicate that he is more or less likely to uphold the American values of liberty and equality?

In general, what does accommodation of religion in public life mean in the context of religious pluralism with varied moral perspectives in a multicultural context? Are there core values and a fundamental moral base that America should preserve for its future? If not, on what do we base law and public policy decisions? If so, do such core values have any moral authority in a world of many views about how society should be organized? Is there a fundamental American identity that we should take with us as we assert our interests in the global community? Do the founders' original intentions regarding the role of religion in American public life help us to answer these questions?

As the most combative participants in the debate have clearly recognized all along, the answers to all of these questions by the United States Supreme Court, other courts, the executives and the legislatures of the land will determine the meaning and extent of freedom and the ways in which we Americans can pursue the good—good government, good international relations, good communities, good families, good relations between individuals, and good individuals. The answers will shape the moral fabric of the nation—the very terms on which the debate itself will be conducted—and will have a tremendous impact on our national identity as we interface with other nations in an increasingly globalized world. Consequently, it is not an overstatement to say that these are some of the most critical questions of our time.

Yet every attempt to answer such questions only results in greater confusion about them—in no small part because the various interpretations of the original intentions of the founders do not appear to provide the common ground one might expect to find. Still, one has the sense that the answers might be found there.

On Looking Back to Rediscover America's Moral Foundations

How is it possible that all sides in the debate on these important issues are able to cite the American founders to support their very different views? Is this merely because there were many different people speaking from many different perspectives at the time of the founding of the nation and, therefore, there was no consistent view, as some have claimed? It certainly is the case that the founders' views appear fragmented, disjointed, and contradictory when one listens to accounts of them from the various sides in the debate about the wall of separation of church and state. Still, it is difficult to believe that the founders could have achieved the founding of the United States in the context of such a confused rhetoric. Perhaps something has been missed by those in the contemporary discourse that might make more sense of all of this?

Relying on bits and pieces of rationale based on fragments of American history at the time of the founding of the United States that can be gleaned from our popular and political contemporary debate itself, or from the evolution of ideas since the founding (as some do), is not helpful. Instead, we must go back to the American Revolutionary period and review the primary sources with a sincere desire to understand the moral grounding of the Religion Clauses. As we do so in the chapters that follow, we will discover—or rather rediscover—that the views of the founders were grounded in fundamental ideas and beliefs that differ from the ideas of the participants in the popular and political contemporary debate, although the founders' views may appear similar to this side or that in the contemporary debate when taken out of context.

Reinvestigating strongly held assumptions (our own and others'), we will begin to see the ways in which all sides in the contemporary debate have been relying on meanings of terms that have shifted over the centuries (e.g., "religion" and "secular"), inapt dichotomies (e.g., public/private), and misunderstood concepts (e.g., separation of church and state). At the same time, we will see that the various sides have been harvesting statements from the past in a piecemeal fashion that support a presently held view, all the while obscuring the "original intentions" of the founders.* As a result, the contemporary debate has become confounded and confused.

But when we look back to rediscover America's moral foundations, we will gain several insights that together provide a perspective in the contemporary debate that draws from existing perspectives, but shifts their emphases. Consequently, those who embrace the religious right and those who embrace the secular left, as well as those who identify with the accommodationists, may recognize elements of their views of America's moral foundations in the following pages. But we will see that the ideas expressed here diverge from all those views in many ways as well. And it is these divergences that make all the difference—for it is here that we will find our common ground. We will rediscover the sacred foundations of the American system,

---

* I am not referring to "original intent" regarding the application of the Religion Clauses to any particular issue. Rather, I am addressing the underlying "original intentions," shared by the founders in the establishment of the States and the United States, which, I argue, form the foundations not only of the Religion Clauses, but the entire American System. See Leonard W. Levy, *Original Intent and the Framers' Constitution* (New York: Macmillan Publishing Co., 1988), wherein Levy discusses the difficulty in attempting to glean the "original intent" of the founders for the purpose of determining the meaning of specific constitutional provisions. See also Leonard Levy, *The Establishment Clause: Religion and the First Amendment*, 2nd ed. (Chapel Hill and London: The University of North Carolina Press, 1994), xix.

which are grounded in a simple theology and which imply a basic structure in which participation in public life is to occur. I call this theology and structure "America's Sacred Ground."

Several things follow when we place the contemporary debate on what I maintain is its proper footing on America's Sacred Ground. We will rediscover the difference between, on the one hand, the way to the good (the moral good) as understood by those who seek to impose their will (understood as God's will) on the people, and, on the other hand, the way to the good through the workings of America's Sacred Ground. We will find that individual freedom of conscience is • the core American civil right, and we will find the founders' belief that, through the collective speech and action of individuals of conscience, a good society can be built.

Significantly, we will discover that the building of a good society on America's Sacred Ground requires a two-tiered public forum for debate and action, which grounds the American system in civic and conscientious moral values. This is what makes possible the pursuit of the good without the coercive force of government. Thus, the good society is not something conceived by those in power at the top of a grand societal hierarchy as an "overarching worldview" to be imposed on the people. Rather, the good society is realized through the debate and action of the people pursuing the good according to conscience from the ground up by virtue of the shared expression of the plurality of their perspectives. In this way, America's Sacred Ground preserves maximum liberty while making possible pursuit of the good. Consequently, the whole idea of freedom was not intended by the founders to be freedom to pursue self-interested happiness, nor was freedom a vacuous concept only to be filled with policy-makers' ideas of what is to be pursued, but it was *freedom to be and do good according to one's conscience.* •

We also will discover that there are ways in which the contemporary discourse can be reframed based on America's Sacred Ground. And if the discourse were reframed in this way, it would be possible to begin to unravel the confused rhetoric of the contemporary popular and political debate, which has sent all sides in directions never intended by the American founders. Significantly, we will find that if the debate about the application of the Religion Clauses to particular issues were reframed in light of America's Sacred

Ground, there would be wide-reaching implications for the discourse about the role of religion in public life, in general, and, specifically, the ways in which religion was and was not intended by the founders to participate in the shaping of American values. And, in turn, America's Sacred Ground would contribute to all debates about the ground of American liberty and the pursuit of the good. That is, America's Sacred Ground would inform contemporary conversations, popular and political, about the moral ground of the American legal/political system, itself, and therefore, the direction it should take as we go forward in the twenty-first century. Most important, we will find that if we fail to take account of America's Sacred Ground, we risk eroding the very foundations of the American system, which have made the debates, themselves, possible in the first place.

Alasdair MacIntyre in his pivotal 1981 work *After Virtue: A Study in Moral Theory*, identified what he viewed as the main problem of the public discourse, which makes understanding and compromise about moral issues so difficult: Americans have no common moral language.[10] I submit that we do. However, the moral discourse in America has become disconnected from that language because we have lost our foothold on what truly grounds the American system. And the only way to become surefooted again is to reclaim our American heritage. We need to reorient the discourse about liberty and the good by reaching back into history and placing ourselves in the shoes of the founders. We need to walk on the ground they walked on. And it is imperative that we do this because, just as those participating in the debate sense, all that makes the American system unique *is* truly at stake.

And when we do reach back into that history to reclaim our American heritage, when we walk in the shoes of the founders, we find that there *is* a moral base that we should hold on to that makes America *America*. We rediscover the heartfelt hope of the founders that America would be fertile enough for the good to take root, grow, and flourish in a lively, free, and open forum for debate about religion and morality—not by force, but by choice. We rediscover America's Sacred Ground.

A Few Definitions

Before we turn to Part I, it is important to note that a few key definitions have been provided in Appendix A. There, the reader will find definitions for and, in some cases, brief discussions about, "religion" and "secular," and related names, terms and concepts, "God" and the "sacred," as well as "the good," "moral relativity," "overarching worldviews," "secularization," and "freedom." Those readers not concerned, at this point, with such details may refer to these definitions while reading the main text as questions about the terms arise. However, those readers interested in coming to a preliminary understanding may turn to Appendix A now and begin to glean hints of some of the aspects of the theory presented in this work that we will be exploring as we go forward.

Now let us turn to our project. Before turning to the American founders, we must reach farther back into history—to the American founders' starting point. We must rediscover the roots of America's Sacred Ground in John Locke. *How shallow a root*

Part I

Looking Back

to Rediscover

America's Sacred Ground

CHAPTER 2

Rediscovering the Roots of America's Sacred Ground in John Locke

Nobody therefore, in fine, neither single persons, nor Churches, nay, nor even commonwealths, have any just title to invade the civil rights and worldly goods of each other, upon pretence of religion. Those that are of another opinion would do well to consider with themselves how pernicious a seed of discord and war, how powerful a provocation to endless hatreds, rapines, and slaughters they thereby furnish unto mankind. No peace and security, no, not so much as common friendship, can ever be established or preserved amongst men, so long as this opinion prevails, that dominion is founded in grace, and that religion is to be propagated by force of arms
—John Locke, *A Letter Concerning Toleration* (1685)

JOHN LOCKE: PROPHET OF AMERICA

It is well accepted that John Locke's philosophy provided the background on which the American republic was established. Nathan Tarcov calls Locke "*our* political philosopher,"[1] and George W. Ewing notes that Locke has been credited as providing "almost

23

scriptural authority" for eighteenth-century thought.[2] Others refer to his work as a "political gospel," and to Locke himself as the "principal guide" to Americans.[3] Evidence of Locke's influence on the founding of the United States is pervasive, his main principles having been embodied, as we shall see, in the Declaration of Independence itself.

In considering this influence, some have read Locke as being ultimately "atheistic," "secular," and "a deist." However, although acknowledged by a few in the academy, what is often overlooked or acknowledged only in passing in the popular and political discourse is the part religion plays in Locke's thinking.[4] In fact, it is clear from Locke's work that he was a deeply committed Christian. True, he did much to criticize the Christianities of his day. Nevertheless, his writing reveals, not a hostility or contempt of religion in general, or of Christianity in particular, as some, for example Leo Strauss have contended, but rather a sincere belief, "an authentic piety."[5]

Therefore, instead of reading Locke's theory of government without regard to Locke's religious views, which were central to his life, in this chapter we will read Locke from the perspective of his theological stance. As George W. Ewing has pointed out, "[n]o man's system of thought can be accurately known without a consideration of the religion that of necessity limits and binds it."[6] And this is no less true with John Locke, for it is the elements of Locke's "authentic piety" as they appear in Locke's political theories that provide the underlying foundation for his mature work, and, consequently are of central importance to the founding of the United States—to such a degree that it is fair to say that John Locke was a prophet of America.

John Dunn claimed in his work *The Political Thought of John Locke* that Locke's philosophy is outdated and unuseful because it is framed in terms no longer recognizable to us.[7] Yet these terms were very much a part of the lexicon of the American founders. Consequently, the fact that these terms have become unrecognizable is *the very reason it is necessary to reclaim them*. Otherwise, we cannot grasp the intellectual framework, and more important the theological underpinnings, that shaped the founding documents of our nation. Without rediscovering John Locke's political theology, we cannot rediscover America's Sacred Ground.

LOCKE'S POLITICAL THEOLOGY: LOCATING THE SACRED CENTER IN EACH INDIVIDUAL'S RELATIONSHIP WITH GOD

Locke's era, the seventeenth century, was one of religious strife and warfare as Catholics and Protestants alternatively vied for power in England. On the one hand, some saw the establishment of a state church as necessary to the civil order. On the other hand, there were a few who scorned the abuses of church and civil authorities and their efforts to bring together "Priest and Prince" against those in society that church and civil authorities deemed in their absolute power to be subversive.[8] Originally, Locke sided with the former camp, finding little in reason or common consent, on which to secure a foundation for society.[9] But his experiences led him to a change in view,[10] culminating in those works that were to prove to be especially profound influences on the American founders—the *Two Treatises of Government* and *A Letter Concerning Toleration.*

The views Locke proffered in these works stood in sharp contrast to the views of those in authority at the time of their publication.[11] Locke challenged the traditions, customs, and hierarchies of the churches, as well as the right of rulers to make laws with respect to ecclesiastical matters. He wrote in favor of separation of church and state and the widest toleration of religious freedom and dissent. These works were so controversial that he published many of them anonymously and went into exile in Holland from 1683 to 1689 to avoid the executioner's rope, which had met other dissidents.[12] What was so threatening to the authorities, both religious and civil, about his work? As we shall see, it was those very things that comprise the theology underlying his writings that were subversive to those in power.

When we peruse these mature works of Locke, we see that there are certain fundamental beliefs that form the framework of his theological perspective. First, it is a theological rather than a theoretical position because it is grounded in a central assumption: There is God. Locke does not tell us the nature of God—for example, whether God is a Being or Being itself, or what constitutes the many attributes of God. Yet we do know one important thing, probably the most fundamental to Locke's theology, and, therefore, his thought: God communicates to individual people. Not only has God made revelations in the Bible, but also the "Spirit of God" in the Scriptures is our "infallible guide" when the text itself is not clear,[13] and Locke acknowledged that Jesus proclaimed the "Spirit of truth" guides believers to truth.[14] Reason is "natural revelation,"[15] which not only serves to aid one in ferreting out the implications of divine inspiration, but is "the voice of God" in human beings.[16] Furthermore, Locke accepted that supernatural revelation can come directly from God to an individual, as Locke contended the Bible so provides.[17] Thus, Locke's famous empiricism extends to personal revelation and personal interpretation of written revelation, the validity of which, Locke held, is judged by reason.

> Reason is natural revelation, whereby the eternal father of light, and fountain of all knowledge, communicates to mankind that portion of truth which he has laid within the reach of their natural faculties: revelation is natural reason enlarged by a new set of discoveries communicated by God immediately, which reason vouches the truth of, by the testimony and proofs it gives, that they come from God. So that he that takes away reason, to make way for revelation, puts out the light of both . . . .[18]

Significantly, Locke abandoned all appeals to tradition and custom.[19] This was a radical step as it challenged the authority of the ecclesiastical hierarchy. Nevertheless, Locke was convinced that tradition and custom do not offer security as to what is or is not pleasing to God. Instead, each individual must conduct his own private "search and study" to discover God's inspirations in order to understand what is to be done.[20]

> Some perhaps may object that no such society [i.e., congregation] can be said to be a true Church, unless it have in it a bishop, or presbyter, with ruling authority derived from the very apostles, and continued down unto the present times by an uninterrupted succession.
>
> To these I answer, in the first place: let them show me the edict by which Christ has imposed that law upon his Church. And let not any man think me impertinent if, in a thing of this consequence, I require that the terms of that edict be very express and positive. For the promise he has made us that 'wheresoever two or three are gathered together in his name, he will be in the midst of them' (Matt. 18.20) seems to imply the contrary.[21]

It follows from all this, and it is by now axiomatic to claim, that Locke's philosophy is "individualistic."[22] What is important for us to recognize for our purposes here, however, is that Locke's individualism was derived directly from his theological belief that God's concern is not with society or any group but with *each individual* whose duty it is to do what is in accord with independent conscience imbued with God.[23]

Accordingly, Locke eschewed the view that enforced conformity is required in order for society to properly reflect religious values—a view held by Catholics and members of various Protestant sects, as well as by those in other religious groups at the time.[24] Instead, he adopted radical tolerance of all the religions as he considered tolerance to be "the chief characteristical mark of the true church."[25] Thus, he argued for tolerance of religious people of all kinds, including those in all sects of Protestant Christianity (naming the most controversial of his day),[26] Catholics,[27] Jews,[28] Muslims or "Mahometans,"[29] Native Americans,[30] and pagans.[31*]

---

* See footnote on page 41 regarding the extent of toleration.

[I]f solemn assemblies, observations of festivals, public worship be permitted to any one sort of professors [i.e., religious people], all these things ought to be permitted to the Presbyterians, Independents, Anabaptists, Arminians, Quakers, and others, with the same liberty. Nay, if we may openly speak the truth, and as becomes one man to another, neither pagan, nor Mahometan, nor Jew ought to be excluded from the civil rights of the commonwealth because of his religion.[32]

Locke advised that even "idolatry, superstition, and heresy" and "heathens" should be tolerated.[33]

Significantly, Locke claimed that at its core Christianity *requires* toleration of others: "If the Gospel and the apostles may be credited, no man can be a Christian without charity, and without that faith which works, not by force, but by love."[34] And this is love with a *this-worldly* focus. Love is not to be misconstrued so as to permit physical torture or imprisonment for the sake of the victim's eternal salvation. Love is to reflect real concern for the well-being of others here and now. In this regard, Locke was well aware of the twisted arguments made by certain Christians who professed love while participating in persecutions, and Locke condemned them:

That any man should think fit to cause another man whose salvation he heartily desires to expire in torments, and that even in an unconverted state, would, I confess, seem very strange to me, and, I think, to any other also. But nobody, surely, will ever believe that such a carriage can proceed from charity, love, or good-will.[35]

Moreover, Locke viewed these practices as hypocritical. Noting that religious authorities often overlook the actions of those within their own flocks that blatantly violate the rules of the church, he contended that the persecution of heretics could not truly be to save their souls.

For if it be out of a principle of charity, as they pretend, and love to men's souls, that they deprive them of their estates, maim them with corporal punishments, starve and torment them in noisome prisons, and in the end even take away their lives; I say if all this be done merely to make men Christians, and procure their salvation, why then do they suffer 'whoredom, fraud, malice, and such like enormities' (Rom. 1), which (according to the apostle) manifestly relish of heathenish corruption, to predominate so much and abound amongst their flocks and people?[36]

[W]hilst he is cruel and implacable towards those that differ from him in opinion, he be indulgent to such iniquities and immoralities as are unbecoming the name of a Christian, let such a one talk never so much of the Church, he plainly demonstrates by his actions that 'tis another kingdom he aims at, and not the advancement of the kingdom of God.[37]

Locke's belief that God's concern is with each individual and not society as a whole, or even any particular religious institution, led Locke to the conclusion that the only thing that counts as "true religion" is sincere faith in God. Here is where the sacred is revealed, not in church doctrine. Thus, Locke emphasized that "true religion consists in the inward persuasion of the mind."[38] Only personal conviction counts as being truly religious: "It is only light and evidence that can work a change in men's opinions."[39] True faith cannot be the blind "faith" of going along with what a religious group's authority asserts is truth. Faith is *really* believing. Consequently, if an individual is coerced into complying with the things that her society requires of her in religious matters, then she is betraying her own conscience—what she believes to be God's will. Accordingly, by complying, the individual may avoid the charge of "heretic" by civil and ecclesiastical authorities; yet she is, in effect, a "heretic" to her own convictions—that which is dictated by conscience imbued with God.

Consequently, Locke roundly condemned all religious persecution as it is unreasonable to conclude that anyone has authority to dictate the conscience of others. The persecution of others to that end makes no sense, he claimed. Moreover, Christians (who were the persecutors of others in Locke's society) have no biblical authority for persecution, Locke reasoned.

> [T]he Gospel frequently declares that the true disciples of Christ must suffer persecution; but that the Church of Christ should persecute others, and force others by fire and sword to embrace her faith and doctrine, I could never yet find in any of the books of the New Testament.[40]

Significantly, there is no evidence that civil or ecclesiastical authorities are more likely to be correct about what is "true religion" that is pleasing to God than is the individual, Locke argued. He points out that there is no authority for the supremacy of ecclesiastical doctrine in the Bible.[41] But even if such authorities are correct, Locke reasoned, if the individual does not believe it, it can be of no avail to him. Because God's concern is with the individual, the outward conforming of an individual's actions to the dictates of authorities (but which are contrary to that individual's conscience) cannot be pleasing to God. Accordingly, such compliance is hypocrisy, nothing more, and, therefore, it cannot provide succor to one's soul.

On the other hand, if the authorities are wrong in their assessment of the right path to God, then the individual who goes against his conscience (in order to conform to the dictates of such authorities) has adopted untruth, rather than truth. He has, in effect, traded possible salvation for blasphemy.

> [N]o man can so far abandon the care of his own salvation as blindly to leave it to the choice of any other, whether prince or subject, to prescribe to him what faith or worship he shall embrace. For no man can, if he would, conform his faith to the dictates of another. All the life and power of true

religion consists in the inward and full persuasion of the mind; and faith is not faith without believing. Whatever profession we make, to whatever outward worship we conform, if we are not fully satisfied in our mind that the one is true, and the other well pleasing unto God, such profession and such practice, far from being any furtherance, are indeed great obstacles to our salvation. For in this manner, instead of expiating other sins by the exercise of religion, I say in offering thus unto God Almighty such a worship as we esteem to be displeasing unto him, we add unto the number of our other sins those also of hypocrisy, and contempt of his divine majesty.[42]

It is important to recognize that Locke held that ecclesiastical and civil authorities are *less likely* than the individual to be correct in their assessment of what is pleasing to or required by God. The reason is that church and state often are motivated by factors other than the care of souls. Each wishes to increase its stature and power and, thus, the one serves to corrupt the other in the performance of its duties to its constituents.

[I]t appears what zeal for the Church, joined with the desire of dominion, is capable to produce; and how easily the pretence of religion, and of the care of souls, serves for a cloak to covetousness, rapine, and ambition.[43]

And Locke readily pointed out that the prince is likely to grant authority to that church whose doctrines are in accord with his own persuasions, and that churches are likely to sway their doctrine in order to attain approval of the prince.[44] As Locke said:

The English history affords us . . . examples, in the reigns of Henry the 8th, Edward the 6th, Mary, and Elizabeth, how easily and smoothly the clergy changed their decrees, their articles of faith, their form of worship, everything, according to the inclination of those kings and queens.[45]

Evidence that ecclesiastical authorities have no greater claim to legitimacy in determining the right path to God can be found in the very fact that so many of them have significant disputes over doctrine, Locke asserted. The result is that there are many options from which the individual must choose and, therefore, the individual is led inevitably back to his own conscience.

> [P]ray observe how great have always been the divisions amongst even those who lay so much stress upon the divine institution and continued succession of a certain order of rulers in the Church. Now their very dissension unavoidably puts us upon a necessity of deliberating, and consequently allows a liberty of choosing that which, upon consideration, we prefer.[46]

Similarly, the various "princes" choose different faiths to support. Consequently, the mere fact that the prince favors one ecclesiastical authority over another provides no security whatsoever to the individual that the prince's choice is sound.[47]

> Would an Israelite, that had worshipped Baal upon the command of his king, have been in any better condition, because somebody had told him that the king ordered nothing in religion upon his own head, nor commanded anything to be done by his subjects in divine worship, but what was approved by the counsel of priests, and declared to be of divine right by the doctors of their Church?[48]

For all these reasons, Locke held that the individual, left to his own conscience—the concern for his own soul—is *more likely* to make a correct assessment of God's will than is an authoritative body governed by others. And even if the individual does not find the right way, it cannot be provided by force because it must be freely chosen in order to have any positive effect.

> How great soever, in fine, may be the pretense of good-will, and charity, and concern for the salvation of men's souls,

men cannot be forced to be saved whether they will or no. And therefore, when all is done, they must be left to their own consciences.[49]

Significantly, as David Wootton has noted, Locke even suggested that the "true church" may take many forms.[50] Consequently, the things that individual conscience dictates may be directed toward any one of many forms and, still, the individual may have chosen a right path. The fact that various groups' practices and beliefs differ may be of no account in substance, Locke suggests. Such conflicting practices are likely to be "indifferent," that is, in effect, of no concern.[51] Further, Locke was no supporter of creeds and orthodoxies. He especially saw them as confounding the plain and simple message of the Christian scriptures,[52] or worse, being used as a basis for charges of heresy by Christians against other Christians who eschew such church doctrines but take the scriptures at face value.

Still, even if there is only one way to salvation, Locke held that just as "no man can be forced to be rich or healthful," so "God himself will not save men against their wills."[53]

I cannot be saved by a religion that I distrust, and by a worship that I abhor. It is in vain for an unbeliever to take up the outward show of another man's profession. Faith only, and inward sincerity, are the things that procure acceptance with God.[54]

The only way for an individual to find the right way to God and truth is to permit "every private man's search and study" so he "discovers it unto himself."[55]

In summary, Locke's political theology is based on the fundamental principle that God's concern is with each individual, not with society as a whole or any church or other group. Accordingly, religious beliefs and practices are properly left to individual conscience. No authority, civil or religious, nor any person, has any greater claim to know the true path to God than does the individual himself. Significantly, a "blind" faith and outward show cannot bring one salvation, Locke contended; it is only sincere and deeply held conviction, which necessarily is the province only of the individual, that is pleasing to God. Accordingly, no one but the individual has any legitimate authority as to how to worship God or function in the world in a manner pleasing to God.

> Whatsoever is not done with that assurance of faith, is neither well in itself, nor can it be acceptable to God. To impose such things, therefore, upon any people, contrary to their own judgement, is in effect to command them to offend God; which, considering that the end of all religion is to please him, and that liberty is essentially necessary to that end, appears to be absurd beyond expression.[56]

⚜

THE SOCIAL CONTRACT AS SOCIETY'S SACRED GROUND

Why was Locke so concerned with freedom of conscience? Because Locke had seen the disastrous results of the efforts of those individuals and groups (in his society all Christians of one sort or another) who claimed to be the mediators of conscience and then sought to impose their "unifying" moral visions for the common good of society as a whole—their overarching worldviews—on the people. Clearly, experience had shown that reliance on such claims did not produce the peaceful and harmonious society they promised. Rather, such reliance produced wars, conflicts, persecution and torture. Locke, a committed Christian, was convinced that the ethic that could bring about peace and goodwill among human beings was right there in the scriptures, particularly the New Testament. Yet, as George Ewing has written, Locke saw that "seventeen centuries of Christianity had not produced the society that a perfect ethic should."[57] Why not? Locke proposed a new approach—one that addressed that very question. Like the church authorities he criticized, Locke had a vision of the common good that he sought to promote. The difference was his means for attaining it.

Locke often is interpreted as having provided no "ends," no "good" at which to aim, but only "means" to ends in his theory of government—a criticism laid on Enlightenment thinkers in general by such scholars as Alasdair MacIntyre in *After Virtue: A Study in Moral Theory*.[58] But Locke clearly had "ends" in mind. Although he did not seek to impose them, he provided the context within which there is a possibility that they could be realized, if the "means" he provided were instituted. Moreover, he was hopeful that the good *would be* produced because he believed that reason—the "natural law," which is "the voice of God" in human beings—would prevail.

And what does reason dictate, according to Locke? It dictates Locke's political theory set forth in the second of his *Two Treatises of Government*.[59] The *Second Treatise* asserts that individuals are fundamentally free and equal in the "state of nature" as provided by God;[60] that is, they are by nature free and equal—governed only by the "law of nature," that is, God's law, which is discernible through reason.[61] The fundamental principle of that law is the mutual obligation to love.[62] Because we are created by God, we are God's property; therefore, we do not have liberty to harm ourselves. Furthermore, because we are all equal and independent in a state of nature, "no one ought to harm another in his life, health, liberty, or possessions. . . ."[63] Otherwise, there is a "state of war" between people where there is only "enmity and destruction."[64]

The only justification for harm to another is punishment for a transgression of the law of nature (that is, the law of freedom and equality and against harm), and then only "to retribute to him . . . so much as may serve for reparation and restraint."[65] And everyone in the state of nature, being equal, has the equal right to punish a transgressor of that natural law. However, the problem in the state of nature is that there is no impartial judge of disputes about violations of the natural law. Moreover, there is no common settled law to give effect to the natural law and no power to execute sentences.[66]

Consequently, government is necessary for the purpose of preserving liberty (which includes freedom from harm) and equality, which are human beings' "natural" rights, and to provide an impartial judge to address disputes. In other words, the natural law of freedom and equality is to be reflected in society's law in order to avoid a "state of war" in the "state of nature," which at best gives rise to the eventual establishment of a king, who is unlikely to recognize or enforce the law of nature.

While Locke emphasized in the *Second Treatise* that the purpose of government is to protect private property, by "property" Locke meant much more than material goods and estates; he meant the property of each individual in "one's person, life, liberty and religion"[67]—all that one has a right to enjoy in the state of nature. Thus, under Locke's theory, government's main purpose is the preservation of the individual liberty of men and women to realize full personhood to the extent that such liberty does not interfere with the liberty of others (which would be harm and, thus, contrary to the law of nature).[68]

Though not emphasized in the *Second Treatise*, Locke's *Letter Concerning Toleration* makes clear that freedom of religion, or freedom of conscience imbued with God, is a central liberty, which is essential to the realization of full personhood. Accordingly, rather than civil authorities using coercive power to enforce religious *doctrine*, they are to use their power to preserve the greater probability of authentic religious *conviction*. They are to ensure each individual's maximum chance to find his and her way to God by keeping individual conscience free.

Accordingly, Locke had a vision of the common good. It was the creation of a societal context within which people are free to hear "the voice of God"[69] and act in accordance with that call. That societal context is created by the mutual consent of the people—a social contract where government is a trust for the benefit of the people to ensure their liberties and their safety.[70] This contract was seen by Locke as the only reasonable means to ensure freedom because it provides for a government that does not impose religion and morality on individuals by asserting an overarching worldview. The only exception is the imposition of the moral values *reflected in the social contract itself,* which are necessary to provide the context within which people can be called to reason—where people are free to turn conscience, not to churches or civil authorities, but to God.

One may argue that Locke did not provide for ends because Locke's theory does not provide an injunction that people turn toward reason or to God. True. But when we read Locke from the perspective of his works on religion, we see that while the context within which people can be called to God—the social contract—does not allow coercion (except to give effect to the social contract itself), it does allow *persuasion.*

Locke expressly encouraged the creation of an open forum—within the context of the social contract—to provide the means for the realization of the true and the good. For while no one has a right to "magisterial care" of souls, that is, the right to compel by punishment, "a charitable care, which consists in teaching, admonishing, and persuading, cannot be denied unto any man."[71] Locke exhorted Christians, in particular, to use persuasion and not coercion to bring others to truth and goodness, as did Jesus:

> If, like the captain of our salvation, they sincerely desired the good of souls, they would tread in the steps, and follow the perfect example, of that prince of peace who sent out his soldiers to the subduing of nations and gathering them into his Church, not armed with the sword, or other instruments of force, but prepared with the gospel of peace, and with the exemplary holiness of their conversation. This was his method.[72]

Moreover, not just Christians but *everyone* is bound by the social contract to refrain from coercion of others and to use persuasion to bring others to one's own conception of how one should believe or act.

> Anyone may employ as many exhortations and arguments as he pleases towards the promoting of another man's salvation. But all force and compulsion are to be forborne. Nothing is to be done imperiously. Nobody is obliged in that matter to yield obedience unto the admonitions

or injunctions of another, further than he himself is persuaded.[73]

It was clearly Locke's expectation, however, that if people lived in a societal context where they *could* be called to truth, they *would* be called to truth because all human beings have the "light of reason" in them. Certainly, as history has shown, compulsion is not an effective means to truth, Locke reasoned. Consequently, the conscience of a free people is the only hope—only then does truth have a real chance to prevail.

> For truth certainly would do well enough, if she were once left to shift for herself. She seldom has received, and I fear never will receive, much assistance from the power of great men, to whom she is but rarely known, and more rarely welcome. She is not taught by laws, nor has she any need of force to procure her entrance into the minds of men. Errors indeed prevail by the assistance of foreign and borrowed succours, but if truth makes not her way into the understanding by her own light, she will be but the weaker for any borrowed force violence can add to her.[74]

Thus, for Locke, the common good is constituted in the social contract, which serves to preserve freedom and provide a forum for persuasion. And because a central purpose of the social contract is to provide a context within which people of God and reason, or as Locke says "God and nature"[75] may exemplify the good, the common good is the means to the good. Hence, Locke's means lead to an end. That end is "peace, good will, mutual assistance, and preservation,"[76] "peace, equity, and friendship," "peace and goodwill toward all men," and honesty, peaceableness, and industriousness.[77] All of these are fostered by the social contract itself, which is derived by Locke through reason by appealing, first, to God. Consequently, while the role of Locke's civil government is a worldly one, it is nevertheless religiously grounded.

That is why Locke held that those "who deny the being of God" ought "not at all to be tolerated" because the denial of God threatens the "[p]romises, covenants, and oaths, which are the bonds of human society" and "undermine[s] and destroy[s] all religion" and so "can have no pretence of religion whereupon to challenge the privilege of toleration."[78] In other words, in Locke's view, for atheists, there is no appeal to conscience, truth, and goodness. Therefore, atheists cannot be good citizens of the government that Locke envisioned because through them, Locke believed, his "ends" could not be realized.*

Traditional Christian political theory, based on the work of Augustine, also provided a religious justification for government. However, traditional Christian political theory was founded on the doctrine of Original Sin. It held that government was necessary in order to restrain the sinful nature of human beings. Clearly this way of viewing things requires the state and the prevailing religious institution to be close allies. Ecclesiastical authority seeks the favor of powerful kings and princes in order to have more effective means to enforce the church's judgments regarding sin; the state uses the sanction of church doctrine to justify its punishment of sin. In effect under this system, theoretically at least, the state is an instrument of religion, as evidenced by the doctrine of the divine right of kings.[79]

But Locke rejected the doctrine of Original Sin[80]—a move that undercut traditional Christian political theory. No longer was the role of church and state to work together to restrain the sinful nature of humankind. Without Original Sin as the basic assumption, Locke could shift the theoretical underpinnings of civil government toward a different religious purpose—one grounded in the relationship of God to individual human beings. Rather than religion informing the structure of society from the lofty reaches of the top of church hierarchies down to the masses as an overarching

---

* As we will see in chapter 3, however, the American founders expanded the idea of freedom to include toleration of atheists, while still maintaining Locke's basic idea for how a good society could be realized.

worldview to live by, as had been the traditional approach, religion is to effect society from the ground up, as individuals of conscience freely express themselves from the perspective conscience gives them.[81] And because it is a society "by the people," rather than an autocracy or oligarchy, an empire or a kingdom, ruling from the top down, it is a "civil society." And "civil government" is government that preserves "civil society."

But what was Locke's purpose in all this?—a society devoid of religion and morality? Clearly not. His purpose was to create the societal structure that he thought would be most likely to bring individuals to consciousness imbued with reason and God. This, he recognized, cannot be realized through coercive force. Instead, it is produced by making possible the individual's reliance on conscience. Then, through persuasion, individuals share with others what they believe conscience directs and, through the workings of reason (the voice of God in human beings), individuals may come to an understanding of what conscience actually directs. In this way, truth is left "to shift for herself," so that she has a greater chance of coming to consciousness.[82]

Clearly, then, religion was not removed by Locke from worldly matters. On the contrary, the social contract itself was derived by Locke from a belief in God. Individual rights are "natural rights." They are derived from reason—in other words, derived from God. Locke's justification for government is based on the need to preserve these rights, and because these rights are protected by the civil government, Locke calls them "civil rights."

So we see, then, that civil government has a sacred purpose: It is to preserve the civil rights, in particular freedom of conscience so that individuals are able to find their way to God. Therefore, for Locke, "civil rights" are not "secular" rights as that term is understood today (that is, they are not devoid of religious content); *they are sacred rights*, and government rightly grounded is *religiously* grounded. Locke's vision was that free individuals with consciences filled by God—consciences that are persuaded by nature (i.e., reason) and God—will seek the good together. They will build their world based on their visions of the good on that sacred ground, not by force, but by choice. In the terms of Locke's own religion, they will "aim for the Kingdom of God."[83]*

AIMING FOR THE KINGDOM OF GOD REQUIRES "JUST BOUNDS" BETWEEN CIVIL GOVERNMENT AND CHURCHES

Locke recognized that under traditional Christian political theory what he had held ought to be two separate and distinct institutional forces—the state and the church—had been, in fact, inextricably intertwined. Central to Locke's thesis, then, was the need for proper delineation of the authority of each.[84]

Locke set out to make this delineation clear: Civil government's proper role is to attend to those matters of this world—preserving the civil rights, in particular freedom of conscience, and maintaining the safety and general welfare of the commonwealth. It is not, as had been the traditional approach, to institute a moral vision of society based on the religious doctrine of an ecclesiastical authority and to impose it on the people from the top down as an overarching worldview.

---

* It is important to note here that Locke is commonly interpreted as not extending toleration to Catholics and Muslims. I contend, however, that this is a misreading of the text. In this regard, see endnotes 29 and 31 of this chapter, and accompanying text, where Locke expressly includes the practices of these religious societies among those to be tolerated. To be sure, Locke expressed concern that Roman Catholics may be swayed by their allegiance to the Pope, and Muslims may be swayed by their allegiance to the "Mufti of Constantinople," to reject the legitimate civil laws of the magistrate, which ensure the preservation of civil society. In other words, because of these allegiances, they may embrace, instead, top-down overarching worldviews, which would be intended to override the fundamentals necessary to preserve the social contract. This, of course, cannot be tolerated, *as it is this sacred ground that makes tolerance possible, in the first place.* However, this is not more or less toleration than Locke would have extended to adherents of any other religion. As the above text shows, Locke would not have tolerated anyone's top-down overarching worldview approach to government, including that of his own Anglican church. Locke, *Letter Concerning Toleration, Political Writings*, 425–426.

For the political society is instituted for no other end but only to secure every man's possession of the things of this life. The care of each man's soul, and of the things of heaven, which neither does belong to the commonwealth nor can be subjected to it, is left entirely to every man's self. Thus the safeguard of men's lives, and of the things that belong unto this life, is the business of the commonwealth; and the preserving of those things unto their owners is the duty of the magistrate.[85]

Accordingly, the civil authority, that is, the "magistrate," is to have no authority in ecclesiastical matters because "the business of laws is not to provide for the truth of opinions, but for the safety and security of the commonwealth, and every particular man's goods and person."[86] The magistrate has no valid authority to compel worship.[87] Further, the magistrate has no valid authority to prohibit it, except to the extent that worship results in a harm to someone else's "life or estate" or "worldly concerns" and, therefore, their civil rights.[88] However, Locke made clear that this exception was to be exercised with considerable caution:

The part of the magistrate is only to take care that the commonwealth receive no prejudice, and that there be no injury done to any man, either in life or estate. . . . [T]hose things that are prejudicial to the commonweal of a people in their ordinary use, and are therefore forbidden by laws, those things ought not to be permitted to Churches in their sacred rites. *Only the magistrate ought always to be very careful that he does not misuse his authority, to the oppression of any Church, under pretence of public good.*[89]

Consequently, laws are valid only if they directly involve a "political matter"—one that furthers the goals of the social contract.[90] Regardless of the magistrate's personal religious convictions, no sect can be provided with privileges granted by the magistrate, and all religious assemblies must be tolerated.[91]

All men know and acknowledge that God ought to be publicly worshipped. Why otherwise do they compel one another unto the public assemblies? Men therefore constituted in this liberty are to enter into some religious society, that they may meet together, not only for mutual edification, but to own to the world that they worship God, and offer unto his Divine Majesty such service as they themselves are not ashamed of, and such as they think not unworthy of him, nor unacceptable to him; and finally that by the purity of doctrine, holiness of life, and decent form of worship, they may draw others unto the love of the true religion, and perform such other things in religion as cannot be done by each private man apart.

These religious societies I call Churches: and these I say the magistrate ought to tolerate.[92]

As we already have seen, civil authority's sacred purpose is to preserve the civil rights, in particular freedom of conscience. To accomplish this, the civil authority is to remain unentangled with churches. In answer to those who claimed that religious uniformity and punishment against those who deviate from it are necessary to maintain the public order, Locke argued that enforced uniformity *is contrary to peace*. All attempts to enforce uniformity have resulted not in a peaceful and orderly society, but in fractionalized interests and armed disputes, Locke showed.

It is not the diversity of opinions (which cannot be avoided), but the refusal of toleration to those that are of different opinions (which might have been granted), that has produced all the bustles and wars that have been in the Christian world upon account of religion.[93]

The result is that those persecuted on account of religion, when they are otherwise lawful citizens, are bound to resist what they rightly perceive to be injustice.

[W]hat else can be expected but that these men, growing weary of the evils under which they labour, should in the end think it lawful for them to resist with force, and to defend their natural rights (which are not forfeitable upon account of religion) with arms as well as they can? That this has been hitherto the ordinary course of things is abundantly evident in history; and that it will continue to be so hereafter is but too apparent in reason.[94]

In fact, then, enforced conformity often is the *direct cause* of civil unrest. Thus, while religious groups are to be tolerated by the magistrate, there is to be no tolerance of religious groups that seek *dominion* over others. In other words, the magistrate is to be intolerant of intolerance.

> These . . . , and the like, who attribute unto the faithful, religious, and orthodox, that is, in plain terms, unto themselves, any peculiar privilege or power above other mortals, in civil concernments; or who, upon pretence of religion, do challenge any manner of authority over such as are not associated with them in their ecclesiastical communion: *I say these have no right to be tolerated by the magistrate . . . .*[95]

Toleration of religion, Locke contended, should extend only so far as religious people are tolerant themselves. Thus, "conscientious dissent" was to be permitted, but not persecution of heretics[96]—the former arising out of individual conscience, the latter being the suppression of individual conscience. The magistrate is to ensure that freedom of conscience in the worship of God is not infringed by anyone, not even if one claims that "conscience" so directs.

> No peace and security, no, not so much as common friendship, can ever be established or preserved amongst men, so long as this opinion prevails, that dominion is founded in grace, and that religion is to be propagated by force of arms.[97]

In summary, the authority for governing power derives from its sacred purpose. In all other respects its power is to be limited. No longer does it derive its sanction from religious institutional doctrine. No longer is its purview the "care of souls." Now, instead, its authority is limited to keeping the peace by ensuring the sacred rights of individuals, and, in that regard, punishing those who do not tolerate others on account of religion.

Furthermore, when it comes to the role of religious institutions, Locke's theory serves to remove entirely the governing authority of religious bodies in civil matters: *The churches are to have no authority whatsoever over civil government; that is churches are to have no jurisdiction whatsoever over worldly matters.*[98] Ecclesiastical authority over the salvation of souls extends only to the enforcement of church rules in its own congregation. Its only legitimate instrument of punishment is excommunication; and this extends only to removing the violator of such rules from the group. It cannot result in the loss of any civil rights.

> I hold that no Church is bound by the duty of toleration to retain any such person in her bosom as, after admonition, continues obstinately to offend against the laws of the [church] society. For these being the condition of communion, and the bond of the society, if the breach of them were permitted without any animadversion, the society would immediately be thereby dissolved. But nevertheless, in all such cases. . . . [e]xcommunication neither does, nor can, deprive the excommunicated person of any of those civil goods that he formerly possessed. All those things belong to the civil government, and are under the magistrate's protection.[99]

REDISCOVERING THE INDIVIDUAL AS THE SOLE AUTHORITY OVER CONSCIENCE AND THE AUTHENTIC RELIGIOUS COMMUNITY AS A FREE AND VOLUNTARY CALL TO CONSCIENCE

So we see that what Locke has advocated is a specific kind of "separation of church and state." He has made the state the authority over worldly moral matters, while the church is to attend to the "salvation of souls" in its own congregation.[100] Yet the church is not the final authority over such matters. The final authority as to the "care of the soul" is the individual him- and herself. Individuals may obligate themselves to the dictates of a particular religious group; however, the church has no authority to enforce its rules, except by excommunication. Similarly, the state has no authority over the dictates of individual conscience. The state's role is to preserve the social contract (which in turn will preserve the peace of the commonwealth) so that individuals remain free to act in accordance with God's will as they believe is required.

Separation of church and state is meant to keep the church from attaining *any power over the individual at all, except to the degree voluntarily chosen by the individual,* and to remove all power of the church to dictate a course to the civil authority. The reason for this is to keep civil authority focused not on the punishment of sin, but on preserving the sacred civil rights. Moreover, separation of church and state is meant to keep civil authorities from corrupting the church, which it had accomplished in the past by, among other things, granting the church favors for providing the civil authorities with religious justifications for its various actions designed to constrain the people.[101]

> But, to speak the truth, we must acknowledge that the Church (if a convention of clergymen, making canons, must be called by that name) is for the most part more apt to be influenced by the court, than the court by the Church.[102]

Instead, if church and state are separated, the church is more likely to remain true to its original inspiration and be an authentic call to individual conscience. Then each individual may participate in the church that is in accord with the dictates of conscience. Hence, the church becomes a voluntary association. In this way, individuals of conscience can form and participate in the religious association as a "free and voluntary," "spontaneous society" that

> neither acquires the power of the sword by the magistrate's coming to it, nor does it lose the right of instruction and excommunication by his going from it. This is the fundamental and immutable right of a spontaneous society, that it has the power to remove any of its members who transgress the rules of its institution. But it cannot, by the accession of any new members, acquire any right of jurisdiction over those that are not joined with it. And, therefore, peace, equity, and friendship are always mutually to be observed by particular Churches, in the same manner as by private persons, without any pretence of superiority or jurisdiction over one another.[103]

That is, the preservation of individual civil rights, particularly freedom of conscience, is necessary so that individuals are able create community consistent with the will of God as conscience directs. Only then can authentic community arise.

SETTING THE "JUST BOUNDS" BETWEEN INDIVIDUAL CONSCIENCE'S MORAL CHOICE AND THE STATE

Because, under Locke's thesis, the church is to have no authority over conscience other than that voluntarily granted by individuals, and the state is to have no authority over the church, the delineation between church and state is clear. It is more difficult, however, to set the bounds between the authority of the state and the authority of individual conscience over moral choice.

Morality, as Locke duly noted, involves the whole range of human action aimed at the good. It inheres in the most personal activities of human beings, as well as those activities of people that reflect their aspirations for society. It inheres, therefore, not only in those things people do voluntarily for the public good, but also in the activities of the institutions of government, no less than in the very structures of government itself, that limit or encourage individual and group action. Therefore, morality is involved in every facet of life. As Locke said, "[m]oral actions belong therefore to the jurisdiction both of the outward and inward court; both of the civil and domestic governor; I mean, both of the magistrate and conscience."[104]

The question for Locke, as it is for us today, was: Which moral actions are properly left to individual conscience and which ones are properly left to civil government? Locke knew full well the difficulty in making a clear delineation between the "jurisdiction" of the civil government and the "jurisdiction" of conscience so that each does not interfere with the proper functioning of the other. As Locke said, "Here, therefore, is great danger, lest one of these jurisdictions entrench upon the other, and discord arise between the keeper of the public peace and the overseers of souls [i.e., consciences]." Still, Locke asserted that if one considers "rightly" all that he has "said concerning the limits of both these governments," "it will easily remove all difficulty in this matter."[105]

The framework Locke prescribed draws the line of moral authority between the two "governors"—the magistrate and conscience—at the point where the temporal good meets the eternal good. That is, those actions that involve "the temporal good and outward prosperity of the society," are in the scope of the authority of the magistrate, and those actions that involve "eternal salvation"—"what [an individual] . . . in his conscience is persuaded to be acceptable to the Almighty"[106]—are reserved to the individual.

But, as Locke knew, there are some activities in the "temporal" realm that pertain to "eternal salvation": How human beings conduct themselves in their daily lives determines to a great extent their salvation. In other words, worldly matters sometimes have eternal consequences. Hence, Locke further refined his delineation between the two.

As we have seen, Locke placed great stress on freedom of the individual, in particular, freedom of conscience because this is how human beings discern their highest duty—their duty to God. Accordingly, when Locke drew the bounds between the two jurisdictions, he weighted it on the side of conscience.

> [T]he observance of [those things necessary to the obtaining of God's favour] . . . is the highest obligation that lies upon mankind, and . . . our utmost care, application, and diligence ought to be exercised in the search and performance of them, because there is nothing in this world that is of any consideration in comparison with eternity.[107]

Accordingly, Locke placed in the jurisdiction of individual conscience everything except what is absolutely *required* for the temporal good, which was reserved to the magistrate. In fact, those things required for the temporal good consist of the very things Locke set out as sacred under his political theology—the social contract, which includes the preservation of the sacred civil rights, in particular the preservation of freedom of conscience, and the safety and general welfare of the people.[108]

> [T]he necessity of preserving men in the possession of what honest industry has already acquired, and also of preserving liberty and strength, whereby they may acquire what they may further want, obliges men to enter into society with one another, that by mutual assistance, and joint force, they may secure unto each other their properties in the things that contribute to the comfort and happiness of this life; leaving in the meanwhile to every man the care of his own eternal happiness, the attainment whereof can neither be facilitated by another man's industry, nor can the loss of it turn to another man's prejudice, nor the hope of it be forced from him by any external violence. . . .
>
> I mean, that provision may be made for the security of each man's private possessions; for the peace, riches, and public commodities of the whole people; and, as much as possible,

for the increase of their inward strength, against foreign invasions.[109]

Locke acknowledged that there may arise occasions where mistakes are made on both sides of the line as to the proper exercise of authority and concluded that in such cases "God alone" may judge. He recognized that as a practical matter the individual may disagree with the magistrate about those matters properly left to conscience and those in the purview of the magistrate. And Locke concluded that, when such a conflict arises, the individual must do what conscience directs, but nevertheless be subject to the punishment accorded by the state. Nevertheless, the state never legitimately treads into the jurisdiction of conscience unless its action involves a "political matter"—one necessary for the magistrate's obligations under, or for the preservation of, the social contract.[110]

⁂

RETHINKING THE PRIVATE/PUBLIC DICHOTOMY IN LOCKE'S POLITICAL THEOLOGY AND THE "PUBLIC" ROLE OF RELIGION

In establishing the "just bounds" between the jurisdiction of the state and the jurisdiction of conscience, Locke has been thought by most to have endorsed a distinction between public and private spheres of moral action,[111] religion being placed in the private sphere. Locke's express designation of the purview of the magistrate as "civil" and the purview of conscience as "domestic," and also as "outward" and "inward," respectively, supports this claim. But I contend that interpreting Locke as designating religion as "private" in a public/private dichotomy obscures the religious purpose underlying Locke's justification for civil governance.

"Public," although not originally intended as such, implies in common parlance "out in the open where people can see," while "private" connotes "in the home or within one's mind where no one can see." In contemporary common usage this has come to mean, respectively, "visible" and "hidden." According to this usage, religion, being relegated to the private sphere, is to be hidden—tucked away in the home where no one can see and where it will not bother others. Yet this clearly was not Locke's intention.

Recall that the temporal good is, for Locke, the worldly common good. That common good is the social contract itself, which is religiously grounded and is the means to the good life. The eternal good is everything else, which is reserved to individual conscience. But this does not correlate to "public" and "private" spheres of moral influence with religion on the "private" side. Rather, Locke expressly reserved a religious voice in these "temporal" public matters—a voice that includes religious arguments justifying and supporting the common good of the social contract.

First, Locke held that religious speech and action is appropriate in defense of the social contract itself and, therefore, the preservation of the sacred civil rights. In fact, it can be said that this is the highest duty of a citizen after the one owed to God, because it is directed toward ensuring one's ability to do one's duty to God. True, Locke asserted that *church* authority is not to impose its purported "God-given" justifications for political institutions on the people.[112] This was the top-down overarching worldview of those who held to traditional Christian political theory, based on Original Sin, which was rejected by Locke. Yet the social contract is justified, according to Locke, by what he holds *is* God-given: liberty and equality and, therefore, the sacred civil rights.

The difference between Locke's justification and the traditional Christian justification is that Locke's religious justification is made by reference to the *individual* who rationally chooses a political system that preserves freedom of conscience—so that he is able to find his way to God and produce the good from the ground up. Consequently, while Locke intended that top-down overarching worldview arguments are not appropriate in civil matters, he expressly sanctioned and even encouraged *ground-up* religious arguments in the public sphere. The reason is that "civil rights" are sacred rights and, thus, their sacred roots are rightly brought to the attention of civil authorities who seek to undermine them. While top-down justifications always lead to corruption of civil and church authority, and therefore undermine what is truly sacred, *ground-up arguments recognize the sacred foundations on which liberty stands.*

Additional support for this point can be found in the *Second Treatise's* express recognition of a place for resistance, rebellion, and even revolution whenever civil rights are ignored or violated by the civil authorities. Locke argued that, as a practical matter, the magistrate will be unable to keep the peace if civil rights are not recognized and preserved because "[t]he people generally ill treated, and contrary to right, will be ready upon any occasion to ease themselves of a burden that sits heavy upon them."[113] They will rise up in an effort to right the wrong. And rightfully so, according to Locke, because the magistrate will have failed in his duty to uphold the terms of the social contract, which require the preservation of these civil rights. In fact, then, it is the magistrate who has begun the rebellion by returning civil society to a "state of war."[114] Argumentation, resistance, and rebellion, which certainly are public, are then, justified. Moreover, because "civil rights" are "sacred rights," as we have seen, the very same religious arguments that were made by Locke are appropriately repeated by those who are resisting, as well as by those who speak on behalf of those who are resisting, in the "public sphere" in an effort to claim or restore such rights.

Further in this regard, Locke maintains that the oppressed hold a special place in preserving civil rights. He suggests that there is an opportunity for expansion of the understanding of the extent of civil rights beyond that which he may have recognized in his time. The oppressed guide us in an ever-unfolding understanding of the depth of these sacred rights, he implies. For "oppression raises ferments, and makes men struggle to cast off an uneasy and tyrannical yoke."[115] Consequently, as the oppressed make themselves known and demand the liberty and equality that is their sacred right, oppression should be rooted out by the magistrate. To do otherwise is to risk the peace and security of the commonwealth.

Just and moderate governments are everywhere quiet, every-where safe. But oppression raises ferments, and makes men struggle to cast off an uneasy and tyrannical yoke. . . .

Take away the partiality that is used towards them in matters of common right; change the laws, take away the penalties unto which they are subjected; and all things will immediately become safe and peaceable.[116]

Certainly, then, Locke could not have meant to silence the calls of the oppressed in the "public sphere" when the oppressed assert that they belong to God and, therefore, are entitled to liberty and equality—arguments that obviously are made on the very same religious grounds used by Locke. It follows, then, that religion, that is, individual free conscience imbued with God, is a proper subject in temporal, that is "public," matters when religious arguments are made in support of the social contract and the civil rights that are preserved by it.

Second, "eternal" matters are not necessarily "private" or "hidden" either. As I have said, Locke intended to create a forum for public discourse in which people can use all methods of exhortation to persuade others of the rightness of their opinions, including their opinions about the right path to God—that is, religion and its moral precepts. To the extent that these matters do not rise to the level of the "temporal" matters involving civil rights described above, these are not proper subjects to bring to the attention of the magistrate for enforcement by civil authority. *However, they certainly are matters for "public" persuasion and voluntary acceptance by individuals in accordance with their own consciences.*

Third, Locke expressly recognized that religion involves "public worship." By this Locke meant to include the worship of God by people together in "religious societies," that is, churches, wherein they "offer unto his Divine Majesty such service as they themselves are not ashamed of . . . ." However, there is nothing in Locke to suggest that "public worship" be kept hidden in an enclosed location set apart from others, but rather that it "by the purity of doctrine, holiness of life, and decent form of worship, . . . draw others unto the love of [what is considered by them to be] the true religion . . . ."[117] Accordingly, Locke expressly acknowledged that "public" worship would occur where it would be seen. However, public religion is subject to the admonition that insofar as it purports to assert its dominance over the civil authority by virtue of its doctrinal justification for a government of another sort, its public privilege would be revoked by Locke. For as Locke said: "[N]o opinions contrary to human society, or to those moral rules which are necessary to the preservation of civil society, are to be tolerated by the magistrate."[118] *

REDISCOVERING THE MORAL GROUND OF LOCKE'S POLITICAL THEOLOGY

We have been discussing the ways in which Locke conceived of the role of religion in "public." Let us turn now to a discussion of the "public" moral stance—the civil moral stance—that is expected of individuals who honor the sacred civil rights of others.

It was Locke's view that the public peace would prevail if people were treated fairly under the social contract by the magistrate, and transgressors of the social contract were punished appropriately. That way there would be no need for individuals to return to the state of nature and reclaim their right to punish such transgressors. In this regard, Locke sets out two fundamental rules.

First, one must do no harm to another in his "life, health, liberty, or possessions"—the fundamental rights of individuals in civil society.[119] With respect to religion, therefore, Locke expressly

---

* As we will see in chapter 3, however, the American founders expanded the idea of freedom to include toleration of all opinions, even those of the intolerant, as being essential to a free society in the search for truth. However, they did not extend this to include toleration of such contrary views to the degree that they would permit harm to the inalienable rights of others through the coercive force of government, which would undermine the Lockean fundamentals that form the basis for the social contract and government.

enjoined the civil magistrate to permit all activity of individuals unless an activity "prejudices," that is, does harm to, another.[120] This is so even if such activity is offensive, sinful, heretical, or otherwise disagreeable in the view of the complainant on account of his religion.

> But idolatry (say some) is a sin, and therefore not to be tolerated. If they said it were therefore to be avoided, the inference were good. But it does not follow that, because it is a sin, it ought therefore to be punished by the magistrate. For it does not belong unto the magistrate to make use of his sword in punishing everything, indifferently, that he takes to be a sin against God. Covetousness, uncharitableness, idleness, and many other things are sins, by the consent of all men, which yet no man ever said were to be punished by the magistrate. The reason is, because they are not prejudicial to other men's rights, nor do they break the public peace of societies. Nay even the sins of lying and perjury are nowhere punishable by laws; unless in certain cases, in which the real turpitude of the thing, and the offence against God, are not considered, but only the injury done unto men's neighbours, and to the commonwealth.[121]

Significantly, in this regard, Locke held to a second fundamental rule, which is in effect a reverse "Golden Rule": Do not do unto others what you would not want done unto you. In addition to supporting the "no harm rule," this reverse Golden Rule is the rule of logical consistency in Locke's argument, which Locke exhibited throughout his work and clearly held is a foundational principle of moral action. In this regard, we must not deny to others what we are not willing to deny to ourselves. To do otherwise would be hypocrisy, which Locke clearly held to be of the greatest offense to reason and God because it is in utter discord with the natural law of liberty and equality.

As regards religion, in particular Locke's *Letter Concerning Toleration* is replete with examples wherein he argues that if anyone expects to have freedom of conscience to do as he pleases under civil law, he must therefore expect the same right for others—no matter how disagreeable he finds the beliefs or actions of others to be. In just one of many examples, Locke states:

> It may be said: What if a Church be idolatrous, is that also to be tolerated by the magistrate? In answer I ask: What power can be given to the magistrate for the suppression of an idolatrous Church, which may not, in time and place, be made use of to the ruin of an orthodox one? For it must be remembered that the civil power is the same everywhere, and the religion of every prince is orthodox to himself. If, therefore, such a power be granted unto the civil magistrate in spirituals, as that at Geneva (for example), he may extirpate, by violence and blood, the religion which is there reputed idolatrous; by the same rule another magistrate, in some neighbouring country, may oppress the reformed religion; and, in India, the Christian.[122]

In other words, a person cannot expect to dictate doctrine to others without expecting that "by the same rule" another doctrine could be dictated to her.

Accordingly, we can conclude that it was Locke's view, in effect, that if the "no harm rule" and the "consistency/no hypocrisy rule" were applied as indicated above, all subjugations would be lifted. All people would be granted liberty and equality, which is their "natural" right, and "will think themselves so much the more bound to maintain the peace of the commonwealth as their condition is better in that place than elsewhere."[123] Peace would reign and real potential for goodness would flourish.

> And all the several separate congregations, like so many guardians of the public peace, will watch one another, that nothing may be innovated or changed in the form of government, because they can hope for nothing better than what they already enjoy; that is, an equal condition with their fellow-subjects, under a just and moderate government.[124]

Thus, Locke said: "we may draw towards a conclusion: the sum of all we drive at is that every man may enjoy the same rights that are granted to others."[125]

DISTINGUISHING LOCKE'S REASONABLE CHRISTIANITY FROM HIS POLITICAL THEOLOGY

As George Ewing has noted, Locke was "steeped in Christian tradition," having at one time stated, "A Christian I am sure I am."[126] There is no doubt that Locke was writing out of a Christian context.[127] And, in this regard, we can readily find the roots of Locke's political views in his reading of scripture. However, while Locke's political theology can be seen as being derived from his Christian roots, he should never be read as advocating the imposition of Christianity on others.

We are fortunate that we do not have to guess about Locke's Christian faith by deriving it from his childhood religious instruction, his education at Christ Church, Oxford, or his political works. Instead, Locke set forth a full account of his views on the Christian faith. He was sixty-three when he published *The Reasonableness of Christianity* in 1695, a work that set forth in simple language his "sole reading of the Scriptures (to which they all appeal) for the understanding of the Christian religion."[128] In turning to that work, we find that Locke's Christianity converges with his political theology in several ways.

Locke held that "true worshipers . . . worship the Father both in spirit and truth . . . as is with application of mind and sincerity of heart. . . ." Thus, temples and special places are not necessary to worship, "which by a pure heart might be performed anywhere." As Locke said, "[E]veryone was to look after his own heart, and to know that it was that alone which God had regard to and accepted."[129] That is why Locke rejected Original Sin and held that "everyone's sin is charged upon himself only."[130] Thus, according

to Locke's understanding of Christianity, God's concern is with individual human beings and not society as a whole or church
groups. This, as we have seen, is a central tenet of Locke's political
theology as well.

Moreover, Locke asserted that Christianity clearly holds that
God communicates with individual human beings through revelation and reason, which provide individuals with knowledge of the
eternal, immutable law, which it is their duty to obey.[131] As Locke
said, the "law . . . cannot be otherwise than what reason should
dictate,"[132] although discovery of truth through reason alone is extremely difficult.[133] Accordingly, it is revelation that provides the
key to truth, whose door can then be further opened by reason once
inspired by revelation. But all morality is derived from both reason
and revelation, which are based on the same eternal law.

Locke's political theology provides that human beings are created free and equal in the state of nature. This, too, is consistent
with his reading of scripture, which provides, according to Locke,
that everyone is created in the image of God and is equally subject
to the eternal immutable law of God and, therefore, has equal dignity before God. Moreover, because Locke believed that all human
beings have equal dignity before God, Locke emphasized the com-
mandment that human beings are to love their neighbors as themselves. Locke's conclusion that no one may harm another is
deducible from this, but is also consistent with certain moral injunctions from scripture, such as the injunction not to kill or steal.

That said, it is important that we not overstate the scope of
Locke's Christianity or his intentions regarding its place in his political theology. In order to understand Locke's Christianity more
clearly and the extent of its impact on his political theology, we
must keep in mind three things. First, Locke was a severe critic of
what he saw as the tendency of various Christian sects to claim
dominance—something he fought vehemently against, as we have
seen. He argued forcefully that this did not exemplify the true
Christian faith, which he contended rightfully promotes peace,
goodwill, and toleration.[134] Second, Locke had a very specific view
of what he considered to be "true" Christianity—one not shared, by

any means, with all Christians.[135] And, third, Locke did not seek to impose on others all that even he considered to be the true core of the Christian faith.[136]

Consequently, while we find that faith that Jesus was the Messiah is central to Locke's Christianity, it is omitted from Locke's political theology as are all matters that Locke considered to be purely matters of faith, such as belief in the miracles of Jesus—that is, matters not verifiable by reason. Locke adhered to the doctrine of justification by faith, but only if one is dedicated to good works.[137] He believed that Jesus restored to human beings what they lost in the Fall—eternal life—and that Jesus will pronounce judgment and reward or punish according to one's works. Yet all of these things are left out of his political theology. Why? The answer is that Locke's goal was not to establish the Kingdom of God as he saw it, but to establish a political framework that makes possible aiming for the Kingdom of God so as to ensure that its progress is not impeded.

CREATING THE POLITICAL CONTEXT FOR THE REALIZATION OF THE TRUE AND THE GOOD

The civil liberties Locke set out in his political works are not for liberty's sake alone. They have a purpose. They are part of a political structure that restrains only those things that impede the *possibility* of goodness. It is a context within which people from many religious persuasions are free so that they may do what conscience directs—what they believe is pleasing to God. That way truth is "left to shift for herself."[138] The good and the true that each individual pursues is not to be *dictated* by civil or religious authorities, but is to be the subject of persuasion and voluntary acceptance. The good and the true are to be *discovered* in revelation and reason brought to the public forum in dialogue with others in a process whose goal is the search for understanding and mutual consent. In this way, the "Spirit of truth" can "guide you into all truth. . . ."[139]

So we see that Locke's political theology establishes a political context within which people are free to be and do good. Consequently, Locke's Christianity is not a claim to the dominance of an overarching worldview. Rather, it provides only certain general principles that ground Locke's political theology, which reflect only the very basic premises of Locke's "authentic piety." That is, Locke's political theology provides the ground in which the seeds of the flowers of true faith can be planted. Yet it does not require one to be a gardener. Still, it does not prohibit the gardener from sharing the beauty of the visage or the scent of his blooms.

CHAPTER 3

The United States Constitution: Establishing America's Sacred Ground

> I esteem it above all things necessary to distinguish
> exactly the business of civil government from that
> of religion, and to settle the just bounds that lie
> between the one and the other.
> —John Locke, *A Letter Concerning Toleration* (1685)

REDISCOVERING JOHN LOCKE IN THE REVOLUTIONARY SPIRIT

John Locke did not, of course, settle the question as to the "just bounds" between the role of civil government and the role of religion once and for all. His own time was fraught with discord on the issue, as we have seen. But clearly it was his intention to leave his legacy so that generations after him might read his works and recognize in them the potential for creating a good society. And that legacy found its way into eighteenth-century thought where it had a substantial and profound impact. Most important for our purposes, Locke provided the formative foundation and language that shaped the American revolutionary mind and emboldened the American spirit.

Americans were in a unique position in the years leading up to, during, and just after the Revolution. They were in the position to set up any sort of government they wished, and they saw themselves as being in the original position of the state of nature of which Locke had written. As Thomas Hutchinson (then Lieutenant Governor of Massachusetts) said in 1764:

> [The colonists] thought themselves at full liberty . . . to establish such sort of government as they thought proper, and to form a new state as full to all intents and purposes as if they had been in a state of nature, and were making their first entrance into civil society.[1]

Being a people who, for the most part, had left behind societies with legacies of tyranny and oppression in both political and, in particular, religious matters, freedom from such persecutions and oppressions was foremost on their minds. While it is true that some came for economic benefit (e.g., the Virginia colony originally was founded as an economic venture), all colonies became, to greater and lesser extents, refuges for those persecuted in their own lands on account of religion.[2] Accordingly, in the years leading up to the revolution, Americans were, with few exceptions, of one mind in their support for establishing a republican form of government that would give effect to Locke's fundamentals.*

We can see from the colonists' expressions on the eve of the Revolution regarding human rights, which they held to be sacred, that there clearly was a debt owned to the writings of John Locke. "The Rights of the Colonists and a List of Infringements and Violations of Rights," drafted by Samuel Adams in Massachusetts in 1772, provides an especially striking example of just how deeply rooted Lockean ideas were in the beliefs of the Revolutionary generation. One of the first documents of the prerevolutionary resistance, it speaks of "Life, Liberty, and Property" as fundamental to the

---

* There is a considerable debate about whether the founding of the nation was based on Lockean liberalism or whether the emphasis on republican principles was more in the forefront. In that regard, I agree with Jerome Huyler that the establishment by the American founders of a republican form of government was not in opposition to Locke's political philosophy, rather it merely provided the "means" for preserving the "fundamentals" of Lockean liberalism. Jerome Huyler, *Locke in America: The Moral Philosophy of the Founding Era* (Lawrence: University of Kansas Press, 1995), 210 *et seq.*

"Laws of Nature," and the "State of Nature" and the contractual nature of society, and it expressly references Locke.[3] In fact, Locke's championing of the preservation of "life, liberty, and property" as fundamental to humankind was accepted, adopted and referenced universally by the American colonists in the formative documents of the states.[4] Furthermore, the phrase "life, liberty, and property" became the slogan that served to rally the populace during the Revolutionary period as it stood for all that Locke had held were the "natural rights" of humankind. For the Americans, then, Locke's ideas were not mere theory; rather they provided the basis for the political framework for the states and the nation—to make possible the good society that Locke had envisioned.

Not all agree with this assessment, however. Locke's influence on the American Revolution has been questioned in recent years by those who eschew America's "secular" and "liberal" foundations. In an effort to reclaim the religious roots of America, many are reconsidering the myth of America's founding by "deists"* and maintaining, instead, that it was evangelical sentiments, not the "rational philosophy" of the likes of Locke, that fed the revolutionary zeal of the late eighteenth century.[5]

But that assessment is based on the erroneous idea that Locke's views had little or no religious import. As we have seen, however, Locke's views were inspired by his "authentic piety," and his political thought is religiously grounded. While some in later generations involved in the political discourse may have stripped Locke of his religious roots, those roots were very clear, visible, and strongly felt on the eve of the American revolution.

Eighteenth-century America was witness to two significant religious impulses that were to provide the rationale for the decision to declare America's independence, as well as the impetus for the popular support of the Revolution—the evangelical movement and the rational religion movement. Significantly, both were fired, in large part, by Locke's political theology.

Nathan O. Hatch, among others, has argued that when the impact and vigor of the first Great Awakening declined after 1742, its

---

* For a brief explanation of deism and elaboration on this point, see pages 70–72 below.

original religious fervor was rekindled in the evangelical spirit that came to align its eschatological expectations with republican ideals.[6] In fact, those who experienced the "new birth" of their evangelical conversions embraced a personal relationship with God. This individualistic religious perspective inspired adherents to stand against authorities who opposed their newfound faith. When British policies became oppressive, this individualistic, "antiauthoritarianism" was readily turned against British officials.[7]

This spirit also was found in dominant religious traditions in the eighteenth-century American colonies. Nowhere was this more true than among the New England Congregationalists who always had a tendency to tie their eschatological hopes to the "New Israel"—America. Now that theme was grafted onto the cause of liberty and the conflict with the British Crown. America became not only a battleground for freedom from tyranny, but for salvation from the "evil power" that was now equated with "oppressive arbitrary civil governments."[8]

Locke's works became the inspiration for impassioned church sermons that linked freedom to God and advocated "natural rights," the "social compact," and the right, even the duty, to resist oppressive arbitrary government.[9] The cause of individual liberty, infused with Locke's ideas, his language, his authentic piety, became a religious cause. For the American religious, then, there was not only a political motivation for rebellion, but a religious impetus to revolution—a "Revolutionary revival,"[10] and that impulse had Locke woven into the very fabric of the revolutionary spirit.

At the same time, another religious trend was afoot in America. The Enlightenment, with its emphasis on reason, was infused into religion. By these lights, emotional religion was considered suspect—its adherents seen as unpredictable and irrational, easily swayed into mob action. All too common were the abuses perpetrated by such "mobs" in Europe, as well as America, when religious zeal gave way to religious persecution. The panacea, according to the rationalists, was calm reflection given over to reason. However, this did not necessarily imply an absence of "real" faith as often has been the charge. Those adhering to "rational religion" were not necessarily "deists" in the sense of eschewing the notion that God is active in the world.[11] Like Locke, who adamantly resisted the efforts of those who wished to place him in the deist camp, many who adhered to the "reasonable" approach to religion found reason and insight to be as much the source of an "authentic piety" as "new birth" at religious revivals around the country.

Obviously, those who espoused this view found a friend in Locke.[12] For Locke, as we have seen, the traditions and customs of institutionalized religion gave way to individualistic religion—*a reliance on individual conscience imbued with God discovered through reason and insight.* That view had led Locke to the conclusion that the only legitimate government is one created by mutual consent of the people so that individual conscience imbued with God would remain free, and never legitimately be infringed by government. And when infringed, the people would have a right to resistance and even rebellion. Clearly, Locke's political theology also was compatible with the sentiments of the religious rationalists as the country moved toward revolution.

So we see that Locke's authentic piety was the foundational force that inspired those who adhered to evangelical religion, as well as those who embraced "reasonable" religion. Locke was not, then, merely a "secular" philosopher for the intellectual elite. He was the prophet of America—the head and heart of the Revolution. Evidence of this is pervasive, but is most notable in the Declaration of Independence itself, which is grounded entirely on Locke:

> We hold these truths to be self-evident: that all men are created equal; that they are endowed, by their Creator, with certain inalienable rights: that among these are life, liberty, and the pursuit of happiness. That to secure these rights, governments are instituted among men, deriving their just powers from the consent of the governed; that whenever any form of government becomes destructive of these ends, it is the right of the people to alter or to abolish it, and to institute a new government, laying its foundation on such principles, and organizing its powers in such form, as

to them shall seem most likely to effect their safety and happiness.

It is clear that the very origins of the revolution are, for the most part, Lockean and are, thus, religiously grounded.* And, as we shall see in the pages to follow, the American political system that was established by the founders is religiously grounded in the same way, as well.

REDISCOVERING THE RELIGIOUS ROOTS OF THE AMERICAN POLITICAL SYSTEM

Central to the new system of government that the colonists envisioned was the preservation of the inalienable right that was recognized almost universally as fundamental—the right of conscience. Samuel Adams's "The Rights of the Colonists and a List of Infringements and Violations of Rights" (1772), referenced earlier, also illustrates that the prerevolutionary colonists followed Locke in asserting the importance of freedom of conscience or religious toleration (which is the same) and held it to be the hallmark of a true Christian, as did Locke:

> In regard to Religeon, mutual tolleration in the different professions thereof, is what all good and candid minds in all ages have ever practiced; and both by precept and example inculcated on mankind: And it is now generally agreed among christians that this spirit of toleration in the fullest extent consistent with the being of civil society "is the chief characteristical mark of the true church" & In so much that

---

* There are some who emphasize other "ideological origins" of the American Revolution. For example, Bernard Bailyn has claimed that oppositional writers such as John Trenchard and Thomas Gordon provided the greatest influence. But it has been credibly argued by Jerome Huyler in *Locke in America: The Moral Philosophy of the Founding Era* (Lawrence: University of Kansas Press, 1995) that the works of Trenchard and Gordon, and other works of the era, were grounded in Lockean fundamentals, as well.

Mr. Lock has asserted, and proved beyond the possibility of contradiction on any solid ground, that such toleration ought to be extended to all whose doctrines are now subversive of society.[13]

In fact, freedom of conscience was everywhere espoused by Americans as central to liberty. Accordingly, it was memorialized in every Revolutionary period state constitution or declaration of rights.* As the *Essex Result* (1778) had declared, using the same reasoning as did Locke and recognizing, too, the link between reason and God:

> [Certain rights] are unalienable, and of that importance, are called the rights of conscience. We have duties, for the discharge of which we are accountable to our Creator and benefactor, which no human power can cancel. What those duties are, is determinable by right reason, which may be, and is called, a well informed conscience. What this conscience dictates as our duty, is so; and that power which assumes a controul over it, is an usurper; for no consent can be pleaded to justify the controul, as any consent in this case is void.[14]

It is readily apparent why a free conscience was so important to the founding generation. For all their diversity, and whether or not church attendance was high or low, they were united in one way: They were a religious people.[15]† In fact, the documentary record is replete with references to God. This is evident in many of the state

---

* See Appendix B for a list of the freedom of religion provisions adopted in the Revolutionary period state constitutions and declarations of rights.

† There is considerable disagreement among scholars as to whether there was a decline in religion in eighteenth-century America, both sides supporting their arguments with credible evidence. See, for example, James H. Hutson, *Religion and the Founding of the American Republic* (Washington, DC: Library of Congress, 1998), 19, 24; Perry Miller, *The New England Mind: From Colony to Province* (Cambridge: Harvard University Press, 1953), 34–36. Apparently, this is considered important in the argument as to whether religion was or was not a significant force in the founding of the nation. In *Rediscovering* the argument is that the nation has a religious ground. Consequently, what is important is the way in which liberty became a sacred cause and the degree to which that sacred cause was embodied in the founding documents of the nation and the political system that was formed, regardless of whether church attendance was strong at the time of the founding.

constitutions and declarations of rights, the debates regarding their formation, and other documentation of the Revolutionary period. For example, the Vermont Declaration of Rights (1777) and the Pennsylvania Declaration of Rights (1776) reference "the Great Governor of the universe";[16] the Massachusetts Declaration of Rights (1780) references "the Great Legislator of the Universe";[17] James Madison's "A Memorial and Remonstrance" (1785) references "a duty towards the Creator";[18] and the list goes on and on. The Declaration of Independence itself references "the laws of nature and of nature's God," the "Supreme Judge of the world," and "Divine Providence." Clearly, the generally held view at the time was that there is God, and, furthermore, whether or not there were dissenters on this point, that the state and federal governments were being founded on this belief.

In fact, the founders saw themselves as being blessed by Providence. The "Letter of Agrippa" (1788), which has been credited to James Winthrop, put this sentiment succinctly: "This [the republican form of government] is the happy form under which we live, and which seems to mark us out as a people chosen of God."[19] But nowhere was it better expressed than by George Washington, himself, in his "Circular Address to the States" (1783) and "First Inaugural Address" (1789):

> The Citizens of America . . . are, from this period, to be considered as the Actors on a most conspicuous Theatre, which seems to be peculiarly designated by Providence for the display of human greatness and felicity; Here, they are not only surrounded with every thing which can contribute to the completion of private and domestic enjoyment, but Heaven has crowned all its other blessings, by giving a fairer opportunity for political happiness, than any other Nation has ever been favored with.[20]

> In tendering this homage to the Great Author of every public and private good, I assure myself that it expresses your sentiments not less than my own, nor those of my fellow-citizens at large less than either. No people can be

bound to acknowledge and adore the invisible hand which conducts the affairs of men, more than the people of the United States. Every step by which they have advanced to the character of an independent nation, seems to have been distinguished by some token of providential agency; and in the important revolution just accomplished in the system of the united Government, the tranquil deliberations and voluntary consent of so many distinct communities from which the event has resulted, cannot be compared with the means by which most Governments have been established, without some return of pious gratitude, along with an humble anticipation of the future blessings which the past seems to presage.[21]

Moreover, because Locke's political theology provided the foundation for the new governments, the "inalienable rights" were, in fact, Locke's "civil rights," which we have already seen were understood by Locke to be sacred rights given by God. And they clearly were understood as such by the founders, as well. "The Rights of the Colonists and List of Infringements and Violations of Rights" (1772) declared that "freedom [is] . . . the gift of God Almighty."[22] The "Address to the Inhabitants of Quebec" (1774) proclaimed that "[l]iberty of conscience in your religion" is something "God gave . . . to you."[23] Robert Yates's "Letters of Sydney" (1788) refers to "that freedom which God has a given you," and, even more directly, James Winthrop, in his "Letter of Agrippa" (1788), speaks of the fundamental rights "which we consider at present as sacred."[24] The Declaration of Independence clearly states that the "unalienable rights" are "endowed by" the "Creator."

Often historians and others have noted the references to God and the sacred rights, but have contended that the framers of the federal Constitution and Bill of Rights were primarily deists and conclude, therefore, that the framers did not really hold what we generally might think of today as a "religious" view. However, there is considerable evidence that the myth of America's founding by "deists" is an unlikely one.

Deism is a form of "rational religion" that rejects the mysteries of revealed religion and, instead, relies on what can be discovered and believed on the basis of reason alone. Significantly, it holds that while God created the universe, God is not active in human affairs. As a consequence, deists generally deny the divinity of Christ and challenge the authority of the Bible and church creeds and doctrines, such as the doctrine of the Trinity. Moreover, deism reduces religion to a system of morality.[25] Benjamin Franklin, Thomas Jefferson, George Washington, John Adams, and Alexander Hamilton often are referred to as deists in general histories of religion and the American Revolution.[26]

While there is support for the claim that such luminaries of the founding of America were adherents of "rational religion"—that is, they subjected revelation and faith to reason—there is little support for the idea that they were deists in the sense that they believed God to play no role in human affairs. In fact, the opposite appears to be the case. For example, Benjamin Franklin was of the view that God supports good religions and fails to support bad ones.[27] Moreover, in his "Motion for Prayers in the Convention" (1787) he stated: "I have lived, Sir, a long time; and the longer I live, the more convincing proofs I see of this Truth—*that God governs in the Affairs of Men.* And if a Sparrow cannot fall to Ground without his Notice, is it probable that an Empire can rise without his Aid?"[28] In addition, when asked what constitutes his religion, he replied:

> Here is my Creed. I believe in one God, Creator of the Universe. That he governs it by his Providence. That he ought to be worshipped. That the most acceptable Service we render to him is doing good to his other Children. That the soul of Man is immortal, and will be treated with Justice in another Life respecting its Conduct in this. These I take to be the fundamental Principles of all sound Religion, and I regard them as you do in whatever Sect I meet with them.[29]

In his "A Memorial and Remonstrance" (1785), James Madison referred to God as "the Governor of the Universe" and "the Universal

Sovereign,"[30] implying that God governs human affairs. And John Adams referred to himself as a "church going animal,"[31] and declared his belief in the intervention of God into human affairs when, in his proclamation for a national day of fasting, he stated:

> [There is] the governing providence of a Supreme Being and of the accountableness of men to Him as the searcher of hearts and the righteous distributor of rewards and punishments [the deep sense and full acknowledgement of which] are conducive equally to the happiness and rectitude of individuals and the well-being of communities.[32]

Moreover, even those whose "rational religion" primarily rested on morality held to the belief in immortality and future rewards and punishments. They maintained, therefore, that, in this way, God can operate indirectly through the conscience of individuals when such individuals perform the duties of conscience.

Jefferson is often cited as the most deistic of the founders. However, even here we find something more than just a rational morality. The opening sentence of Jefferson's "A Bill for Establishing Religious Freedom" (1779) begins:

> Well aware that the opinions and beliefs of men depend not on their own will, but follow involuntarily the evidence proposed to their minds; that Almighty God hath created the mind free, and manifested his supreme will that free it shall remain by making it altogether insusceptible of restraint; that all attempts to influence it by temporal punishments, or burthens, or by civil incapacitations, tend only to beget habits of hypocrisy and meanness, and are a departure from *the plan of the holy author of our religion,* who being lord both of body and mind, yet chose not to propagate it by coercions on either, as was in his Almighty power to do, but to extend it by its influence on reason alone . . . .[33]

This quotation shows that it was Jefferson's view that conscience is formed by reasoning through the "evidence" that is "proposed to their [individuals'] minds." And God, who is "lord of both body and mind," propagates God's "plan" by extending its influence on reason. In other words, as did Locke, Jefferson maintained that reason is divined from God and, through the opinions and beliefs of individuals based on reason, and the actions they engender, reason plays an important role in giving effect to God's plan.

We see, then, that the "rational religion" of these important figures in the founding of the nation was not deist in the strict sense. Rather, it was more akin to the "reasonable" religion of John Locke, which, we have seen, holds that there is God and that God's concern is not with society as a whole, but with individuals, and that true religion is sincere faith in God. Consequently, the founders—those adhering to "rational religion" as well as those following in more traditional religions—were in consensus: There is God, and God is active in history. Even more important: Those adhering to "rational religion," as well as the substantial evangelical population, held that God communicates with individuals—whether through reason and insight or through "new birth" conversion experiences.

Accordingly, both were antiauthoritarian as well, and therefore sought to ensure that individual conscience would remain free of coercion from both civil and ecclesiastical authorities. As the famous evangelical preacher of the Great Awakening, George Whitefield (1714–1770), had held, individual experience of conversion was the core of faith, not official church membership.[34] Others, as well, later preached the same message. For example, James McGready (c. 1758–1817) had said: "In that awful day, when the universe, assembled, must appear before the quick and the dead, the question brethren, will not be, were you a Presbyterian—a Seceder—a Covenanter—a Baptist—or a Methodist; but, did you experience a new birth?"[35] Jefferson, as well, rejected the notion that civil or ecclesiastical "legislators and rulers" have any legitimate authority over "the faith of others." He stated that the imposition of "their own opinions and modes of thinking" has "established and maintained false religions over the greatest part of the world and through all time . . . ." Furthermore,

Had not free inquiry been indulged at the era of the reformation, the corruptions of Christianity could not have been purged away. If it be restrained now, the present corruptions will be protected, and new ones encouraged.[36]

Hence, Jefferson, in accordance with Locke, as well as evangelical preachers, eschewed ecclesiastical authority, as well as civil authority, in matters of conscience, and sought to preserve individual freedom of conscience imbued with God in order that true faith could come to the fore and the good could be realized.

We see, then, that freedom of conscience generally was deemed by those of the founding generation to be the core civil right. However, it was understood that in order to ensure free conscience, and all the rights derived from liberty and equality, which were granted by God in the state of nature, it would be necessary for the new governments being formed to preserve such rights. The only issue, then, was not *whether* these sacred civil rights were to be protected, but *how* best to protect them. In accordance with Locke's political theology, the founders sought to establish a system of government that worked entirely differently than had any before—one that placed the pursuit of the good and a good society, to the greatest degree possible in the hands of the governed, just as Locke had promoted, rather than one that would permit the dictates of governors to override individuals' pursuit of the good.

THE STATES: TOWARD GOVERNMENT THAT ENSURES FREEDOM OF CONSCIENCE AND SEEKS TO PROMOTE A GOOD SOCIETY

As did John Locke, Americans of the Revolutionary period had direct experience of the negative effects of conscience fettered by civil government and ecclesiastical authorities in top-down overarching worldview political systems. Moreover, immediate European history reflected some of the most severe abuses that had been the consequence of the combination of religion and government—even Christianity and government—that history had known. There rather than being free to do what conscience directed, individuals were manipulated into serving the goals of such powers, which often were directed toward things such as avarice and the maintenance of power. And even when intentions were good, untold harms were perpetrated on individuals in the name of uniformity. This had been accomplished by outright force through imprisonment, torture, threat of death, as well as by controlling the information that came to individuals through censorship and indoctrination so that their minds were not free. Civil discord had prevailed where religious establishments reigned and dissenters challenged them, just as Locke had said.

Colonial governments, themselves, had provided ample evidence of many approaches to church and state relations and their various results. On the one hand, there was, for example, the Puritan theocracy of the Massachusetts Bay Colony, which had led to the trials and expulsions of "heretics," such as Ann Hutchinson and Roger Williams. On the other hand, there was the experience of colonies such as Pennsylvania and Rhode Island, which had tolerated many diverse groups of believers, including some considered very subversive at the time, where relative peace had prevailed. For example, Pennsylvania, the home of the Quakers, welcomed a Rosicrucian German group that "lived in caves along the banks of the Wissahickon Creek, awaiting the 'Woman of the Wilderness,' whose arrival would usher in the millennium."[37] And Rhode Island, which had been founded by Roger Williams after he had been forced out of the Massachusetts Bay Colony, welcomed Jews as early as 1658.[38]

It was understood by the founders, then, that individuals cannot flourish unless government ensures freedom of conscience, and that a society has no chance of being a good society unless government ensures the freedom to express conscience through speech and action. At the same time, however, it was also understood that the idea of liberty and equality, itself, had been derived from certain moral and religious precepts. In fact, the documentary record of the founding era is replete with statements declaring the importance of moral virtue in maintaining civil society and the importance of religion in maintaining moral virtue.[39] As John Adams said,

> "Statesmen . . . may plan and speculate for Liberty, but it is Religion and Morality alone, which can establish the Principles upon which Freedom can securely stand . . . . The only foundation of a free Constitution, is pure Virtue, and if this cannot be inspired into our People in a greater Measure, than we have it now, They may change their Rulers, and the forms of Government, but they will not obtain a lasting Liberty."[40]

Consequently, as the states formed their new governments "by the people," they were faced, in effect, with the same question faced by Locke: How can a government ensure freedom of conscience and its expression and nevertheless foster a society that is good?

The Americans sought to ensure that the inalienable rights would not be infringed by government by specifically reserving them in the constitutions and declarations of rights of the state governments they were forming, even though these rights were deemed by the Americans to be inalienable whether or not so delineated in a written constitution.[41] Those framing the new state governments acknowledged the inalienable rights expressly so that future generations would not fail to defer to them.

A majority of the states adopted "Declarations of Rights," New Hampshire being the only state to label its designation of rights as a "Bill of Rights."[42] New York, New Jersey, South Carolina, and Georgia did not have such a declaration or bill, but included provisions regarding the inalienable rights in the body of their constitutions.[43] Whatever the approach, however, the general consensus was that human beings are born free and equal under nature and therefore under God, and that, as a consequence, they have certain rights that cannot be relinquished by "mutual consent" when the social contract to form government is made.[44] As the Virginia Declaration of Rights (1776), which served as the model for eight of the states, said:

> [A]ll men are by nature equally free and independent, and have certain inherent rights, of which, when they enter into a state of society, they cannot, by any compact, deprive or divest their posterity; namely, the enjoyment of life and liberty, with the means of acquiring and possessing property, and pursuing and obtaining happiness and safety.[45]

While the acknowledgment of the inalienable rights took precedence, there was, secondarily, an effort to temper conscience with some caveats to ensure that conscience would be "real conscience" and not mere license.[46] For example, in an effort to focus liberty on the good, certain of the states enumerated moral virtues that were thought to be essential to the continuation of the free government that their constituents hoped they were creating. The "Virginia Declaration of Rights (1976)" stated "[t]hat no free Government, or the blessing of liberty, can be preserved to any people but by a firm adherence to justice, moderation, temperance, frugality, and virtue, and by frequent recurrence to fundamental principles." In addition, it stated that "it is the mutual duty of all to practice Christian forbearance, love, and charity, towards each other."[47] Similar provisions are found in the Pennsylvania Declaration of Rights (1776) and the Massachusetts Declaration of Rights (1780).[48] New York State declared broad rights of conscience, stating in its Constitution (1777), in words reminiscent of Locke:

> [W]hereas we are required, by the benevolent principles of rational liberty, not only to expel civil tyranny, but also to guard against that spiritual oppression and intolerance wherewith the bigotry and ambition of weak and wicked priests and princes have scourged mankind, this convention doth further, in the name and by the authority of the good people of this State, ordain, determine, and declare, that

the free exercise and enjoyment of religious profession and worship, without discrimination or preference, shall forever hereafter be allowed, within this State, to all mankind.[49]

Still, it provided that "the liberty of conscience, hereby granted, shall not be so construed as to excuse actions of licentiousness, or justify practices inconsistent with the peace or safety of this State."[50]

Some were reluctant to unhinge their newly forming governments from their Christian roots, even though they also knew that Christianity had been the support of persecution in the past. Still for many Americans it had been Christianity that had inspired them to travel the path of resistance and liberty in the first place; it had been Locke's own religious ground. Consequently, some states made specific references to Christian or general religious affiliation in an effort to place liberty explicitly within a moral or religious context. For example, the Delaware Declaration of Rights (1776) provided:

[A]ll men have a natural and unalienable right to worship Almighty God according to the dictates of their own consciences and understandings; and that no man ought or of right can be compelled to attend any religious worship or maintain any ministry contrary to or against his own free will and consent, and that no authority can or ought to be vested in, or assumed by any power whatever that shall in any case interfere with, or in any manner controul the right of conscience in the free exercise of religious worship.

Yet it went on to state that "all persons professing the Christian religion ought forever to enjoy equal rights and privileges in this state, unless under colour of religion, any man disturb the peace, the happiness or safety of society."[51]

The Maryland Declaration of Rights reserved full freedom of conscience only to those professing the Christian religion, as did the New Hampshire Bill of Rights, which stated that "every denomination of christians demeaning themselves quietly, and as good subjects of the state, shall be equally under the protection of the law:

and no subordination of any one sect or denomination to another, shall ever be established by law."[52]

Pennsylvania and Vermont took a more inclusive approach. Pennsylvania's constitution did not reference Christianity; however, it did require that one acknowledge the being of God in order to be entitled to full freedom of conscience, stating:

> Nor can any man, *who acknowledges the being of God,* be justly deprived or abridged of any civil right as a citizen, on account of his religious sentiments or peculiar mode of religious worship. . . .[53]

Similarly, Vermont preserved freedom of conscience, but stated that "every sect or denomination of people ought to observe the Sabbath, or the Lord's day, and keep up, and support, some sort of religious worship, which to them shall seem most agreeable to the revealed will of God."[54]

Most states required that there be an oath of office that included a statement with respect to one's religion—the "religious tests" for holding office. For example, the Pennsylvania Declaration of Rights, while expressing moderation in its religion clauses, required the following oath in order for one to serve in the Pennsylvania House of Representatives:

> I do believe in one God, the creator and governor of the universe, the rewarder of the good and the punisher of the wicked. And I do acknowledge the Scriptures of the Old and New Testament to be given by Divine inspiration.[55]

In addition, many people thought that the state should support religion. As Irenaeus wrote in a Massachusetts newspaper in March 9, 1780:

> [A] very respectable part of this Commonwealth look upon it as a duty which God required of Legislators, that they make suitable provision for the support of public worship

and teachers of religion. And not only so, but they esteem it as one of their most sacred and invaluable rights.[56]

In an effort to be more egalitarian in their approach to the support of religion, some states (e.g., Massachusetts, Connecticut, and New Hampshire) enacted "general assessment" laws that required each citizen to support the church of his choice and "nothingarians" to support public education.[57] On the other hand, Baptists who were perennial dissenters before, during, and after the Revolutionary period, as well as some other religious groups, generally were against any sort of state support of religion. As James H. Hutson has noted, the Baptist view was that "the best way for the state to support religion was to do nothing," because history reveals that religion only thrives when government and religion are completely separated.[58] Therefore, the Baptists' view was consistent with Locke's: Religion, if left on its own, would be more likely to remain pure and exemplify true faith.[59]

So we can see, then, that the formative period of the American governments involved some differences in the approach to the "just bounds" between civil government and conscience, which was in evidence in the various approaches of the states. Many, in an effort to ensure that their civil societies would be aimed at the good, took the view that some statement should be made in the state constitutions or declarations of rights as to what their framers believed to be the foundations and goals of freedom. But we should not conclude from this that the framers of the states' constitutions had abandoned Lockean fundamentals.

Whatever various provisions were adopted, and however they were enforced following adoption of the state constitutions and declarations of rights, one thing is most important to cull from all of this: What we, today, may view as limitations on liberty in some of the Revolutionary period state constitutions and declarations of rights, clearly were understood at the time to ensure that the political systems of the states reflected the fundamental ideals that had been derived from Locke's political theology; that is, they were believed to be necessary for the preservation of liberty, particularly freedom of conscience. Many believed, for example, that if public office were not limited to Christians, or in some cases to Protestants, there would be a grave risk of undermining the very fundamentals of the social contract that the framers of the state constitutions and declarations of rights were trying to preserve. That is, such provisions were understood, correctly or not, to enhance freedom of conscience for everyone. Consequently, while there certainly must have been a few holdouts for the traditional top-down overarching worldview approach for religion and government that had prevailed in Europe and some earlier colonial settlements, by the time of the adoption of the state constitutions, forced uniformity in religion was roundly rejected in every state, even in South Carolina, which had expressly established the "Christian Protestant religion" as the state church.

The reason is that, in general, the founders of the states viewed their mission as God's mission, and that mission was to ensure individual liberty, in particular freedom of conscience and its expression, so that there would be the greatest opportunity for society to reflect the good of God, as Locke had urged. And, as we will see, the approach taken in the United States Bill of Rights, which the states eventually were to follow, unequivocally embraced Locke's radical vision for freedom of conscience and its role in the creation of a good society and, in fact, took it even further.[60]

The United States: Toward Government that Ensures Freedom of Conscience and Creates the Context for the Search for the True and the Good

James Madison, known by posterity as the "Father of the Constitution," was the author of the original draft of the federal Bill of Rights, which he first presented to the newly formed United States House of Representatives on June 8, 1789. There is very little in the documentary record regarding the debates in the House and then the Senate, leading up to the passage of the Bill of Rights, nor is there much of a record of the debates in the various states regarding ratification of the Bill of Rights. What we do know, however, is that the Bill of Rights, which became the first ten amendments to the United States Constitution, was passed in substantially the original form submitted by James Madison to the House.*

It is safe to say that freedom of conscience generally was considered by the founders to be the most important of the inalienable rights. In fact, freedom of conscience had been recognized as inalienable in the state constitutions and declarations of rights even before freedom of speech had been so recognized.[61] James Madison stated that the right of "conscience of every man" in religion is "unalienable" because it derives from the "duty towards the Creator" and "[t]his duty is *precedent* both in order of time and degree of obligation, to the claims of Civil Society."[62] Irving Brant, a leading Madison biographer, concluded that "Madison looked upon liberty of conscience as the fundamental factor in freedom of religion, and religious freedom, to judge from the concentrated attention he gave it, as the fundamental freedom."[63]

While there had been considerable variations as to the expression of freedom of conscience among the charters for the colonies and, later, the constitutions and declarations of rights of the states, as well as other documents,[64] the eventual statement of the right

---

* Madison's original draft of what became the First Amendment read: "The civil rights of none shall be abridged on account of religious belief or worship, nor shall any national religion be established, nor shall the full and equal rights of conscience be in any manner, or on any pretext, infringed.

The people shall not be deprived or abridged of their right to speak, to write, or to publish their sentiments; and the freedom of the press, as one of the great bulwarks of liberty, shall be inviolable.

The people shall not be restrained from peaceably assembling and consulting for their common good; nor from applying to the Legislature by petitions, or remonstrances, for redress of their grievances." Bernard Schwartz, ed., *The Bill of Rights: A Documentary History* (New York, Toronto, London, Sydney: Chelsea House Publishers, 1971), 1026.

For other wording that was suggested during the debates on the Bill of Rights, see Appendix C.

in the First Amendment to the United States Constitution was unreserved:

> "Congress shall make no law respecting an establishment of religion, or prohibiting the free exercise thereof . . . ."

In addition, the body of the Constitution expressly provides that "no religious test shall ever be required as a qualification to any office or public trust under the United States" (Article VI). Significantly, the Religion Clauses, themselves, are broadly written. While we have no commentary in the documentary record of the debates on the Bill of Rights that expressly indicates that the clauses were intended to be broadly construed, we readily can deduce this to be true in that the United States Congress did not follow the approach of the state constitutions that had included express moral reservations. Had the framers of the federal Constitution wanted to avoid the obvious implication of broadly construed rights, they could have specified Christianity or belief in God as a requirement for full civil rights as did certain of the states.[65] Furthermore, Madison had said that his goal was to provide "the rights of Conscience in the fullest latitude."[66]

Moreover, there were other commentaries at the time that tended to show that the constitutional framers had to have been aware of the breadth of the rights they were acknowledging. For example, the Constitutional Convention was sent a letter, dated September 7, 1787, by Jonas Phillips, a Jew, wherein he argued for freedom of conscience and against a religious test for office that would exclude Jews.[67] In addition, Madison, in a letter to Jefferson dated October 17, 1788, noted that "[o]ne of the objections [to the United States Constitution] in New England was that the Constitution, by prohibiting religious tests, opened a door for Jews Turks & infidels."[68] And the founders were aware that they were setting the standard for generations to come who may not be as religiously homogeneous as their own generation. In 1787, when Richard Henry Lee argued in favor of the adoption of a bill of rights that included the right to free conscience, he stated: "It is true, we are not disposed to differ much, at present, about religion; but when we are making a constitution, it is to be hoped, for ages and millions yet unborn, why not establish the free exercise of religion, as a part of the national compact."[69]

Moreover, some of the founders unequivocally expressed the view that the inalienable right to freedom of conscience extends to people of all faiths, as did Locke. For example, Richard Henry Lee wrote to Madison: "I fully agree with the presbyterians, that true freedom embraces the Mahomitan [Moslem] and the Gentoo [Hindu] as well as the Christian religion."[70] And Jefferson's "Notes on Religion" (1776) echoed Locke when they stated: "He [Locke] says 'neither Pagan nor Mahomedan nor Jew ought to be excluded from the civil rights of the Commonwealth because of his religion.' Shall we suffer a Pagan to deal with us and not suffer him to pray to his god? . . . It is the refusing *toleration* to those of different opinion which has produced all the bustles and wars on account of religion."[71] Clearly Madison, too, held this view. He defeated a motion to limit to Christians the protections of Jefferson's Virginia "A Bill for Religious Freedom," which stated that "no man shall be compelled to frequent or support any religious worship, place, or ministry whatsoever . . . ."[72] But this view was expressed most eloquently of all by George Washington during the time that state ratification of the federal Bill of Rights was in process. In his "Letter to the Hebrew Congregation in Newport, Rhode Island" (August 18, 1790), he clearly acknowledged the obviously widely held view that, under the federal Bill of Rights, religious freedom was for all:

> All possess alike liberty of conscience, and immunities of citizenship. It is now no more that toleration is spoken of, as if it was by the indulgence of one class of people, that another enjoyed the exercise of their inherent national right. For happily the Government of the United States, which gives to bigotry no sanction, to persecution no assistance, requires only that they who live under its protection should demean themselves as good citizens, in giving it on all occasions their effectual support. . . . May the children of the

stock of Abraham, who dwell in this land, continue to merit and enjoy the good will of the other Inhabitants, while everyone shall sit in safety under his own vine and figtree, and there shall be none to make him afraid. May the Father of all mercies scatter light and not darkness in our paths, and make us all in our several vocations useful here, and in his own due time and way everlastingly happy.

Washington's "Letter to Roman Catholics in America" (March 1790) supports this view as well.[73]

Still, a central question remained for the framers of the United States Constitution, just as it had for those drafting the constitutions of the states: How can a government ensure freedom of conscience and its expression and nevertheless foster a society that is good? When it came to the actual wording, the framers of the United States Bill of Rights made an even bolder choice than did the framers of the state constitutions. Under the federal Bill of Rights, the right to free conscience no longer appeared along with expressions of particular goods. Rather, the federal Bill of Rights (and the United States Constitution as a whole) preserves the right to pursue the good, but does not enumerate corresponding duties.

But that omission was not meant to imply that that duty was not still in effect; as Robert Yates wrote in 1788: "If God hath given us freedom, are we not responsible to him for that as well as other talents?"[74] On the contrary, the expression of the duty was left out because it was believed that a free conscience is the only potential source of truth and goodness. Because political and ecclesiastical power, especially if combined, were deemed to corrupt truth, the good was not considered to be possible when such powers reign over conscience in any way. *Therefore, to the extent that enforcement of any particular good is placed in the hands of such powers, the potential for truth and goodness is thwarted.*

On the other hand, the founders were well aware that religious convictions can be a source of strife. Too often, they knew, religious zeal, just as other passions, can lead to persecution. As James Winthrop cautioned, "It is a just observation of his excellency, doctor Adams, in his learned defence of the American constitutions that unbridled passions produce the same effect, whether in king, nobility, or a mob."[75] And, in his "Address to the People of New York on the Constitution" (1788), John Jay cautioned: "As vice does not sow the seeds of virtue, so neither does passion cultivate the fruits of reason."[76] Consequently, it was understood that something significant was necessary to counter the potential threat of unbridled passions, religious or otherwise, to freedom of conscience and pursuit of the good. If an individual with free conscience is to be certain of the truth of her convictions, she must also be presented with all the points of view of others who also believe themselves to be informed by conscience. Accordingly, the defense against this threat to free conscience and pursuit of the good was to be full and free argument and debate.

It was clear to the founders, then, that the necessary conditions that ensure that truth will have an opportunity to prevail include not only free conscience, but also a political context in which the true and the good for individuals and society can arise out of the common debate of a free people where all are permitted to persuade others of their views. In this vein, Jefferson stated:

> [S]he [truth] is the proper and sufficient antagonist to error, and has nothing to fear from the conflict unless by human interposition [she is] disarmed of her natural weapons, free argument and debate; errors ceasing to be dangerous when it is permitted freely to contradict them.[77]

So, while there is considerable disagreement in today's discourse about the various minor differences between drafts of the First Amendment, a review of the language of the First Amendment, itself, and of prior drafts, together with a reading of the record at the time that does exist, makes clear that the United States Bill of Rights provides the broadest possible scope for free conscience to pursue truth and the goodness that truth engenders—not only for oneself or one's group, but for society as a whole. It does so not only by ensuring that individual conscience is free of governmental restraint whatsoever, but also by creating a political context for the expression of free conscience in speech and action through the complementary rights also granted in the First Amendment to the United States Constitution, which follow the Religion Clauses:

> . . . or abridging the freedom of speech, or of the press; or the right of the people to peaceably assemble, and to petition the Government for a redress of grievances.

In other words, the First Amendment not only preserves freedom of conscience, but also provides (1) that everyone is free to speak his or her conscience, (2) that the press is free of governmental restraint and, therefore, it is to be a forum for commentary that makes sure conscience is fully informed, (3) that the people are able to assemble to express conscience and consider their joint pursuit of the good, and (4) that grievances can be expressed to the government and be addressed. In effect, then, the free speech, free press, assembly, and petition clauses of the First Amendment derive from freedom of conscience in that their purpose is to create the political context within which free conscience can be informed and expressed. Together with the "Religion Clauses," they are the "rights of conscience."

It is not reasonable to conclude, therefore, that the failure of the framers of the First Amendment to reference "conscience" (such as the proposed and rejected "nor shall the rights of conscience be infringed") was meant to imply a limitation or rejection of the rights of individual conscience, as opposed to formal religious group worship. The founders continued to use the phrase "freedom of conscience" for what they had accomplished even after the passage of the Bill of Rights by the First Congress, and individual liberty of conscience had been a primary focus throughout. Clearly, the First Amendment that was passed by the First Congress was meant to preserve the "rights of conscience."*

---

* See, for example, the quotation of George Washington included on page 83–84 above.

This becomes even more clear when we recognize that the word "religion" was not intended to limit the effect of the Religion Clauses to religious institutions and doctrine, as many in our contemporary debate mistakenly contend. On the contrary, the intended effect was to preserve "personal piety or relationship with God," that is, faith and belief—the common meaning of the word at the time. As discussed in the definitional section in Appendix A, it was not until the *nineteenth* century that the word "religion" came to be used commonly to denote "an objective systematic entity," that is, a "church." Accordingly, the proscriptions in the First Amendment against laws "prohibiting the free exercise [of religion] and against laws "respecting an establishment of religion" should be read together as it is now clear that they were designed to ensure that individual conscience would be free from coercion—*not that religious organizations would be free or that only those who are members of religious organizations with systems of beliefs would be free.* Consequently, whatever the founders meant by "an establishment," it is clear that making laws "respecting an establishment" was deemed by the founders to infringe freedom of conscience.[78] Clearly, then, any contemporary debate about "establishments" should be focused on whether individual freedom of conscience or the free and open forum for debate and action is diminished by the proposed interpretation, not what the founders meant by "an establishment," which is, unfortunately, the focus of much of the contemporary debate and is difficult, at best, to discern.[79]

In summary, Madison's fear that a federal Bill of Rights' free conscience provision "would be narrowed much more than they are likely ever to be by an assumed power"[80] was not realized. The United States' expression of Locke's fundamentals was broadly articulated, clear, and unambiguous. Therefore, full and complete toleration where "bigotry [has] no sanction," as George Washington had put it, was acknowledged as the inalienable right of all and was embodied in the Bill of Rights. Furthermore, the First Amendment also created the political context within which conscience could be expressed through speech and action, so that it would be possible for the true and the good to prevail in society. As Jefferson, echoing

Locke, had declared in "A Bill for Establishing Religious Freedom": "[T]ruth is great and will prevail if left to herself."[81]

Significantly, as we have seen, freedom of conscience and the political context for its expression in speech and action is religiously grounded in a political theology. Being derived from God, with all that follows as Locke had anticipated, it is civil society's sacred ground. More specifically, it is "America's Sacred Ground." As John Dickenson wrote in 1788:

> [A] constitution is the organization of the contributed rights in society. Government is the exercise of them. It is intended for the benefit of the governed; of course [it] can have no just powers but what conduce to that end: and the awfulness of the trust is demonstrated in this—that it is founded on the nature of man, that is, on the will of his Maker, and is therefore sacred. It is an offence against Heaven, to violate that trust.[82]

Exploring the Theological Terrain of America's Sacred Ground

The founders understood themselves to be "establishing" a new government, which included the express preservation of the inalienable rights. While, as a part of this, they expressly provided that there be no laws "respecting an establishment of religion," they nevertheless *did* establish America's Sacred Ground in both the states and the United States.[83] And, as we have seen, America's Sacred Ground is religiously grounded because it is based on a theology, which is derived from Locke's fundamentals and which, in turn, provides the foundation for the American political system.[84]

The concepts of the "state of nature," the inherent freedom and equality of all human beings, and therefore their "natural rights," including the right to rebel when the natural rights are infringed, are all derived from this initial theological premise: There is God who created human beings free and equal. And there is a fundamental assumption about God: God communicates the "natural law" through revelation, insight, and nature, including reason, to individuals. Further, God is not coercive. However, while human beings are free, still, they owe a duty to their Creator to be and do in accordance with the natural law. The only legitimate judge, other than God, as to what constitutes this duty and the natural law (other than what is required as the basis for America's Sacred Ground itself) is each individual for himself according to his own conscience. That is why freedom of conscience and its expression in speech and action are inalienable rights. That expression may lead to the development of "spontaneous societies," as Locke called them, which will be authentic communities because, like God, they are not coercive. Moreover, through free argument and debate, conscience will be tested and revealed as "truth shifts for herself," making possible the realization of the good society through the speech and action of the people from a variety of perspectives.

While the establishment of America's Sacred Ground was not an establishment of Christianity, to claim that it owes no debt to Christianity is to ignore the history of Western thought. Certainly, the general and simple theology of America's Sacred Ground was derived from Locke's "reasonable Christianity," as well as the Christianity of the founders. But as I pointed out in chapter 2 with regard to Locke, and is now also clear for the founders in chapter 3, Locke and the American founders held Christian religious beliefs that were more extensive than the basic theology of America's Sacred Ground. For example, Locke, as was shown in chapter 2, was a devoted Christian and active member of the Church of England throughout his life, and John Adams, too, was committed to his Christian faith. Yet neither based his political ideas on all that constituted his faith. Rather, America's Sacred Ground was founded only on those things considered at the time to be generally applicable, universal principles, regardless of any particular faith. Some may have concluded, as did John Adams, that those principles were the general principles of Christianity.[85] But even when they did hold that the principles of the republic were the general principles of Christianity, they were not referring to a tradition of Christianity aligned with any particular church. Rather, John Adams (and others) admonished all not to "look backward" but "forward" in the Enlightenment tradition of, for example, Hume and Locke.[86] Whatever Adams or others may have meant by the "general principles of Christianity," it was not the view that Christianity should be imposed on the masses *en toto* in order to enforce uniformity.

Accordingly, although the general fundamentals of the American system are derived from Christianity, they are not all that any particular Christianity has ever been.[87] Therefore, we can say that America's Sacred Ground consists of elements in common with some forms of Christianity (e.g., not all forms of Christianity hold that God's relationship is with individuals or that human beings are free). But we can also say, in the case of those forms of Christianity that do hold elements in common with America's Sacred Ground, that America's Sacred Ground and those forms of Christianity are not coextensive either; the latter inevitably provides a more elaborate theology than the simple theology of America's Sacred Ground. Consequently, America's Sacred Ground provides that no one's particular vision of "God's plan" is to be imposed on society as a whole as is the case with top-down overarching worldview justifications for a social order—not any particular Christian vision, not even John Locke's own vision of Christianity, nor the vision of any particular founder.

Just as was the case with Locke's fundamentals, America's Sacred Ground can be readily distinguished from the religious overarching worldview approaches to government that Locke and the founders sought to avoid. A religious overarching worldview provides a unified vision of all the specific ways in which a conception of the "divine order" should be reflected in the social order. This is the approach of such religiopolitical systems past and present that combine a particular religious doctrine with the force of law from top to bottom, for example, medieval Catholicism and the Holy Roman Empire, the Church of England and the seventeenth-century British Crown (which Locke opposed), Neo-Confucianism and the eleventh- and twelfth-century Song Dynasty in China, Islam and Saudi Arabia today.* While it is true that the American system is religiously grounded, too, its theological premises are grounded, not in a conception of a divine order to be reflected in the social order, but in the individual and her relationship to God. Consequently, to the degree that coercive power was granted by the founders to governmental authorities, its objective is theological—to protect and preserve God's relationship with individuals and the expressions of conscience that derive from it, but not to determine what conscience should direct.

COMPARING THE MORAL TERRAIN OF AMERICA'S SACRED GROUND WITH THE MORAL ORDER OF OVERARCHING WORLDVIEW APPROACHES TO GOVERNMENT

The "overarching worldview" versus "sacred ground" terminology is not merely a change in metaphor that amounts only to form without substance. Rather, embracing America's Sacred Ground involves a completely different way of thinking about how a society should be structured so that it will be a society with the greatest chance of being morally good. Under an overarching worldview approach, a "unifying" order—whether understood as having been derived from a "divine order" or another source—is deemed to be *morally right* by the authority in power; all that is in discord with that unifying order is deemed to be *morally wrong* by that authority. Then, when that authority enforces that moral order through the coercive power of the state, it is a moral order dictated by the state.

---

* Of course, nonreligious movements may promote top-down overarching worldviews as well. For example, Karl Marx was a major critic of religion; however, his own communist ideology was an overarching worldview that functioned much as did the religious overarching worldviews referenced above, at least as it was applied.

True, such an authority actually might have the best of intentions and even have good ideas about what is morally correct, Locke and the founders allowed. The problem is that when *any* authority is provided with the instrumentalities of political government and law, so that coercion can be used to enforce a unifying order in the social order, such authorities are prone to corruption, even when that unity is asserted as a means to promote public peace and safety. Moreover, the use of coercive mechanisms for the purpose of establishing an overarching worldview is *ultimately* corrupting, Locke and the founders held, because it is an attempt to usurp the will of God, which is directed to each individual and not to such authorities—who can never know what God intends for others.

As a consequence, top-down overarching worldview approaches to government, even when intentions are good, ultimately lead to oppression through dominance, which, in turn, results in uprisings by those who are oppressed (and their advocates)—and social discord follows. Therefore, societies based on such approaches *never, ultimately, are good.* That is why the founders clearly sought to establish a political system that avoided the use of coercive power to the greatest degree possible. This view is evidenced in George Washington's "Letter to the Hebrew Congregation" quoted on pages 83–84. And it is also how Jefferson understood it:

> [A]ll attempts to influence it [conscience] by temporal punishments, or burthens, or by civil incapacitations, tend only to beget habits of hypocrisy and meanness, and are a departure from the plan of the holy author of our religion.[88]

To understand more clearly how America's Sacred Ground differs from such top-down overarching worldview approaches to government, it is necessary to examine more closely the political context created, in effect, by the founders' Constitution. This is the context within which conscience is to be expressed—the "Public Forum." When we look more closely, we find that it actually is comprised of two levels or fields of moral inquiry. The first is the forum for debate about and action in support of things that preserve, endorse, reveal, clarify, and expound on America's Sacred Ground. Also, those things that are deemed to undermine America's Sacred Ground are discussed, clarified, and rejected. Accordingly, this is the forum about the extent and limit of America's Sacred Ground, which preserves the sacred civil rights, in particular freedom of conscience and the Public Forum, itself. This forum was incorporated as fundamental to the American system through the founding documents of the nation. I call this level the "Civic Public Forum."

The second level or field of moral inquiry is the forum for debate and action that involves those matters left to individual choice—where the moral and immoral are as understood by individuals themselves.* This is where everyone is permitted to use all means of persuasion in the context of America's Sacred Ground to convince others of the truth of one's convictions and the rightness of one's moral code of action, or to be persuaded in the debate as to the truth of the convictions and program for moral action of others. I call this the "Conscientious Public Forum."

Only matters involving the Civic Public Forum can be the subject of governmental force of law, regulation, and judicial decisions. The reason is that the preservation of the sacred civil rights, especially freedom of conscience and its expression in speech and action, as well as the Public Forum itself, is essential to create the context for the discovery of truth and, therefore, the realization of the good. Then, the actual realization of the good is a matter of persuasion and voluntary choice in the Conscientious Public Forum. Of course, the line between these two fields of moral inquiry is a matter for debate as well. However, the existence of the basic framework of America's Sacred Ground is sacred and inviolable.

Clearly, then, instead of having a system setting out from top to bottom how society should be structured and then using the

---

*It is important to point out here that while I am focusing on the "religion and values debate," this is not the only subject-matter for the Public Forum. All that is created, spoken, or acted in the Public Forum contributes to society—art, dance, music, and so on. In other words, the Public Forum is not only the realm for the potential realization of the true and good, but of the beautiful as well.

force of law to ensure uniformity, as is the case with overarching worldview approaches, America's Sacred Ground leaves nearly all of the judgments about what is morally right and wrong to individuals. This is the vast moral landscape left to individual pursuit of the good in the Conscientious Public Forum where people build, create, believe, debate and take action on America's Sacred Ground—where the "moral order" is left to the collective individual contributions each person makes to society.

The Civic and Conscientious Morality of the Two-Tiered Public Forum

But there is more to the moral landscape of America's Sacred Ground than this. There are, in essence, certain fundamental principles that arise out of the Public Forum and its two levels of moral inquiry. While nearly all moral judgments are left to individuals, two fundamental civic moral principles must be upheld in order to preserve America's Sacred Ground—and, therefore, they belong to the Civic Public Forum and have the force of law behind them. First, no one may harm another in his life, liberty, or property. That is, the sacred civil rights of others must not be infringed. The American understanding of this is embodied in the provisions of the Constitution and should be reflected in the laws of the land. The interpretation of laws, and the enactment of other laws in furtherance of America's Sacred Ground, are matters for debate in the Civic Public Forum, but the fundamental principle of "no harm," itself, which was derived from Locke and embodied in the Bill of Rights, is sacred.[89]

Of course, it is necessary for law to be concerned with the safety and general welfare of the people. But this really falls within the scope of the "no harm" principle, as well. In other words, such purposes must always have in view the main goal, which is to preserve conscience and its expression in speech and action up to the point where such expressions infringe on the rights of others. Therefore, such purposes are only legitimate, if the law based on them does not limit conscience and its expression, except to the limited degree necessary to preserve these rights for all.

The second principle is related to the first; it is the law of consistency/no hypocrisy. As Locke argued, to deny others what one is not willing to deny oneself is contrary to the fundamental principles of liberty and equality, which derive from God. Accordingly, a law producing such an effect can never be legitimate under America's Sacred Ground.

It is important to point out here that there are certain elements of Locke's work that would have involved limitations on the Public Forum that were not adopted by the founders. First, full civil rights were not limited by the founders to those who profess a belief in God, as Locke had proposed and as had been the approach in certain states. Second, Locke argued that civil authorities should not tolerate intolerance. But as Jefferson noted, the founders went further than Locke in these regards:

> Locke denies tolerance to those who entertain opinions contrary to those moral rules necessary for the preservation of society; as for instance, . . . [those] who will not own and teach the duty of tolerating all men in matters of religion; or who deny the existence of a god (it was a great thing to go so far—as he himself says of the parliament which framed the act of toleration but where he stopped short we may go on).[90]

Accordingly, intolerance was not prohibited by the founders, except to the degree that it rises to the level of harm to others in their life, liberty, or property—their sacred civil rights—where the prohibition of intolerance is warranted to preserve America's Sacred Ground. And atheism was not made a bar to being accorded full civil rights.

In addition, it is important to acknowledge that in their own time the founders did not reflect the full import of the Bill of

Rights in their legal system, and, to the degree that they did not, they violated their own principles. For example, women were not accorded the full reach of the sacred civil rights, and slavery was not abolished, although many had spoken against it. Jefferson had included a criticism of it in his original draft of the Declaration of Independence, and elsewhere he had warned that God's justice would not permit the institution of slavery to continue:

> Nothing is more certainly written in the book of fate than that these people are to be free.

> I tremble for my country when I reflect that God is just; that his justice cannot sleep forever . . . .[91]

Yet even Jefferson failed to free his own slaves and believed that, when freed, the former slaves should live separate from whites.

But we should not conclude that, because the founders violated their own principles, those principles were not still fundamental to the American system. On the contrary, what those who understood the full reach of America's Sacred Ground did not accomplish at the time of the founding was nevertheless inherent in the system, itself, and has remained there as a latent force continually moving toward its full realization.

In fact, the founders left the Civic Public Forum open to the principles of America's Sacred Ground, expressly stating in Amendment Nine of the Bill of Rights: "The enumeration in the Constitution, of certain rights, shall not be construed to deny or disparage others retained by the people." In other words, the particular enumerations and, I would add, interpretations of them at any particular time, do not preclude a reinvestigation of them based on the political theology undergirding them as the discourse in the Civic Public Forum evolves. Furthermore, we may recall that inherent in Locke's political theology was the understanding that those who remain oppressed will rise up to right the harms against them. This was understood, as well, by the founders. As Jefferson stated: "[It is] no wonder the oppressed should rebel, and they will continue to rebel and raise disturbance until their civil rights are full[y] restored to them and all partial distinctions, exclusions and incapacitations removed."[92] Accordingly, the oppressed hold a special place for America's Sacred Ground, as they did for Locke, because they guide America to an ever-unfolding understanding of the depth of the sacred civil rights—as has occurred throughout American history.

America's Sacred Ground implies moral rules for the Conscientious Public Forum as well. These do not, of course, involve the force of law and so are matters for persuasion and voluntary compliance. Nevertheless, they are moral principles derived from Locke's political theology for the Conscientious Public Forum that one *should* follow if the political system devised by the founders is to realize its full potential and not be usurped by an individual's or group's overarching worldview.

The founders established America's Sacred Ground for a purpose—to make possible the pursuit of the good society through the debate and action of individuals of conscience from a plurality of perspectives. Consequently, regardless of the fact that we, the people, cannot be forced by law to comply, we, nevertheless, have conscientious moral obligations in the Conscientious Public Forum.

The conscientious moral principles recall our discussion of Locke and are the heart of the Conscientious Public Forum. Before I set out these principles, however, it is important that it be understood as background that everyone is a participant in the Public Forum. Whatever each individual says or does *is his participation*, no matter how "public" or "private" that individual's contribution or lack of contribution to society. Participation is inherent in the American political system itself; it is, to a large extent, what freedom is for. And because the American political system is "by the people," what the people collectively do with it (or not) is what it is.

With this in mind, and recognizing the importance of conscience and the goal of the founders to make possible a good society, we can readily anticipate the first conscientious moral precept: Each individual has a duty to move beyond one's own wants and desires, and to broaden one's sights to the "universal" or, if one prefers, the whole collective (however understood, whether religiously or not) and try to reflect on and discern through conscience (however conceived) what it is that promotes the good for society within the context of the Public Forum of America's Sacred Ground.

The second is related to the first. Each individual has a conscientious moral obligation to do one's best to contribute, within the context of America's Sacred Ground, to the development of a good society. This is done not only though one's own speech and action, but by listening sufficiently to "take in" and understand the views of others, so that conscience is informed and the good can be revealed or reconfirmed.

If enough of us do not adhere to these conscientious moral principles, then we will end up proving our founders wrong: a society of free individuals does not promote the good—not even the good as separately conceived by society's various constituents; it promotes a licentious society where individuals have no regard for their nation and its future, only themselves. When that happens— when we have lost sight of what freedom was for—we will surely be in danger of losing the liberties that the founders and all of our forbears fought so hard to give to "ages and millions yet unborn."[93]

So now we can see that while many of the founders argued that moral virtue is of central importance in the maintenance of civil society, they also upheld liberty. Edwin Gaustad has written: "Adams stood for morality, but he also stood for liberty, and that has never been an easy distinction to maintain . . . ."[94] But, on the contrary, the founders' theological ground does not require that a distinction be made between liberty and morality. Rather, the founders saw liberty and morality not in opposition but as complements, leading to the same end—the possibility of a good society. And so when we come across the many assertions of the founders regarding the importance of morality to the legal/political system they adopted, this does not necessitate the conclusion that they held all moral values to be matters appropriate for coercive action on the part of the state. Rather, first they sought to establish and preserve America's Sacred Ground. And, second, to the degree that the founders asserted moral values beyond what is required for that purpose, they were using persuasion for voluntary compliance at the level of the Conscientious Public Forum.

THE ROLE OF RELIGION IN THE PUBLIC FORUM AND IN THE PURSUIT OF THE GOOD

Now that I have clarified the basic framework of the Public Forum and its moral principles, it is important to set out just what is to be the role of religion in it. To do so we need to distinguish America's Sacred Ground from a widely held view that contrasts the "public" from the "private," and then limits the role of religion in "public" life accordingly.

Just as they do with Locke, scholars often hold the view that the founders provided for "public" and "private" spheres of moral action. Those matters that pertain to the "public" sphere are matters for law, regulation, and judicial decisions. Those matters that pertain to the "private" sphere are matters that are exempt or "free" from such governmental coercive force. Under this dichotomy, religion, being free, is therefore a matter for the "private" sphere.

While such scholars are correct, of course, that certain matters are the appropriate subject of laws and others are not, the choice of terminology is unfortunate because it is misleading. These terms— "public" and "private"—not only have a specified meaning for academic discourse, but they have metaphoric significance in popular and political discourse, as well. Their metaphoric meanings are problematic because they obscure the obvious intentions of the founders and confound the popular and public debate about religion's role in shaping moral values in society and, therefore, making possible the pursuit of the good. As said in chapter 2, the common usage of the term "public" implies "visible" to people in general, while "private" has come to mean "hidden" from people in general. According to this metaphoric usage, religion, being relegated to the private sphere, is to be hidden—tucked away in one's home or church where no one can see and it will not bother others. This clearly was not the intention of the founders.

As was so with Locke, the founders' clear intentions were that religion (in the sense of individual conscience imbued with God, including through reason) was to be free of restraint and that the force of government was never to be afforded to religious authorities so as to ensure that conscience would remain free. However, it was also clear, as was so with Locke, that the founders not only permitted, but encouraged religious people's contributions in the public sphere: How else could truth "shift for herself"? *Accordingly, religious participation belongs at both levels of the Public Forum.*

Religious people certainly are appropriate and significant participants in the Civic Public Forum. After all, the American founders grounded it in God, just as did Locke, and, therefore, the civil rights are sacred rights. It follows then that no one can rightly argue that religion is not a subject for public debate at this level. In fact, religion has a very important role to play at the level of the Civic Public Forum in preserving, clarifying, and promoting liberty and equality. And, if the oppressed (and those who advocate for them) are to perform their role in guiding America to an ever-unfolding understanding of the depth of the sacred civil rights by rising up to right the wrongs against them, then argumentation, resistance, and in severe cases, even rebellion, *which certainly are public*, become necessary. When this is so, the underlying religious roots of America's Sacred Ground are rightly brought to the attention of the civil authorities who may be undermining them or not fully recognizing the extent of them.

There are numerous examples of religion's participation at this level, where religious arguments have been used in support of the clarification of the fundamental principles underlying America's Sacred Ground. One example involves the Quakers. The Quakers were active participants in the Civic Public Forum in the years leading up to the Civil War and before as advocates for the abolition of slavery. They used religious arguments in the Civic Public Forum in support of their view that the fundamental principles of America's Sacred Ground—freedom and equality under

God—necessarily must include Africans. A second example involves the "holiness" movement of the mid-nineteenth century. This was an evangelical movement that spawned the likes of Elizabeth Cady Stanton and Phoebe Palmer, who argued in favor of women's rights. Stanton and Palmer used religious arguments in the Civic Public Forum in support of their view that the fundamental principles of America's Sacred Ground—freedom and equality under God—necessarily must include women.[95]

Turning now to the Conscientious Public Forum, recall that it is the greater part of the pursuit of the good. This is where, as Locke envisioned and the founders provided, all manner of persuasion may be used to convince others of the rightness of one's views; this is where one is free to be and do all that one believes reflects the true and the good, so long as one is not in conflict with the fundamentals of America's Sacred Ground. Certainly, religious voices were intended by the founders to play an important role at this level, as well. Here, religious people are invited to share the sincerity of their convictions and the certainty of their truths in an effort to convince others, or to be persuaded by others, as to what is the right path for making a better world and to ensure personal salvation. The role of religion at this level also has been exhibited throughout history when those of various religious convictions have argued for such things as greater church attendance, ways of structuring the authority within the family, and the importance of certain virtues, such as chastity, temperance, and forbearance, for promoting a good life here and now—as well as for eternity.

In summary, then, religious people are to be important participants in the Public Forum at both levels because America's Sacred Ground and its sacred civil rights are based, in large part, on the theological conviction that each of us owes a duty to our Creator to do according to the natural law as each individual conscience discerns it through revelation, spiritual insight, and reason. And that discernment includes contributing one's views, as well as fully considering the views of others, in an open and free forum for debate and action—the two-tiered Public Forum—in a deliberative process through which God reveals or reconfirms to conscience what one's duty entails. The individual, because free, is able to act in accordance with that call, constrained only by the principles embodied in America's Sacred Ground. In this way, God's plan can be revealed, discovered, and grasped by a free people participating in the creation of the good society. It can be built one brick at a time from the ground up on America's Sacred Ground.

AMERICA'S SACRED GROUND: THE FOUNDATION FOR PLURALISM AND MULTICULTURALISM THAT REFUTES THE CLAIMS OF MORAL RELATIVITY

Many philosophers, political scientists, legal theorists, and others may argue that the founders' original intentions, as described in this work, are no more credible as a source for the foundation of the American system as any other. This is just one framework among many possible choices that could make a claim on "general and/or universal" grounds that, in fact, is as morally relative as any other, they might say. By way of example, they might point to problems with the foundations of Locke's own thinking. Locke argued that matters of faith are not legitimately enforced by civil government. Yet he would not have permitted full civil rights to those who do not believe in God—an enforcement of faith. Moreover, his whole system, which was adopted by the founders, begins with God—a matter of faith. In addition, it is widely held that "conscience," which is at the center of the America's Sacred Ground, is formed in one's social context and, therefore, does not have the universal referent that the founders and others in their day assumed it had. Instead of "rediscovering" an American foundation (or ground), such critics might hold that, as problems arise, we should be open to new ideas and ways of thinking about society, and look for solutions that can have effective practical applications. In addition, some of these critics may argue that any foundational claim, including America's Sacred Ground, threatens the existence of the plurality of views we now enjoy, many of which arise out of the various multicultural perspectives that thrive in the contemporary United States.

In my view, however, all these critics take for granted what it is that permits the very things such critics hope to preserve. That is, they do not recognize that they are assuming unwittingly the very foundational context within which the conversations about those perspectives are occurring. Accordingly, they are assuming the fundamental values that ground the very debates about moral relativity, pluralism, and multiculturalism in which they are participating.

What is often missed is that, once America's Sacred Ground was established, it created the forum for debate about the social good. And that debate has developed to the point where it now has an inherent foundational "catch-22" logic to it: Arguments against America's Sacred Ground must fail at their outset because the existence of America's Sacred Ground is what allows for all of the arguments to be raised in the first place. Accordingly, *to assert the moral foundationlessness of the American political system is to risk the silencing of one's own voice in the debate.* This is so, particularly for anyone making an argument that all such foundational claims are relative—with no ethical foundation more credible than any other claim in the plurality of perspectives in our multicultural society.

To elaborate: In a society governed by a top-down overarching worldview, there would be no place for the moral relativist's views. In fact, such views would be likely to be highly censored because they would contravene the overarching worldview in power. Therefore, such a system is not an alternative to America's Sacred Ground for the moral relativists' participation. But the moral relativist might argue: What about a system framed around the concept of moral relativity itself? Wouldn't such a system provide the widest acceptance of all views because it would not value any one more highly than another? The answer is that such a system, if it were possible to conceive of one, most certainly would be an anarchistic return to a "state of war" in the "state of nature" where competing forces vie for dominance. There would be no foundation to hold in place *the value of acceptance of all views* that such an argument purports to hold; any moral or other claim could prevail in the competition. Consequently, there would be a high risk that the prevailing claim would result in an overarching worldview that would prove to be the demise of the relativist's participation, as well as the participation of those with any other of the plurality of perspectives not consistent with the one then in authority. Clearly, this is not what the founders intended, but more significantly for the discourse today, it is doubtful that this is what is intended by the moral relativists themselves—or the pluralists or multiculturalists either, for that matter.

From the beginning of the nation, liberty has been conceived of as "ordered liberty"; that is, everyone is to have maximum freedom up to the point where one's freedom infringes on the liberty of others. In other words, liberty is given full sway up to the point where it results in "harm." This is the only way that there can be a society that is free for *all*, and not a "*free-for-all*" akin to what occurs in the state of nature. Only the ordered liberty of America's Sacred Ground preserves the value that it is "good" to have all voices expressed and considered, and all actions not otherwise in violation of America's Sacred Ground accomplished.

Clearly, the only framework within which the moral relativist's argument is welcome is the one that creates the widest possible participation for everyone—America's Sacred Ground, the one that holds in place the basic moral foundation of the Public Forum and individual participation in it. In effect, then, America's Sacred Ground is the foundation on which antifoundationalist/moral relativist arguments can be made. It is the foundation that makes pluralism and multiculturalism possible. No other of the plurality of perspectives, including the moral relativist's perspective, can make this claim. Accordingly, the moral relativist's argument against the moral foundation of America's Sacred Ground is without justification as it is inconsistent with itself and promotes results at odds with its own primary assumptions.

This can be seen more clearly when we recognize that the moral relativist's argument does not threaten America's Sacred Ground, properly understood, as it does overarching worldviews; rather, the relativist's argument supports America's Sacred Ground. The reason is that with every participation in the Public Forum, the relativist is validating the system that permits its voice to be heard. What is validated is *our foundation—our Sacred Ground.* This forms the basis for the fundamental values of the American system, which have served from the beginning and have come to the fore ever more prominently as their full import has been played out as our history unfolds. This, of course, includes the value that it is *good* to provide a forum where all views can be expressed, even the views of moral relativists, and where many religiocultural expressions are possible. We must not forget this. To undermine America's Sacred Ground in the name of moral relativity is to bring about the demise of what it is that makes the expression of a plurality of perspectives, including those of moral relativists, possible in the first place.

America's Sacred Ground as the Common Good: Where Religious Voices Are Prominent and Truth Can Shift for Herself

The prevailing view of the founders—the one that was given effect in the First Amendment—was that freedom of conscience is at the core of truth and truth is the herald of the good. And the good only prevails, it was held, in a free forum for debate and action where truth can "shift for herself." If, and only if, the Public Forum is free and open, and conscience is expressed, can it be said, as it was said in the *Essex Result* (1778), that "[t]he voice of the people is . . . the voice of God."[96] There is no other political system under which this can be the case because, as Locke said (and Jefferson echoed): "[I]f truth makes not her way into the understanding by her own light, she will be but the weaker for any borrowed force violence can add to her."[97]

Thus, freedom of conscience was not preserved as a kind of benign right for the private benefit of individual people. Rather, the expression of the free consciences of the people in the Public Forum was deemed to be central to the entire American enterprise because it was to be not only an end for individuals, but the *means* to a good society. That is, while freedom of conscience is private and voluntary (Madison)[98] and thus "solely between man and his God" (Jefferson),[99] *freedom's function is to promote the public, as well as the private, good.*

It follows, then, that civil government's jurisdiction involves only that which preserves American's Sacred Ground, in particular, freedom of conscience and the two-tiered Public Forum for debate and action—the subject of the Civic Public Forum. Everything else is left to the jurisdiction of individual conscience and its expression in speech and action in the Conscientious Public Forum. Of course, the Civic Public Forum requires debate and the enactment of laws that provide for the safety and general welfare of the people as well, as Locke also provided, which creates issues as to when such matters promote or detract from America's Sacred Ground. But what we must always remember is that America's Sacred Ground, itself, is sacrosanct. It must never be supplanted with any group's or individual's conception of the divine or other unifying order as a top-down overarching worldview (in whole or in part) for all to live by—for this can never produce a good society, as history has shown.

That is why under the federal Bill of Rights, the good was not expressed by the founders as any particular good. Instead, an underlying concept of the good prevailed—one derived from Locke: The social contract, now in the form of a republican government that preserves the inalienable, sacred civil rights, and therefore expressions of conscience, *is the common good* through which the realization of an even greater good is possible.

> The common good, therefore, is the end of civil government, and common consent, the foundation on which it is established.[100]

Part II

Rooting the Contemporary Debate

in Sacred Ground

CHAPTER 4

Taking Sides and Looking Left

Litterary talents may be prostituted and the powers
of genius debased to subserve the purposes of
ambition or avarice; but the feelings of the heart
will dictate the language of truth, and the
simplicity of her accents will proclaim the infamy
of those, who betray the rights of the people, under
the specious, and popular pretence of justice,
consolidation, and dignity.
— Elbridge Gerry, *Observations of the New Constitution
and the Federal and State Conventions* (1788)

UNRAVELING THE CONTEMPORARY DEBATE

Now that we have rediscovered America's Sacred Ground, we can
explore the contemporary debate about religion and moral values
in public life in light of it. In coming to terms with the various perspectives competing in the debate, we will gain a very clear understanding of how those perspectives shape the debate and how they
compare/contrast with America's Sacred Ground. To accomplish
this, we will be looking back to works from the last decade that are
good representatives of three "sides" in the debates—secular left, religious right, and the accommodationists, who generally view themselves as taking a more moderate or "middle" approach than the
extremes.

In so doing, we will find that we have discovered a key to unraveling the confused and potentially damaging rhetoric of the current debate that has skewed the discourse—sending all sides in directions never intended by the founders of our nation. In this way, the debate can be placed on its proper footing—the only one that keeps open the two-tiered Public Forum for debate and action, which, as we have seen, is at the core of the American system. To fail to do this is to risk eroding the sacred foundations of the American system, which have made the all of debates possible in the first place.

EMBRACING THE FEARS AT THE EXTREMES: LEFT AND RIGHT

James Hunter, in his influential 1991 book *Culture Wars: The Struggle to Define America*,[1] and Alasdair MacIntyre, in his often-cited and pivotal 1981 book *After Virtue: A Study in Moral Theory*,[2] as well as many other writers, have assessed the debate about moral values in America as being a problem of competing "worldviews" or "metanarratives," each vying for dominance. For example, Hunter defines the problem in terms of it being a "cultural conflict" that is a "political and social hostility rooted in different systems of moral understanding." He goes on to conclude that "[t]he end to which these hostilities tend is the domination of one cultural and moral ethos over all others."[3] Of course, Hunter and MacIntyre are correct that there is a contentious debate going on. But I hold that the very framing of the debate in this way—as competing worldviews vying for dominance—represents a failure of such writers to recognize that all sides in the debate, and those attempting an analysis, such as themselves, are ignoring what should be the common ground—America's Sacred Ground.

Hunter explores the "polarizing impulses" in the debate and identifies one of the main problems as being "extremist rhetoric" on both sides of the "cultural divide" between what he refers to as the "traditionalists" and the "progressivists," roughly the religious right and the secular left, respectively. In an effort to push a political agenda, each side, in effect, demonizes the other, Hunter argues, making real engaged dialogue an unrealizable hope. The result is that the views of those "in the middle of these debates" (who Hunter presumably believes would be more reasonable) are left unheard.[4]

Having been involved in a number of discussions with people of both the secular left and religious right about the role of religion in public life, I have come to believe that one of the main reasons for the polarization of the positions in the debate that Hunter identifies is not the need to grandstand for fundraising or other purposes, as Hunter argues, but the failure of each side to adequately address the fears being brought to their attention by the other. The result of this failure is more and more extreme expressions of those fears in an effort to have them recognized and understood. As these extreme fears are expressed, the opposite side's fears are raised even higher, leading those on that side to express more fear in order to prevent the worst they fear from being realized by the other. As each side continues to ignore what are perceived to be the central issues by the other, a real, and in my view, reasonable concern develops by those who have been unheard that prevents even the most modest of compromises: *If the other side cannot see the fearful potentialities I see, how can I trust them in a compromise that moves even a little bit closer to the eventuality of that fear?* The result is a ping-pong effect, the consequence of which is the complete eroding of any possible common ground.

While I agree with Hunter that engaged dialogue may be our only hope, I do not agree that it will occur, as Hunter implies, by having each side step off the grandstand of the extremist views it expresses in mailers for fundraising, in the polarized media debate on issues, and so on. Rather, as Hunter hints at the end of his book, I contend that engaged dialogue will occur only if each side addresses the real fears of the other side.

Significantly, it is by examining the extremes that we can begin to see the ways in which the failure to rediscover and embrace

America's Sacred Ground confounds the debate, making authentic dialogue unlikely. This can been accomplished by closely examining representatives of the two "sides" in the debate. Certainly, there are many participants in the debate with more tempered views than some of those I have chosen as representatives. However, I believe that by examining the extremes and then starkly contrasting them with America's Sacred Ground, we can more readily grasp the ways in which America's Sacred Ground, if rediscovered, provides a common ground on which real, engaged discourse among those holding the various perspectives, including the more tempered ones, could occur. In doing so, we will see that by failing to walk on America's Sacred Ground in the discourse, both extremes gradually undermine it. The result is that both are walking down the same road—one that leads away from America's Sacred Ground and toward an end that no one ultimately desires, one that leads to the dominance of someone in the debate—someone who might not represent oneself.

Let us turn now to an examination of representative perspectives from the secular left and religious right and address the issues just raised.

Thomas W. Flynn is a self-proclaimed "militant" secular humanist, author of *The Trouble with Christmas*,[5] editor of *Free Inquiry*, a "free-thought" periodical, and co-founder of the *Secular Humanist Bulletin*. He argues in his 1996 article, "The Case for Affirmative Secularism," for a "militantly" strict separation of church and state. In his view, public life should be devoid of "religious language, symbols, and subject matter" and the "public square" should be "naked" because this is the only way to appropriately accommodate America's increasingly "religiously diverse population."[6] I have chosen this article as representative of the extreme secular left as it summarizes many of the most radical arguments on that side of the debate and is representative of the polarized position most feared by the religious right.

Flynn asserts that his goal is the preservation of religious freedom. The central and fundamental fear he expresses in that regard, however, is that Christianity, with perhaps an accommodation of

Judaism, will continue to be a dominant force in public life, or perhaps even enhance its dominant position. Accordingly, minority religions and atheistic secular humanists, such as himself, will be suppressed. In this regard, Flynn decries "that infrastructure of unjust preferences" for Christianity that he believes pervades American public life.

> A century and a half ago, America was like a music hall in which a Protestant bully, having seized the stage, kept the microphone all to himself. Today the Protestant bully has allowed Catholic and Jewish sidekicks to join him onstage—no small reform. But this Judeo-Christian oligopoly behaves as disgracefully as the Protestant monopoly it succeeded, stiff-arming unbelievers, Muslims, Hindus, Buddhists, and whomever else might want to mount the stage and speak a few words into that coveted microphone. That is the context in which Christians' claims about their rights to "free religious expression" need to be evaluated.[7]

But Flynn's fears do not end there. Unless religion is removed entirely from public life, Flynn contends, the demographic shift to a greater and greater plurality of religious groups will lead to tremendous discord—even "religious violence"—as various religions, which are inherently uncompromising, are offended by others' religious speech.[8] He provides examples from history where religious dominance has led to social harms—the Southern Baptist Conference's defense of slavery in pre–Civil War America, the atrocities of Christians during the Crusades, and there are others. His point is that religion is a danger to the public peace. When any particular religion dominates, it has a tendency toward harm of those who disagree. When there is a plurality of religions, there is the potential for conflict among them, which can lead to violence. Moreover, even if violence does not result, the religious are unable to participate in any democratic dialogue, he contends. "Democracy demands compromise," he writes, "and absolutist religious faith, zealously held is the antithesis of compromise." Conse-quently, the religious cannot be "good democrats."[9]

In order to have an orderly and reasonable dialogue, we must remove religious speech and action from public life, Flynn argues. Only through the complete "secularization" of public life, making the public sphere a "religion free, value-neutral" zone, is real dialogue and compromise possible.

> The public square must be stripped so bare of religious references that Americans of all faiths can occupy it in com-fort and with realistic expectations of equality. . . . [T]he alternative is the near-certainty that America's public institutions will become battlegrounds between Christian traditionalists and New Outsider militants.[10]

Quoting a colleague, he argues that secularization does not "threaten" the rights of Christians to free religious expression, as they have contended, but is "simply an attempt to put an end to the privileged position that religion [has] enjoyed."[11] Flynn sees that the current trend is not toward secularization, however, and states that "the price of this failure is a future of religiously mediated social unrest," and when this occurs "there will be little secularists can do about it except to say, 'We told you so.'"[12]

When we look at various publications by people of the religious right, we see that there is little attempt to address concerns such as those raised by Flynn and others in his camp. The religious right generally fails even to acknowledge such fears, setting them aside as rhetorical fictions. Rather, they move directly to critique, thus con-firming Flynn's assessment that they are uncompromising and blind to the intolerance and potential social unrest to which reli-gious dominance leads. I recall, in particular, one typical response on the part of a writer of the religious right to secularist attempts to remove religious speech from public life. Instead of addressing the concerns raised by such secularists, the response moved to a cri-tique: If all kinds of other speech, even offensive and pornographic speech, are permitted in the public sphere, how can religious speech legitimately be denied a voice? The writer argued.

The question . . . [is], notwithstanding the general constitutional principle that forbids government discrimination
among viewpoints, how much worse does the Establishment Clause allow (or require) states to treat believers than
non-believers? The question, put differently by Justice
Scalia, is whether piety is on a par with pornography,
whether (in my words) the Madonna is on a par with
Madonna.[13]

While this is wonderful rhetoric when one is "preaching to the
choir," this does not address Flynn's concern that religion can lead to
real and tangible harm. In other words, Flynn's view might be that *the*
Madonna should *not* be on a par with Madonna because Madonna
has not been used as a justification for the persecution of countless
thousands, while *the* Madonna has. In other words, it does not address the concern that religious persecution and social unrest is perceived by the Flynns of the world as nearly inevitable whenever *any*
religion holds sway with the governing power structure. Instead,
the religious right continues to assert its place in the public life with
ever-increasing vigor, thus, proving to the Flynns of the world that
the religious right, in fact, *is* a threat because the religious right
fails to see the real dangers that the Flynns fear. Consequently, the
Flynns fight even harder against the religious right.

At the other extreme, fears are raised that, similarly, are not addressed by the secular left. M. Stanton Evans is a former chairman of
the American Conservative Union. Evans's book, *The Theme Is
Freedom: Religion, Politics, and the American Tradition*, published
by Regnery Publishing, a well-known conservative publisher, provides a perspective from the religious right.[14] I chose this book because it is especially representative of a spate of books on the side of
the debate that argues for a privileged place for Christianity in the
public discourse, and because in some ways his argument appears
to be similar to my own. However, as we shall see, it differs in fundamental ways. Evans probably would not see himself as representative of an "extreme" conservative position (and he attempts to

distinguish himself from it), and perhaps not even as a member of the religious right. Nevertheless, the views he presents support the extreme position of the religious right and, therefore, provide a theoretical basis for it.* Moreover, in his book, Evans purports to present a reasonable historical and political analysis rather than an emotional faith-based justification for the religious right, and so he provides a plausible intellectual argument, which makes it particularly troublesome for the secular left.

Evans, similarly to Flynn, asserts that his goal is the preservation of freedom. Evans's basic theme is that the founders sought to preserve freedom from governmental interference. Accordingly, their focus was limited government.[15] The primary freedom the founders sought to preserve, Evans implies, was economic freedom. Thus, Evans laments the burgeoning central government of the United States and argues in favor of "free market" economics and Christian moral values. He claims this as a "conservative" cause that opposes the "liberal" push for more governmental programs and, therefore, greater governmental control.[16] I will be leaving aside an analysis of the defense of "free market" economics on such grounds, among other things, for a later work.[17] What is pertinent for our purposes here is Evans's argument in favor of a prominent role for Christianity in the preservation of freedom and in shaping American moral values.

The central and fundamental fear Evans expresses is that "liberal," Enlightenment-based ideology is inherently threatening to freedom. He contends, in this regard, that the secularism that it has spawned "is in fact a substitute form of religious faith."[18] Specifically, Evans claims that Enlightenment ideology is equivalent to the "radical agenda" of the "class/struggle/imperialism" theories of those who promote Marxism "in the guise of 'multiculturalism,'

---

*Evans does attempt to distinguish himself from "big government conservatives who think the state should inculcate virtue in its people" (Evans, 96), but he fails to explain precisely how his thesis can be distinguished from theirs. His promotion of Christianity *en toto* as America's overarching worldview and his argument that there are no bounds between church and state, in fact, cuts more in favor of such "big government conservatives" than toward the freedom he purports to preserve.

radical feminism, Afrocentrism, and the like."[19] This perspective is based on philosophical materialism, he reasons, which rejects God as the absolute foundation of reality. Evans is particularly concerned that such ideas support Marxist conclusions that "religion and morality are merely expressions of dominant economic interests, and [therefore religion and morality] need to be attacked and overthrown precisely for this reason."[20]

But his fears are more far reaching than Marxism. He is expressing concern about moral relativism itself. It is Evans's view that a failure to acknowledge God as the moral foundation of our freedom results in a potential for totalitarian ideologies to arise.[21] Nihilistic and skeptical theories about moral foundations give rise to "secular" ideologies that fill the void that remains when the foundation of freedom is removed, he contends. These ideologies take over "at the level of religion," trading "secular" determinism for the "theological determinism" that provided the former foundation.[22] When secularist views are permitted to replace the original "theological determinism" of the founders, he contends, "spiritual freedom" is lost.

> When religious value is denied in the realm of spirit, but reasserted in the secular order, dominion over every facet of life converges in a single center; the political regime becomes both church and state, and claims authority over faith and conscience.

When faith and conscience are denied, Evans contends, totalitarianism is not far behind.[23]

When we look at publications by people of the secular left, we see that there is little attempt to address concerns such as those raised by Evans and others on the religious right. The secular left generally ignores such fears and moves directly to arguments that the Evanses of the world are merely attempting to assert Christian dominance. The effect is that those on the religious right are ever more fearful that so-called secularists do not see the potential of their own ideology to suppress freedom. One typical response from the secular left is that of Ronald A. Lindsay. Instead of addressing concerns raised by the religious right, he moves directly to critique.

> What is going on here is whining: whining by individuals and groups who have been deprived of the truly privileged position they once enjoyed. For most of this country's history, theism, in particular Christianity, has enjoyed favor. . . . The courts have put an end to some, but certainly not all, of the collaboration between church and state. In doing so, the courts have upset many who assumed that this was the proper way of doing things, the American way of doing things, and who did not see anything coercive, let alone unconstitutional, about such practices.[24]

Again, this is great rhetoric for "preaching to the choir," but it does not address Evans's concern that secularizing away America's biblical foundations will lead to harm—even totalitarianism. Rather, the extreme secular left continues to assert that the neutralizing of the public sphere of religious influences is the means to freedom, thus, proving to the Evanses of the world that the secular left is a real threat to freedom because it fails to see that "neutrality" amounts to suppression of those who are religious and, ultimately, suppression of others as well.

Neither side "engages" the other's fears. Rather, both merely brush aside those fears with misstatements of the issues and assertions that they are not valid concerns. For example, Flynn asserts: "Christians' claims that secularization threatens their 'rights' to free expression are no more credible than those of the Jim Crow–era Southern whites that integration endangered their rights to self-determination."[25] Or, the religious right ignores the concerns altogether and uses heightened rhetoric to drive home a point. For example, Evans contends that secularist ideologies ultimately are informed by a "species of neopaganism" that was fused into Enlightenment ideologies and involve "the immersion of human existence in the cycles of physical nature."[26]

The first thing that strikes one about the debate at the extremes, however, is that both extremes are in essential agreement at the core of their arguments: Freedom must be preserved; oppressive dominance must be avoided. Significantly, each sees itself as the best guardian of freedom, and each believes the other to be disingenuous in this claim.

When we look at the arguments from the perspective of America's Sacred Ground, however, two things are revealed. First, we see that *the fears of both sides are justified.* Second, we see that both sides are undermining the very thing that *does* preserve freedom—America's Sacred Ground. They, in fact, exemplify the "cultural conflict" of "competing moral languages" that Hunter and MacIntyre address in their works. And both undermine America's Sacred Ground by asserting a dominant overarching worldview, in an attempt to exclude the other from the Public Forum, and by obscuring the foundations of our freedoms with argumentation that seeks to support their own dominance.

RECONSIDERING THE SECULAR LEFT FROM THE PERSPECTIVE OF AMERICA'S SACRED GROUND

If there is ever to be a debate on common ground, the extreme secular left must come to understand the ways in which its perspective differs from that of America's Sacred Ground. A starting point is to take account of the fears expressed by the religious right that the secular left is asserting an ideology at the level of religion that claims dominance and excludes others. It is my view that because the secular left perceives secularism to be the best guardian of freedom, it is blind to its own potential for dominance, just as the right has argued.

There is a reason why it perceives itself to be the best guardian of freedom. The reason is that it sees itself as the only one in the debate who is really concerned about the rights and interests of nonbelievers and those of marginalized minority perspectives. To preserve those rights and interests, the secular left, including the believers in its midst, promotes a nonbeliever—devoid of religion—public life.

In order to understand this perspective, we must remember that nonbelievers have been an especially suppressed group historically. Consequently, they have good reason to fear that any dominance (other than their own), particularly religious dominance, necessarily will result in suppression of *them*. Because nonbelievers are free under the current system and social climate, which limits religion in public life, the secular left mistakenly perceives this system and social climate as being freer for everyone. What they fail to recognize, however, is that freedom for nonbelievers has been gained by them through the suppression of others—the religious.

Because those in the secular left fail to recognize this, they perceive their position as being one of "neutrality." However, this "neutral field" is, in actuality, another overarching worldview—something not missed by those on the other side, as we have seen. The top-down nature of their perspective is revealed in that they assert a kind of uniformity in the public arena. The secular left attempts to accomplish this by eliminating certain expressions—religious expressions—from the public square. Its uniformity is "naked" of religion and values: It is devoid of God and morality.

The result is actually an unwitting attempt to establish an overarching worldview to provide an order akin to the divine moral order discussed in chapter 3—albeit here it is an amoral order because its goal is to eliminate religion and morality in public life altogether. We saw in chapter 3 that, under the divine moral order approach, an overarching worldview is the doctrine of truth and goodness of those in power. Everything else is immoral (or perhaps amoral). Specifically, when Protestant Christianity is asserted as the dominant overarching worldview, its doctrine of truth and goodness is the overarching worldview and everything else—the secular and the doctrines of truth and goodness of all other religions—is immoral. Secular humanists, like Flynn, wish to avoid this result. Hence, they promote their own ideological perspective. As a result, the secular humanist perspective takes the place of the overarching worldview and becomes the dominant ideology, eschewing everything else, not as immoral, but as irrelevant, that is all religion and morality—except insofar as they are entirely "private."

What becomes abundantly clear, then, is that there is an erroneous, underlying, unstated assumption in Flynn's argument. That assumption is that, if religion is privatized entirely so that it is no longer a participant in public life, *nothing much is lost.* The reason for this assumption is that religion is understood by Flynn, a nonbeliever, in a sociological sense, as referring to the religious institutional structures that promote theologies and foster traditions of ritualized practices. It never is thought to involve a real experience of God and what is created in response to God—because Flynn holds that there is no God. Thus, religion is deemed irrelevant because he judges it to be inherently false. With Flynn's approach, however, the overarching worldview, that is the "neutral," is secular humanism—the perceived locus of truth. Accordingly, Flynn's extreme secular left perspective is every bit as much an overarching worldview as any religious one that the extreme secular left opposes. This is entirely contrary to America's Sacred Ground, which does not determine truth or untruth, except in the limited way necessary to preserve the system itself. Rather, it creates an open Public Forum where truth can "shift for herself," where everyone participates, according to conscience, in a public dialogue about truth and goodness.

From the perspective of America's Sacred Ground, proposed "truths" promoted by the extreme secular left may provide important contributions to the Public Forum. The mere fact that those in the secular left promote a nonbeliever approach to public life does not necessitate a conclusion that their contribution to the public dialogue is of no account. Recall that the underlying theology that is America's Sacred Ground holds that God communicates to individual human beings through nature and, therefore, reason, as well as revelation. Consequently, according to America's Sacred Ground, the secular humanist is in the same position as the religious person who proposes his or her vision of truth and goodness in the Conscientious Public Forum of persuasion and voluntary acceptance. But the neutralizing arguments of the secular left do not belong at the level of the Civic Public Forum because at that level they involve dominance of one overarching worldview over others.

Clear evidence that the secular left's perspective is a top-down overarching worldview is its justification for the elimination of religion from the Public Forum. This is the very same justification used by the uniformists in Locke's day—the public peace. The problem is that the "keeping-the-peace" justification for the promotion of an overarching worldview/unifying moral order was rejected outright by both Locke and the founders. History had shown them that when a people do not have free conscience, and the freedom to be and do in accordance with conscience, they rise up in protest. Consequently, the goal of avoidance of discord is always thwarted under such an approach. Rather than promoting peace, it promotes *unrest* because the dissenters strive to overcome the effects of their oppression. Accordingly, forced conformity and suppression of dissidents is more likely to be the *cause* of civil unrest than of the advancement of peace and orderliness in society. As Locke said:

> [W]hat else can be expected but that these men, growing weary of the evils under which they labour, should in the end think it lawful for them to resist with force, and to defend their natural rights (which are not forfeitable upon account of religion) with arms as well as they can? That this has been hitherto the ordinary course of things is abundantly evident in history; and that it will continue to be so hereafter is but too apparent in reason.[27]

It is no wonder, then, that a movement of religious people has arisen in the United States to confront those who would silence them.

Significantly, the participation that the Flynns would eliminate— religious participation—was deemed by Locke and the founders to be of utmost importance. In fact, Locke would have eliminated the participation of nonbelievers. While Locke sought to extend freedom of conscience to even "heretics" and "heathens," he expressly excluded those "who deny the being of God" from such right. He argued that they ought "not at all to be tolerated" because the denial of God threatens the "[p]romises, covenants, and oaths, which are the bonds of human society" and "undermine[s] and destroy[s] all religion" and so "can have no pretence of religion whereupon to challenge the privilege of toleration."[28]

It is true, however, as noted in chapter 3, that the founders went further than Locke in this regard, granting freedom to even those who "deny the existence of a god." Clearly, nonbelievers were to be included in the Public Forum by the founders. But to assert that a nonbelieving secular humanist perspective should be *privileged* in public life is entirely contrary to the roots America has in Locke and contrary to the documentary record of the founding generation. Both Locke and the founders considered religion to be foundational to "human society" and to the idea of toleration, itself, and, therefore, freedom. Moreover, the cornerstone of our freedom is a theological ground, and its centerpiece is freedom of conscience and its expression. Therefore, the founders never meant to exclude religious people from public life. Rather, it was expected that religious people would be prominent contributors to the public dialogue about truth and goodness.

Flynn no doubt would assert that his neutral public field preserves free conscience because conscience can remain freer in a "religion free zone" where no one is disturbed by religious arguments that offend one's religious sensibilities. But freedom of conscience, as we saw in Part I, is not for freedom's sake alone. The purpose of a free conscience is to permit each individual to express that conscience through speech and action in the Public Forum. Otherwise, how can truth "shift for herself"? How can the voice of the people ever be the voice of God? Or, in secular humanist terms, how can the voice of the people ever be the voice of reason?

While unbelievers should never be accorded secondary status in America's Sacred Ground, it is incumbent on them to ensure that their reasonable fear of being suppressed does not lead them to suppress others. The goal is an open and free public forum, not one dominated by any person or group in particular—not even "neutral" secular humanists.

The secular left, in its effort to ensure its own freedom, has violated the principles underlying the Civic Public Forum—the forum for law and government action, which must preserve America's Sacred Ground. It has violated those principles by claiming dominance; it has advocated a silencing of religious voices in the Public Forum— a clear harm to liberty and the other sacred civil rights. Moreover, it has violated a fundamental moral rule of the Civic Public Forum— consistency/no hypocrisy. It has sought the aid of the law in order to deny to others what it does not wish to deny itself.

The secular left may argue that it has not taken an inconsistent/ hypocritical stand. Because it advocates a "neutral," "value-free" forum, its own voice is silenced in the Public Forum in the same way as is that of others. But this would be a specious argument because its conception of the public good is one where morality and religion are not discussed in public. Rather than being neutral, it is an assertion of a particular notion of the public good that overrides America's Sacred Ground. Consequently, it is not a valid argument in the Civic Public Forum. Instead, it is an argument that is properly raised only at the level of the Conscientious Public Forum— the forum for persuasion and voluntary compliance. In other words, the secular left may promote such views and form voluntary associations exemplifying them, but it is fundamentally immoral from the perspective of America's Sacred Ground for those representing the views of the secular left to promote such views as appropriate for governmental coercive action, as they have done. This is all the more clear when we recognize that what the secular left is advocating amounts to intolerance.

Often, the secular left claims that its position is only intolerance of intolerance. That may be true to the degree that it seeks to eliminate intolerant religious voices in the Public Forum. However, while Locke might have agreed that intolerance should be excluded from the Public Forum, that was not so for the founders. Rather, this too is where the founders expanded freedom beyond Locke. Significantly, *it was the very extension of freedom by the founders of freedom of expression of all views, even those that are intolerant, that also accorded atheists the freedom they now enjoy.*

Flynn and others on the extreme secular left need to recognize that their views, if given full effect, would actually undermine the

Conscientious Public Forum of America's Sacred Ground by limiting participation. For example, Flynn laments recent court rulings in favor of the Boy Scouts, who have, in Flynn's words, "taken up what amounts to a nationwide purge of atheists"[29] and, more recently, homosexuals, I might add. But arguments and actions in favor of "morality" of a nature more restrictive than what is allowed by the Civic Public Forum are to be permitted in the Conscientious Public Forum.* This necessarily must be the case; voluntary associations that are independent of government must be permitted to adopt "moral rules" consistent with the consciences of their constituents. Otherwise, the only morality in American society would be that which is set by law. Then the only "value" is freedom itself. And when that is achieved, virtually anything that is an expression of freedom is hailed. Thus, freedom becomes license—a result never intended by Locke or the founders.

We see, then, that the secular left has failed to distinguish between the Civic Public Forum and the Conscientious Public Forum. The purpose of the law of the Civic Public Forum is to ensure freedom so that individuals and the associations in which they participate can develop moral rules in the Conscientious Public Forum consistent with the free consciences of their constituents. If they are Christians, they can aim toward the Kingdom of God. The Conscientious Public Forum always was intended to include a place for "teaching, admonishing, and persuading" others as to the rightness of one's convictions, beyond what is required for the Civic Public Forum, in terms of doctrines, ideas, and beliefs, as well as morals. To exclude such activity from the Conscientious Public Forum is to subvert the process of the Public Forum as a whole and its goal—the discovery of truth and, therefore, the realization of a good society.

Most important, the arguments of Flynn and others of his persuasion are particularly disturbing from the perspective of

---

* Of course the issue is not as easily parsed as I have indicated here when public funds are provided to certain groups. The exploration of this issue is beyond the scope of this work, however, which is intended to clarify the framework for the debate, not examine the issues raised at the dividing lines.

America's Sacred Ground because their attack on the other side has some legitimacy. There *is* a danger that religion can assert a claim to dominance and establish an overarching worldview that will eventually limit or eliminate the freedom of others. However, the secular left's attempt to eschew religious participation in the Public Forum flies in the face of the historical record of the founders' many references to God and the great emphasis they placed on moral values. Thus, the secular left leaves the door wide open to those who wish to argue that religion, specifically Christianity, should be America's overarching worldview.

Because the religious ground of America is so clear from the historical record, along with the many references to moral values and the conduciveness of Christianity to a republican form of government, the failure of the secular left to provide an analysis of it *at all* gives an argument that *does* address it a degree of plausibility. As a result, the view that Christian values and American values are co-extensive appears to be the only credible explanation. The reason is that it is abundantly clear that the many references by the founders to religion and morality could not have been of *no significance*, as would have to be the case if secularists' views were adopted. In arguing otherwise, the secular left discredits its own argument and, in so doing, contributes to a self-fulfilling prophesy—the assertion of Christian dominance because Christians see themselves as suppressed dissenters, which, under the secular humanist unifying overarching worldview consisting of a "religion and value free zone," *they are*.

Furthermore, the entire basis for the secular left's approach is specious because it misconstrues the original meaning of a "secular" society. As discussed in the definitional section in Appendix A, "secular" originally did not mean what it has come to mean— devoid of religion. It originally was meant to distinguish between the temporal matters of this world and those eternal matters of the next. In other words, a "secular" civil government was to be one that concerned itself with the well-being of human beings here and now. Judgments about matters pertaining exclusively to heaven were to be left for heaven to judge. Yet, for Locke and the founders, civil government is grounded in God, and the rights that flow from that ground—the civil rights—are sacred because they are derived from God, while, at the same time, they have a "this-worldly" focus. Therefore, Locke's civil society is sacred. And because the American political system, following Locke, is grounded in God, those institutions of American civil government that are cultivated on that ground, and those principles rooted in that ground, are sacred, too. Consequently, what is referred to today as "secular" society is—to the degree it is consistent with America's Sacred Ground—sacred, too.

Alarmingly, however, as the religious right has been quick to note, the secular left has come to the erroneous conclusion that "secular" government (understood as nonreligious government) is what was intended by the founders because of the founders' fear of the dominating tendencies of religious institutions. As a result, there is a belief among those adhering to the secularist position that if institutions of government are "secular" (in the sense of being nonreligious), then the activities they pursue are more "legitimate" or, at least more "democratic."

But this is entirely false. *Any* governing dominance was suspect for the founders—religious or nonreligious. And the nondominating religious ground of the American system—America's Sacred Ground—was their remedy. This is the way the founders sought to preserve individuals' ability to discern the will of God (or reason, if you prefer) and the ability to be and do in accordance with conscience. This is not the "theological determinism" that Evans speaks about, but rather it ensures that no "determinism" will override the foundation that the founders believed would be most likely to result in a world reflective of God.

To counter the historical record, some on the secular left claim that arguments based on the original intentions of the founders have no greater merit than any other arguments.[30] Hence, the references of the founders to God and the grounding of moral values in God should be given no great accord, they contend. The problem with this assertion is that it leaves us with no argument that any one view is more legitimate than another; that is, it leaves us with no foundation at all. The result is moral relativity—a certain threat to liberty, as we have already seen in chapter 3, which would leave us with an unanchored Constitution that could drift toward anyone's interpretation and, potentially, away from America's Sacred Ground, which ensures everyone's liberty and the potential for the pursuit of the good.

But it is not only the extreme secular left in tracts like Flynn's that threatens America's Sacred Ground; it is also those who have considerable credibility and influence in the ivory towers of the academy as well. The famed political theorist, John Rawls, provides an example.

⚜

JOHN RAWLS: COMPROMISING AMERICA'S SACRED GROUND WITH PUBLIC REASONS

In earlier works, Rawls joined those who sought to eliminate religious participation from public life, just as does Flynn (who no doubt has been influenced in his thinking, directly or indirectly, by scholars such as Rawls). More recently, however, Rawls takes a more moderate approach. In a 1997 law review article entitled "The Idea of Public Reason Revisited," he refers to his approach as the "wide view of public reason," which permits religious participation in public life—*if* such participation fulfills certain criteria.[31] In the article, Rawls asks the question: "Can democracy and comprehensive doctrines [i.e., roughly, what I call overarching worldviews], religious or nonreligious, be compatible?"[32] He answers with a qualified "yes" and, in so doing, draws some distinctions and makes certain claims that have some convergence with America's Sacred Ground. But his views resemble Flynn's much more closely than he and other liberal academics probably would like to believe.

Let us begin with Rawls's description of what he refers to as "public culture." Public culture is the realm of Rawls's "political conception." That is, for him, public culture is the basic framework for a society's political, social, and economic institutions.[33]

Participation in Rawls's public culture requires one to exercise "public reason."[34] Public reason, in turn, requires adherence to a "criterion of reciprocity":

> The criterion of reciprocity requires that when . . . terms are proposed as the most reasonable terms of fair coopera-tion, those proposing them must also think it at least rea-sonable for others to accept them, as free and equal citizens, and not as dominated or manipulated, or under the pres-sure of an inferior political or social position.[35]

When free and equal citizens, as "fully cooperating members of so-ciety over a complete life,"[36] adhere to public reason and its crite-rion of reciprocity, then laws based on majority opinion are "legitimate law." That is, "when all reasonable citizens think of themselves ideally as if they were legislators following public rea-son, the legal enactment expressing the opinion of the majority is legitimate law."[37] And the whole process of public reasoning leads, in Rawls's thinking, to "constitutional essentials,"[38] and, therefore, a "constitutional democratic regime" and public traditions resem-bling those found in the United States.[39]

While Rawls holds that the adoption of a comprehensive doc-trine would not be appropriate for the functioning of public cul-ture, he acknowledges that citizens do hold comprehensive doctrines—religious and nonreligious. His idea of public reason would permit the introduction of such comprehensive doctrines into the political discussion of public culture as long as "public rea-sons" are provided for the position one is taking in public culture on the basis of one's comprehensive doctrine. Those comprehen-sive doctrines capable of public reasons are, then, "reasonable com-prehensive doctrines." And all such doctrines, together, result in a "reasonable overlapping consensus of comprehensive doctrines," which, in turn, affirms "equal basic rights and liberties for all citi-zens, including liberty of conscience and the freedom of religion."[40]

Throughout, Rawls's goal is to justify and/or explain the American system—or, rather, a theoretical system that is like it—without reference to "grounding reasons" for "the ideals and principles of public reasons and political conceptions of justice."[41] And, therefore, he proposes a system that he holds is "freestanding"[42]—that is, free of comprehensive doctrines, a main characteristic of which is grounding reasons. But his attempt to fulfill that goal results in several outcomes that are problematic from the perspective of America's Sacred Ground.

What Rawls is doing, of course, is spinning out a hypothetical political conception. In the realm of the abstract, he can assume perfect reasonableness and the outcomes derived from it (although one wonders why, in that case, there is a need to account for unreasonableness to begin with). However, the application of theory to actual political systems often has consequences not accounted for by theory.

In this regard, note that Rawls's theory uses an abstraction as the primary mediator of public decision-making: public reason. As a result, Rawls speaks of public reason, itself, as "seeing" whether the ordering of values that results from the application of public reason is reasonable.[43] But *who* sees? In practice, it would be citizens who "think of themselves ideally" as following public reason[44] that would do the "seeing" as they make decisions about the reach of the coercive power of government. While it is arguable that a law would be "legitimate" if the public reason of a hypothetical majority had produced it, in practice what we would be left with is citizens who "think" they are acting reasonably when, in fact, they may not be. Consequently, to the degree that citizens would not *actually* be reasonable, the concurrence of a majority would not produce Rawls's legitimate law even according to his own theory, and could in fact produce a law that would undermine such constitutional essentials as freedom and equality. Yet the majority might well claim legitimacy for its law and assert, as Rawls's system would allow, that there is no right of resistance to such a law by those oppressed by it.[45]

Of course Rawls does not say that a majority, who believes it is acting in accordance with public reason, could go so far as to, for example, repeal the First Amendment. Rather, he presumes that a

Supreme Court, acting as an "exemplar" of public reason, would be likely to prevent that.[46] Still, he leaves much latitude for "reasonable citizens," including those in a Supreme Court, to interpret the First Amendment in ways that would serve the majority to the detriment of those deemed by them to be "unreasonable." Then the broad liberty of conscience rights, which Locke and the founders sought to preserve (rights extended even to Anabaptists and Arminians, Muslims and Hindus, pagans and heathens, as well as those who practice idolatry, superstition, and heresy—that is, those most likely to be deemed "unreasonable" by the majority at the time), might be subjected to a majoritarian consensus of citizens who believe they have public reason justifications for curtailing some of those rights.

Rawls allows that "[n]o institutional procedure exists that cannot be abused or distorted" and this is no less so for his own political conception, he acknowledges.[47] But what I am arguing here is that, in fact, his political conception leaves vastly *more* room for abuse than Rawls seems to recognize. The reason is that his theory lacks the grounding reasons that would serve as a "beacon" to the American public when they exercise political power in their various capacities. In effect, he would be maintaining a value-free zone in which a majority of the people (or the United States Supreme Court), acting in accordance with public reason, would vote on a "complete ordering of political values"[48] *that could go anywhere*. In other words, without a sense of what freedom is *for*, the contentless public realm has no anchor—and so it can drift from its ground into the sea of relativity, or at least well beyond the shores of the democratic ideals Rawls presumes to justify, even while the majority public rhetoric remains consistent with the bare words of the First Amendment.

This becomes especially clear when we look closely at Rawls's own language in this regard. For example, he speaks of a "constitutional regime" as fully ensuring rights and liberties for "all *permissible* doctrines,"[49] which, of course, leads one to be concerned as to what or who will be considered "impermissible" by those who hold themselves to be "reasonable." In fact, Rawls contends that

the religious liberty of some citizens may be denied if there are public reasons to do so.[50] In other words, those deemed to be unreasonable by the purportedly reasonable majority would not be accorded
full liberty under Rawls's political conception in practice.[51]

Of course, in Rawls's hypothetical society, those who public
reason "sees" as being unreasonable would only be limited in their
religious (or other) freedom in that they would not be permitted
(1) to establish a comprehensive doctrine as the comprehensive
doctrine for all of society or (2) to maintain "a certain degree of
success and influence" through political means.[52] But, as we can
now readily see in the actual application of Rawls's political conception, there is every possibility that these "limitations" would not
in actuality be very limited. And when we consider this on the scale
of Rawls's "overlapping consensus of comprehensive doctrines," the
assumption that, in practice, there would be an affirmation of
"equal basic rights and liberties for all citizens"[53] becomes less and
less plausible. Rather, there is every likelihood that the overlapping
consensus would resemble an overarching worldview that imposes
itself on the masses *en toto* in the name of reasonableness. Instead of
Rawls's political conception *actually* being informed by public reason, there would be a substantial risk of a return to the state of nature where various factions battle by words and deeds until one, or
a consortium of several, attain political power sufficient to suppress
the remainder. Then, the prevailing political system, although it
would claim to be "reasonable," would be, in practice, very much like
the ones John Locke and the founders fought so hard to overcome.

Moreover, because Rawls does not appear to recognize that
freedom is not for freedom's sake alone, Rawls does not fully grasp
the significant role the Conscientious Public Forum plays in the
American system. This is evident even in his choice of terminology
for what remains after public culture determines its reach; he calls it
the "background culture." While this certainly is not "private," and
rather is the realm of what Rawls refers to as "nonpublic reasons,"[54] it
nevertheless is in the "background" for Rawls.

Like the Conscientious Public Forum, Rawls's background culture is the realm of associational and individual activities. However,

Rawls assumes that, if peoples' contributions to society on the basis of their comprehensive doctrines—religious or nonreligious—do not fall within the realm of Rawls's public culture, then they are not ones that we "expect others to share."[55] Further, he says that we speak from various conflicting comprehensive doctrines, but "do not assert the premises from which we argue . . . ."[56] But, as we have seen, the sharing of such "premises" is precisely what the Conscientious Public Forum permits and, in fact, encourages. Otherwise, how can "truth shift for herself"? How can individuals, and the associations they create, pursue the good?

Other scholars have criticized Rawls's political conception because it does not recognize "the need for full and open discussion in the background culture," and Rawls answers that he recognizes that need.[57] However, it is evident from his overall discussion that, whatever it is that occurs in the background culture, it does not hold great import under Rawls's theory and can be diminished for public reasons, even though he claims that it is preserved by his political conception. While his claim may have some validity in theory, what is reserved to the background culture would be threatened in practice. The application of Rawls's political conception would end up with a kind of imposed uniformity under a canopy of reasonableness that requires "complete" and "wholehearted" adherence in order for one to be a participant in the overlapping consensus of reasonable comprehensive doctrines.[58] This would be a society where religion would be irrelevant because it would have no place at all (except in the background), unless it subjected itself to "public reasons." Consequently, there would be no reason to have the religious message expressed in public in the first place. Religion would be "neutralized" or "secularized" through the workings of public reason.

The neutralization of religion by Rawls through "public reasons" is also problematic on other bases than those already mentioned. Since the 1980s, the United States Supreme Court has couched a "neutrality" argument in "civic religion" terms as justification for upholding religious practices that have a "secular" nature.[59] Apparently, if the practice is one that has a long history and an established tradition, then it is "neutral" enough for state support, according to the Court. However, this really begs the question because it is, in effect, saying that, if the majority religions are sufficiently "established" in the nation, then their practices can be endorsed by the state—and if not, then they will not be equally endorsed. Under this view, history, tradition, and the invocation of "civic religion" will favor the religions deemed by the Court to be the religions of history and tradition, that is, certain forms of Christianity and Judaism.* Doing so will be detrimental to new sects within mainstream religions, as well as new religious movements, including those that are new in the United States, but are "traditional" elsewhere in the world. In other words, "neutrality" becomes a justification for majoritarian impulses—in this case from the majority "traditional" religions. When one considers this development in the Court, one can see that Rawls's neutralized "public reasons" may, in effect, support majoritarian dominance from a direction he may not have intended.[60]

It is not overreaching to conclude here, as I did with Flynn, that Rawls assumes nothing much is lost when neutralization has been accomplished. It appears that Rawls, like Flynn, has a fear and belief that the godly can more readily justify oppression and violence than can those who justify their actions by reason. If so, then he has forgotten that those who *believe* themselves to be reasonable can be just as deadly. One need only recall the many purportedly reasonable justifications that were used in Nazi Germany or in Stalin's Soviet Communism, when those in power did not use reasons grounded in God's relationship with each and every human being, whether that relationship is embraced as a matter of faith or, at least, accepted as a grounding idea.[†]

Furthermore, even if one were to agree that Rawls's intricately woven reasonable system could justify the American system without

---

* The appeal to history and tradition may not have the effect intended by those asserting this view. One could certainly argue that the traditional and historical religions of America are those practiced by native Americans.

† Often scholars will argue that Nazism and Stalinism were, in effect, "religions." But this really just begs the question by equating religion with fanaticism, fascism, or both.

grounding reasons, it is not one that would be effective in practice for another reason: While Rawls speaks of public reason as an "ideal" to strive for,[61] there is nothing in it that could inspire people to strive for that ideal—and this is precisely what would be needed if public reason were to fulfill the function Rawls assigns to it. Clearly, it is not likely that masses of people would rally to a cause to participate "reasonably" in public culture. Recall, instead, that we are overwhelmingly a religious people. And what Rawls has missed is what the secular left (and the religious right as well) seems always to miss: There is a political conception *with* grounding reasons that is not a comprehensive doctrine (i.e., not an overarching worldview), and which *does* have the potential to call to America's people now just as it has done time and again throughout America's history. It is one that does not need to obscure the obvious pitfall that an approach like Rawls' exhibits: The failure to recognize the ground that supports the central underlying assumption of the American system—the inherent worthiness of each and every human being as messengers of God through conscience. This political conception is not found in the expediency of a misguided appeal to the public peace (recall John Locke's view of appeals to the "public peace"); nor is it found in the universalized self-interest of Rawls's original position*—it is found in God.

Secular liberal philosophers, like Rawls, may try again and again to find a way to justify America without its ground, but when they do they end up with something more likely to bring about its demise. In this regard, it is interesting to point out that Richard Rorty, another famed philosopher, has interpreted Rawls as recognizing that democracy is "prior" to philosophy, a conclusion with which Rorty agrees.[62] The idea is that philosophy cannot justify democracy; rather, democracy provides the practical framework for

---

* Rawls's "original position" is a hypothetical situation wherein no one knows one's natural abilities, one's preexisting views and opinions, one's economic class or social position, and the like, because everyone is under a "veil of ignorance" about such matters. It is Rawls's view that, when one is in the "original position" and considers social policy decisions from that perspective, a self-interested analysis will lead one to think in terms of everyone—because one could be anyone.

unfettered philosophical inquiry, such as that exhibited by Rawls. However, as we have seen in these pages, under the American system there is something that is even prior to democracy. It is America's Sacred Ground.

So we see that, in all the ways discussed, the secular left has obscured America's Sacred Ground. Rather than working to preserve the framework that protects everyone's sacred civil rights, it has attempted to subordinate that framework to its own purposes. As a result, it has become just one of many factions asserting on overarching worldview that competes for dominance in public life and undermines what it is that provides for its own participation in the first place.

CHAPTER 5

Looking Right

The rights of conscience we never submitted, we
could not submit. We are answerable for them
to God.

—Thomas Jefferson,
"Notes on the State of Virginia" (1781–1785)

RECONSIDERING THE RELIGIOUS RIGHT FROM
THE PERSPECTIVE OF AMERICA'S SACRED GROUND

If there is ever to be a debate on common ground, the religious right
must address the ways in which its perspective differs from that of
America's Sacred Ground, as well. A starting point is to take account
of the fears expressed by the secular left that the religious right's assertion of Christian dominance is inherently threatening to liberty. In
fact, M. Stanton Evans is clear in *The Theme is Freedom* that his goal
is to claim Christianity's rightful (and dominant) place in American
public life. However, he claims this because Christianity, he contends, is the best guardian of freedom. Evans locates the source of free
government in the Christian faith and argues that Christianity is inherently "compatible with free institutions."[1] In this regard, Evans asserts that if we lose the Christian foundations of our freedom, we risk
the loss of freedom altogether.[2]

What everyone in the debate needs to acknowledge before we
can get to common ground, however, is that the religious right has

some basis for believing this. As we have seen, the founders were, in large part, Christians. And even those who took a "reasonableness" approach to religion were steeped in Christian tradition. To deny this history is to ensure that any conclusions contrary to the ones of the religious right will be rejected by them—and for good reason: This *is* a part of American history. But as my analysis of the historical record has shown, Evans's claim for a Christian America is overstated. While America's Sacred Ground embraces certain elements derived from the West's "Judeo-Christian" heritage,* it does not involve all of anyone's particular version of Christianity and, moreover, it does not involve all that Christianity has ever been.

In this regard, it is important that the religious right come to terms with the fact that Christianity is not monolithic, as Evans's argument seems to assume—a fact of which the founders were well aware. Evans cites the work of certain theologians in support of his position, for example, Augustine and Aquinas.[3] However, he fails to acknowledge that there have been many interpretations of the theologies of those whom he cites that do not support his claim, and more important there are many Christian theologies that vary vastly from those he cites. In fact, the very reason for the founders' focus on freedom of conscience was to accommodate the many variations of Christianity (some of which were extremely foreign to those framing the Constitution and the Bill of Rights), as well as Judaism and other religious faiths.

So Evans's argument leaves us with the question: If Christianity were to have a rightful claim to dominance, as he contends, which Christianity should prevail? If, on the one hand, his answer is Christianity as interpreted by him or his church, then he is advocating a return to the thinking that preceded the founding era, where various Christian sects claimed dominance. Clearly, this would be contrary to the goal of the founders, which was to establish a

---

* I am using this term as it is one Evans embraces; however, it is important to acknowledge that this term denotes a concept that is not embraced by all Jews, nor Christians for that matter. Its use has been criticized by some as an effort to subsume a Christian interpretation of Judaism into an overall Christian ideology, while others embrace the term as a recognition of certain common values.

system that accommodates them all. If, on the other hand, his answer is that it is the "general principles" of Christianity that are to govern, then we are left with the dilemma: Who shall determine which principles are general?

But this is a question we do not need to answer because, as already shown, the founders have chosen them for us. There is no need to reiterate them here as they have been adequately explained in chapter 3.[4] What is important to recognize, however, is that the claim of Christian dominance is not consistent with the founding documents of the nation and, therefore, it is not consistent with America's Sacred Ground. Moreover, asserting this claim today only serves to reopen many of the same questions the founders asked and answered. Consequently, doing so results in an unwitting undermining of America's Sacred Ground.

The problem is that, just as is the case with the secular left, Evans and the rest on the religious right have failed to recognize the difference between top-down overarching worldviews and America's Sacred Ground. The foundational principles of America's Sacred Ground—liberty and equality, which are derived from God—dictate that *no one* has a rightful claim to dominance. The mutual consent of each individual to the social contract extends only to governance on the part of the state that preserves the sacred civil rights and the Public Forum, which, in turn, requires general safety and welfare. All top-down overarching worldviews imposed as doctrines of truth and goodness are contrary to the consciences of those who question the validity of such doctrines. Therefore, no religion—not even Christianity—or any other unifying overarching worldview can ever dominate legitimately. Rather, America's Sacred Ground is a uniquely open form of government that provides for maximum freedom of conscience and its expression within a context that is, itself, the foundation for freedom to pursue the good.

Although Evans does recognize that his Christianity is a top-down overarching worldview—in his terms, a form of "theological determinism"—he assumes that some form of "theological determinism" is required for any society.[5] Accordingly, he concludes that "there is, and must be, an 'establishment of religion' in our society, or any other" and "[t]he question being fought out today is, quite simply, which religion shall be established."[6] But by this he means there must be an establishment of an overarching worldview. Because he does not recognize the uniqueness of America's Sacred Ground, which is not just another top-down overarching worldview, his analysis involves a choice among competing "theological determinisms." When he looks, then, to history, he concludes that a Christian "theological determinism," that is, top-down overarching worldview, is the best because it is the source of freedom. Evans contends that if we do not recognize Christianity as the source of our freedom and establish it as America's overarching worldview, some other competing overarching worldview that does not provide for freedom will take that place.

Evans is specifically concerned that secularist ideologies resemble, or are in fact linked to "pagan" ideologies, which he contends are inherently threatening to liberty. They are threatening to liberty because they tend toward "the immersion of human existence in the cycles of physical nature."[7] As a consequence of this way of viewing human existence, "[i]n the usual case . . . pagan cultures united religious and secular functions in the state, thereby precluding the ideas of limited power, foreclosing the notion of any higher loyalty, denying refuge to the spirit."[8] Obviously, what Evans is describing here is what I have referred to as top-down overarching worldviews that involve a unified vision of all the specific ways in which the divine order should be reflected in the moral order. An example is classical Hinduism, which generated the caste system as an expression of *dharma* (society's moral order) as a reflection of *rita* (the divine order).

Evans goes on to argue that secularist ideologies ultimately are informed by a "species of neopaganism" that was fused into Enlightenment ideologies. Consequently, "modern theory," which was derived from such notions, rejects the "theological determinism" of Christianity, which Evans contends informs the American "political order."[9] Inevitably, this will lead to the demise of the American political system and the adoption of such "pagan" approaches to government, he contends.

Significantly, Evans is right to be concerned that those in America who embrace "secularist" ideologies do not seem to recognize the ways in which the religious and moral precepts underlying the American system are essentially different from such "secularist" ideologies. What Evans and others of the religious right need to understand, however, is that *they, themselves, do not recognize the ways in which the religion and moral precepts of America's Sacred Ground differ from their own, either.* As a consequence, they do not understand that Christianity is as capable of generating top-down overarching worldviews that override individual freedom as are classical Hinduism and modern secularist ideologies. In addition, "pagan" religions, such as Hinduism, are capable of theologies that embrace an individualism that is compatible with America's Sacred Ground. After all Hinduism and secular ideologies are not monolithic either. So the threat to liberty is not found in labels such as "pagan," nor is its preservation found in labels such as "Christian" or "evangelical." Rather, the threat is found in claims to dominance, and preservation is found only in a commitment to America's Sacred Ground.[10]

It is my view that because the religious right perceives Christianity to be the best guardian of freedom, it is blind to its own potential threat to freedom. And, as with the secular left, this is because of its own history of being suppressed. Like the nonbelievers of the extreme "secular left," the Christians of the religious right have a history of being dominated and suppressed. The beginning of Christianity is a story of oppression. Significantly, the original American settlers were Christian refugees of religious persecution. As a result, many Christians were dissenters to the majority at the time of the founding of the states and the United States, and, therefore, were prominent voices in the cause of liberty. More immediately, those who claim "new birth" in Christ today have been ridiculed, and their voices have been stifled in public life. While this is beginning to change for the better, it has only come through tremendous effort and sacrifice on their part.

We can see, then, that Christians of the religious right have experienced an immediate history of oppression that comports with a history of oppression of Christians, and a history of overcoming that oppression. As a result, Evans and others on the religious right see themselves as having a great appreciation of freedom. Consequently, they exhort us to take account of our history and point out that "we [Americans] take our liberties for granted." Evans urges us to "count our blessings" but more important "to understand them." He warns us that the failure to take account of our history is to risk the loss of those freedoms.[11]

When Evans looks at history, he finds that the source of free government is the Christian faith, and concludes, therefore, that Christianity is inherently "compatible with free institutions" as the overarching worldview for our political institutions.[12] And, as a result, he contends that "*[i]f we want to grow orchids instead of weeds, it is well to know what kind of climate, soil, and nurture are congenial to orchids*; ignorance of or indifference to these matters will predictably result in failure."[13]

But Evans and others on the religious right leave out much history that informs the debate. While Christianity has experienced a history of *being* oppressed, it also has been a *cause* of oppression when in history it has held a dominant position. Locke's ideas regarding tolerance arose out of his own witnessing of abuses by Christian church authorities in England and the rest of Europe in his day, and out of his knowledge of the immediately preceding centuries, where untold tortures were performed in this world for the purpose of freeing the victim's eternal soul for the next. And, of course, the American founders were well aware of this history, too. As Benjamin Franklin said, "If we look back into history for the character of present sections in Christianity, we shall find few that have not in their turns been persecutors, and complainers of persecution."[14]

Moreover, while Christian historians are right to acknowledge that America's first settlers were Christian refugees of oppression, what they also need to remember is that their oppressors *were Christians too*. Significantly as well, while the founders were steeped in Christian tradition, they too had witnessed firsthand the strife created by religious conflict resulting from the failure to grant freedom of conscience to all. That is why every state and the United States embraced freedom of conscience as the cornerstone of liberty.

Even those states that made general statements of particular goods and continued "religious tests" for holding state office nonetheless embraced the general principle of freedom of conscience.

My own experience is, however, that when the history of Christianity *as oppressor* is raised in a discussion with someone from the religious right, the response is anger and the conversation is halted abruptly. The raising of such concerns is perceived as mere secular leftist rhetoric that is not "constructive" to real dialogue. Presumably, this is because such arguments are considered by them, as one colleague on the religious right informed me, to be very remote concerns that have no real bearing today.[15] But this is really sidestepping the central and critical issue for the secular left: How can the religious right claim that Christianity is conducive to freedom in the face of this history? Where is the assurance that, if Christianity regains dominance, it will not gradually over time undermine freedom and prove that history repeats itself? Evans barely mentions this part of Christian history in *The Theme Is Freedom*.[16]

Rather, Evans makes an argument that serves as his attempted rebuttal of any history that emphasizes Christianity as oppressor: The seeds of the notions that eventually led to representative government derive from medieval church doctrine that the "natural law" is a "higher law" than the law of princes. Later, those seeds were also derived from Christian church doctrine in England, which promoted the idea that "the king is under God—and under the law." Even the Puritans favored limited government subject to the "higher law," Evans points out (while at the same time he ignores the Puritan's persecution of dissenters). Evans concludes that Christianity's basic theology supports freedom and, therefore, Christianity serves the cause of freedom.[17]

> Rather than finding political freedom rising in opposition to the religious values of the West, we see exactly the reverse: ideas of personal liberty and free government emerging in Christian Europe; institutional development of such ideas in the Middle Ages; vigorous defense of these in England, on the basis of medieval doctrine; the translation

of such ideas and institutions to America by a religious people, and the persistence of this connection in our life and thought long past the founding era.[18]

Significantly, Evans holds that, as the notion of the prince being subject to the higher law took hold in English history, the "conceptual space vacated" was filled with "spiritual awareness and instruction" by the Christian churches. And the "biblical focus on religious virtue as a matter of will and conscience likewise constricted the authority of the state."[19]

What Evans and others who make similar arguments fail to realize, however, is that the promotion of God's law over the prince's law during the Middle Ages involved a struggle between two powers—church and state, both of which asserted dominance over the populace. God's law in that context was not the pure "natural law" that the founders were referencing. It was God's law *as interpreted by church authorities.* Consequently, the arguments Evans promotes here as leading to religious freedom actually involved freedom of church *authorities* from state interference.[20]

The founders, on the contrary, following Locke's lead, sought to place the "governing" power for conscience, that is, the determination of what constitutes the "higher law," into the hands of each individual to the greatest extent possible. So while it is certainly true that the notions of limited government were derived in part from the church doctrine Evans cites, the history of Western thought on the subject did not stop there. Rather, the founders followed Locke in reserving freedom of conscience for the individual— *not the churches.*

Thus, for Locke and the founders, the question of the proper delineation between the state and religion is not between the state and the church but between the state and individual conscience. Freedom of conscience is an *individual* inalienable right. It is not a right of churches or sects. Ecclesiastical authorities are to have *no sway* over individual conscience except through persuasion because adherence to church doctrine and, therefore, interpretation of the "higher law" is to be a matter for the individual to decide. The role of the state is to preserve free conscience by not aligning itself with any ecclesiastical authorities or the doctrines they espouse. Therefore, churches are to have no governing role *at all*—not in matters regarding the maintenance of the order of the commonwealth and not in setting the standard for moral values, *except to the extent that the force of their message draws individuals into their folds voluntarily.*[21]

Because those in the religious right misread the historical record, they go on to claim a privileged place for Christianity in shaping American moral values and therefore in the pursuit of the good society. In support of this claim, the religious right, as exemplified by Evans, cites the many instances where the founders referred to the importance of moral virtue to republican government, and to the role of Christianity in instilling virtue. The religious right concludes, therefore, that the founders could not have intended to bar religion from public life. Because freedom derives from Christian religion, the uniting of "Christian value" with American politics is not only permissible but a necessity, Evans contends.[22] Thus, Evans argues in favor of limited government, but one grounded in biblical values as the underlying "premise of our politics."[23] Accordingly, Evans challenges the "liberal history lesson" that teaches that there is a "clash between religious precept and the practices of freedom"—a "conflict between faith and freedom." Moreover, he challenges the validity of the "liberal" doctrine of "the 'wall of separation' between our religious and political institutions."[24]

Evans is correct, as shown in chapter 3, that the founders perceived no "conflict between faith and freedom." *However, they most certainly did see a conflict between individual faith and coercive force of church authorities aligned with the state.* Consequently, while the founders encouraged moral virtue as being important to representative government, they did not, as Evans's approach implies, seek to have moral virtue be something determined by the churches and enforced by the state. This is the meaning of separation (or what I have called, following Locke, the "just bounds") between religion (as free conscience) and the state—not the "religion-free, value neutral zone" favored by the extreme secular left, nor Christian value determined by the churches and imposed by the state as favored by the far religious right. There appears to be a great deal of confusion about this on the part of those on the religious right. They look at the American history of the founding era, see Christian moral virtue espoused, and conclude that the founders never intended churches to be excluded from matters of the state.

We can see this view reflected in James H. Hutson's Library of Congress publication, *Religion and the Founding of the American Republic*,[25] although few would categorize Hutson as a member of the religious right based on this work. Rather, this work appears to be intended, for the most part, to bring to light in a balanced manner the importance of religion, particularly evangelical Christianity, in the founding of the states and the United States. Of course, that general assessment is clearly correct: Religion did play an important role in the founding of the nation. But throughout Hutson's work certain statements are made, and conclusions drawn, that leave the reader with the impression that the founders never intended the separation of church and state. For example, Hutson claims that there was "an intense debate about the possibility of constructive engagement of government and religion which is often neglected in popular histories of the [founding] period." He claims that the failure to acknowledge this leaves one with "the impression that the Declaration of Independence loosed a widespread loathing in the new nation for state involvement with the churches, leading to the swift and decisive banishment of the government from the religious realm."[26] But Hutson distorts the historical record. Certainly there was a debate in the states about the degree to which the force of law should or should not be used to coerce citizens to support their own churches financially (the "general assessment laws" controversy). However, all debates about the degree to which religion, generally, or Christianity, specifically, should be fostered by the coercive power of the state were substantially resolved during the Revolutionary period (and in many cases even before the adoption of the United States Bill of Rights) in favor of minimal or no involvement on the part of the state.[27] So, Hutson's implication that church and state were "constructively engaged" to effect broad societal goals is an overstatement, at best.

Along these same lines, Hutson asserts that the thinking of the founding generation was imbued with a syllogism: "virtue and morality are necessary for free, republican government; religion is necessary for virtue and morality; religion is, therefore, necessary for republican government."[28] He is correct only in part, however, because as we have seen, the founders clearly held that free conscience is required for religion to reflect the good (of God). Hutson's logic is, therefore, short one step and should read instead: virtue and morality are necessary for free, republican government; religion is necessary for virtue and morality; freedom of conscience is necessary for religion to reflect virtue and morality, that is the good (of God); freedom of conscience is, therefore, necessary for republican government. Without the additional step, the implication is that what is meant by "religion" is "the churches" and that they should be "engaged" with the state, as Hutson has suggested. Nothing could be further from the documentary record, as shown in chapter 3. Rather, moral virtue is to be found in the free and open forum for speech and action, where everyone is free to pursue the true and the good within the context that is the common good—America's Sacred Ground.

The religious right no doubt will argue, however, that unless freedom is infused with a counterbalancing sense of responsibility, freedom becomes license for an "anything goes" society that ultimately undermines the freedom to speak and act in accordance with conscience. In this regard, the religious right perceives society as having gone too far in the direction of license, resulting in a society with no standards to live by at all. Therefore, as Evans asserts, the right proposes a return to "tradition"—"the safeguards of religion, custom, and morality."[29] For example, Evans maintains that the very core of American culture is at stake because, as "liberals" disparage religion and promote "secular, permissive themes in media entertainment" and push their presumption "that religious doctrine entails repression and stagnation,"[30] the very foundations of our freedoms and our cultural ethos are being undermined.

Against this pervasive backdrop, the idea that one can favor both religious belief and individual freedom must inevitably seem a hopeless contradiction. Choose our republic and its values, and you accept the secular-Enlightenment doctrine on which it all was based; choose religious tradition of the West, and you reject the premises of our nation. You may have one or the other, but may not consistently have both.[31]

But Evans and others fail to recognize that the "safeguards" of tradition can, themselves, become oppressive when they are imposed from the top down as an overarching worldview by the state. That is why Locke, and the founders after him, abandoned appeals to tradition and custom in the Civic Public Forum (the forum for law and government action, which must preserve America's Sacred Ground).[32]

The religious right may well be correct that American culture is at stake in the licentious environment that is now being generated. It is my view, however, that if this is so, it is because the extreme secular left has been successful in closing down the public conversation about religion and moral values in the last few decades— particularly in the all-pervasive media. Once the Conscientious Public Forum (the forum for persuasion and voluntary compliance) is fully reopened to all perspectives, however, the call to moral virtue will be a large part of the call to truth. As truth "shifts for herself," I believe that a sense of responsibility will freely arise that will provide the counterbalance to freedom that is needed to keep freedom from becoming license. But if it does not, then it will not be found by imposing it from the top down as a overarching worldview. History is our witness that this does not work; rather, it leads to oppression and untold harms. I repeat Locke's warning, "If truth makes not her way into the understanding by her own light, she will be but the weaker for any borrowed force violence can add to her."[33]

We see, then, that because of its misreading of the historical record, the religious right has misconstrued the nature of the Public Forum established by America's Sacred Ground. And it is no wonder, since many in the religious right have been effectively and wrongly suppressed in that forum by others. As a result, they conflate their Conscientious Public Forum arguments with their Civic Public Forum arguments in the public debate.

But it is also important to remember that the religious right has made important contributions as well. It has done much work recently on the level of the Civic Public Forum in its efforts to re-open the Public Forum to participation by the religious. The religious right has made a critical and essential contribution with its "religious speech" arguments in Supreme Court and other cases, which have moved law more toward the realization of the fundamentals of America's Sacred Ground. In addition, the religious right has made considerable contributions in the Conscientious Public Forum. Through persuasion, it has broadened the Conscientious Public Forum conversation not only to include religious voices, but to prevent the silencing of the public moral discourse by those who seek to shut down the Conscientious Public Forum debate altogether. As a result, there is considerably more public conversation about these matters than there was just a few years ago.

Now that the religious right is regaining its own rightful place in the Public Forum, however, it must not use its participation to assert its own dominance. The religious right must not gain its own freedom through the suppression of others. To do so would involve all the same violations of the rules of the Public Forum that have been committed by the extreme secular left against the religious right. Freedom of conscience is for all and, therefore, conscience and its expression must not be dictated through the coercive force of law, except to the limited extent necessary to preserve conscience for all, as well as the ability to express it in speech and action.

Rather, those in the religious right should use all methods of exhortation in the Conscientious Public Forum that are respectful of others' freedom and equality through "teaching, admonishing, and persuading" in order to convince others of the rightness of their convictions. And they should form voluntary associations that exemplify their values and aim for the Kingdom of God. But arguments and actions in favor of a "morality," beyond what supports and preserves America's Sacred Ground and that are intended to be imposed on others through the coercive force of government at the level of the Civic Public Forum (including by promoting the appointment of judges who will not uphold the principles of America's Sacred Ground), involve claims to dominance; these involve attempts to impose an overarching worldview on American society.

Significantly, Evans has gotten caught in the moral relativity trap that undermines all such claims for dominance. In fact, Evans places all overarching worldviews on a par with the "theological determinism" of his own Christianity, asserting, in effect, that his is just one of many overarching worldviews competing for dominance. As a consequence, the only justification for asserting his overarching worldview is tradition. His justification amounts to this: Christianity was the religion of the founders; our founders were for freedom; freedom is at the core of the American system; therefore, Christianity is at the core of freedom.

But even more important, the arguments of Evans and others of his persuasion are particularly disturbing from the perspective of America's Sacred Ground because their attack on the other side has legitimacy. There *is* a danger that the secular left's "neutrality" provides an overarching worldview that will dominate the faithful and eventually limit or eliminate the freedom to be and do good according to conscience imbued with God. However, the religious right's misconstruing of the historical record in an effort to assert dominance discredits its own arguments, which favor a voice for morality in public life. Because the religious right has failed to address the authoritarian abuses in Christianity's own history, and has not shown how it will not rise to undermine freedom again, the right has left the door open for the secular left to discount the right's entire argument. The secular left, in effect, takes Evans's justification and turns it against him: Our founders were for freedom; freedom is not (as the right asserts the historical record shows) compatible with Christianity; *therefore, the founders could not really have been Christians.* And this is the rationale that has prevailed at the extreme left side of the debate for some time now. What is most unfortunate about the religious right's having left the door open for the secular left to discount its arguments, not only for Evans, but for all American Christians as well, is that it obscures and trivializes the real contribution that Christianity *has* made to America's Sacred Ground. More important, it contributes to the trivialization of all religion in the public discourse by providing yet another example of religion's tendency to assert its dominance.

When Christians, such as Evans, claim dominance, they run headlong into the secular left's charge that if religion is given any voice at all, it always will attempt to monopolize the podium. Instead, Christians should take pride in the contribution Christianity has made to the underlying theology of America's Sacred Ground, commit to speech and action in the Civic Public Forum conducive to the continued preservation of the America's Sacred Ground's Public Forum, and place the rest of their values debate where it belongs—in the Conscientious Public Forum.

In summary, just as is the case with the secular left, the religious right has misconstrued the foundations of our freedoms. Unlike the secular left, however, the religious right does not mistake its claim to ideological supremacy as "neutrality." Rather, it claims dominance outright based on a misreading of history. Evans is correct that there must be "an 'establishment of religion' in our society" and there is—America's Sacred Ground. However, it is not an overarching worldview that involves a "theological determinism" that sets moral standards for all. Rather, it provides the context within which individuals have the freedom to hear the voice of God (or reason) and do according to conscience in the search for the true and the good.

So, the question being "sought out today" is not "which religion shall be established?" as Evans contends.[34] The question is whether all sides in the debate will continue to erode America's Sacred Ground, making possible the totalitarianism Evans fears or the inquisition Flynn fears, or whether they will recognize that America's Sacred Ground is the very foundation that provides the freedom for them to be arguing all these points in the first place. This is why it is incumbent on Evans and others in the religious right, when they look back to history, to make sure that they have properly identified the sacred ground of their freedoms. Otherwise, *they may plant orchids, but grow only weeds.*

ACCOMMODATION: COMPROMISING AMERICA'S SACRED GROUND BY MEDIATING THE EXTREMES

By the end of the 1990s, many had become exhausted and extremely weary of the heightened rhetoric of the battle between the secular left and the religious right. Taking assessment of the contentious discourse of the extremes, and concluding, probably correctly, that no compromise is possible in such an atmosphere, many began to call for greater "civility" in the discourse.[35] Along with the call for civility, there was also a search for some kind of middle ground, where compromise *could* be found.

Many sought a tempered approach to the issues in the accommodationist view that earlier had captured the imagination of moderates in the debate. Stephen L. Carter's 1993 book, *The Culture of Disbelief: How American Law and Politics Trivialize Religious Devotion,* was a very influential work in this vein and remains so today.[36] It has become one of the most read accounts of the accommodationist position and, therefore, is an appropriate choice for analysis of that view.[37]

Significantly, Carter's message has been compelling to many readers from both left and right (including former President Clinton, I understand) because Carter put his finger on the pulse of a major problem in America—the trivialization of religious belief in public life. Recognizing that such trivialization has resulted in the suppression of religious voices, Carter understands that something is wrong. His proposed solution is a mediated compromise that in his words "preserve[s] the separation of church and state without trivializing the religious convictions tens of millions of us hold dear."[38] But, as we will see in the pages to follow, this accommodationist trend is as misguided as the extremes—and, in my view, much more threatening to America's Sacred Ground.

The extremes of the secular left and religious right appear as polar opposites at each end of a continuum—a secular/religion continuum—that runs from those who promote total secularization of society to those who promote particular Christian (or Judeo-Christian) religious views for society as a whole. In this sense, they exemplify the extremes in the contentious debate on moral values described by Hunter and MacIntyre. But as I have shown, the two sides have much in common. Each perceives itself as preserving freedom in the face of oppressive trends in society; each considers itself to be the best guardian of freedom; because of this, each sees the other as disingenuous in its claim to be the best guardian of freedom; and, most important for our purposes, each is making a claim to dominate public life with its own top-down overarching worldview as the unifying moral force in America. Interestingly, while their overarching worldviews are of different natures, making them appear oppositional, they, in fact, are merely two sides of the same "coin"—both undermining what was sacrosanct to the founders: America's Sacred Ground.

The vast majority of Americans, including their representatives, are unlikely to take up the position of either extreme. Rather, they are much more likely to attempt to find some mediated compromise somewhere along the secular/religion continuum. When that mediated compromise swings too far to one side, the other side raises the dire warnings of its fears in protest, and so the pendulum tends not to swing far to the left or right. What gets lost as the pendulum swings from left to right and back again along this continuum, however, is that, because it is a continuum running between two extremes that claim dominance, *every single stopping place along the way is a claim for dominance as well.*

In just this way, one gets the sense, when reading *The Culture of Disbelief,* that Carter perceives himself to be wading through the ambiguities between the secular left and the religious right and mediating some reasonable concessions. But because he is mediating between two forces that seek dominance, his compromise amounts to limiting the dominating efforts of one side while accommodating the dominating efforts of the other side. He is making a choice between the religious and secular visions of the good as to which will dominate:

> Indeed, it is not easy in a nation committed to religious liberty, to understand why the risk that the religions might try to impose on secular society their religious visions of the good life is more to be avoided than the risk that the state and its powerful constituents might try to impose on the religions a secular vision of the good life.[39]

There is a fundamental problem with the secular/religion continuum along which Carter strives to mediate an accommodation of religion, however: One cannot effect a compromise between the extremes on the secular/ religion continuum without serving the same erroneous end at which the extremes are aimed—dominance.

As we have seen, the extremes have misconstrued the Religion Clauses of the First Amendment of the United States Constitution. First, both have adopted an erroneous interpretation of the word "religion" in the Religion Clauses. As discussed in the definition section in Appendix A, the "religion" of the Religion Clauses does not refer to religious institutions. Rather, it refers to one's personal piety or relationship with God, or at most one's system of beliefs, ideal or actual, derived from that relationship. Of course, this does not mean that individuals were not intended to form groups, including churches. Rather, it was understood that there would be free associations that would be communities of conscience, and individuals representing such groups would be free to express their views in the Public Forum. However, such a group was not to have the government on its side. Rather, it would be, as Locke envisioned, a "free and voluntary," "spontaneous society" that "neither acquires the power of the sword by the magistrate's coming to it, nor does it lose the right of instruction and excommunication by his going from it."[40] As a result, it would be an authentic community because it would not be coerced. Second, "religion" in this sense is not oppositional to the "secular." "Religion" in this sense includes the "secular"—the "this-worldly" matters addressed by

America's Sacred Ground from which the inalienable individual right to freedom of conscience is derived.

The erroneous interpretation of the Religion Clauses is also evident in Carter's work, as he seeks accommodation along the secular/religion continuum. Carter's definition of religion along these lines is his starting point:

> [R]eligion . . . [is] a tradition of group worship (as against individual metaphysic) that presupposes the existence of a sentience beyond the human and capable of acting outside of the observed principles and limits of natural science, and, further, a tradition that makes demands of some kind on its adherents."[41]*

Carter concludes that the purpose behind the Religion Clauses is "corporate freedom."[42] He then goes on to argue that religious institutions were intended by the founders to be accorded privileged status in society by the state.[43] *However, the documentary record of the founders does not support such a claim, and significantly Carter does not offer any such support.*

What the documentary record does show is that the founders gave great deference to religion as being critical to the development of the good moral character of individuals so that they would be good citizens who pursue the good according to conscience. However, the churches were not intended to have a privileged function in society vis-à-vis the institutions of the state. Rather, the founders sought to prevent all claims to dominance that would interfere with individual freedom of conscience *from both churches and the state.*

---

* In *God's Name in Vain*, Carter adds that, in order to be a legitimate "religion," the organization in question must "stand the test of time and community" and be involved in a "narrative activity." Carter, *God's Name*, 174. Apparently, Carter is unaware that history, tradition, and "tests of time and community" provide no guard whatsoever against religious practices that are an anathema to the American ideal of civil rights. Such practices as slavery, female genital mutilation, prostitution, and oppression of factions within communities, among other things, have been justified around the world by various entrenched religions with very long historical "community" traditions with "narrative activities."

The reason churches were not given a privileged position is that the founders, following Locke, understood something that many Americans today seem to have forgotten: Religious institutions can serve good or ill. And religious institutions can be as oppressive as any other associations granted the coercive power of the state to effect ends not legitimately (according to America's Sacred Ground) in the state's authority. Therefore, the only way that good and not ill can be served is to preserve freedom of conscience to the individual who is then free to choose the church whose community exhibits those characteristics consistent with that individual's conscience. Then the individual is able to stand alone, if need be, to assert what he or she believes is right in the face of a majority that holds a different view, without risking the loss of civil rights. This is not to say that "individualism" is a goal that seeks to marginalize community interests. Rather, it is to say that individualism is a prerequisite to authentic community and, therefore, the pursuit of the good in society as a whole.

Yet Carter's vision appears to be that religious institutions, privileged by the state, will serve a mediating governing function as an additional "check" on state authority. In this regard, he says:

> Accommodation is therefore closer to Tocqueville's (and the Founders') conception of religious groups as autonomous moral and political forces, intermediate institutions, separate heads of sovereignty, vital to preventing majoritarian tyranny. Thus, the reason for accommodation becomes not the protection of individual conscience, but the preservation of the religions as independent power bases that exist in large part in order to resist the state.[44]

But in light of what we found in Part I, Carter's claim that religious institutions should serve a "proper democratic role of mediating between the individual and the state"[45] as "independent centers of power"[46] that should be accommodated by the state is without merit from the perspective of the founders of the nation, and it is a gross misunderstanding of the documentary record of the founding era. Having adopted the secular/religion continuum and its definition of "religion," Carter has unwittingly provided an erroneous theoretical justification for a power grab by the majority religious institutions in contravention of the clear intentions of the founders.

This all becomes abundantly clear when we recognize that defining "religion" as "religious institutions" and then privileging them as such requires a test of legitimacy. It becomes important to distinguish "religion" from the "secular" so we can determine exactly where we are along the continuum. The question becomes: Is this or that a "religion," or is it "secular?" This requires one to make a determination as to what "legitimately" is religion for the purposes of the Religion Clauses, something that can never be done without prejudice to individuals of conscience who are not in the majority.[47]*

The question of legitimacy is problematic from the perspective of America's Sacred Ground because the only point of reference for such a determination is what is readily identifiable by the majority as being *a* "religion." And what is identifiable as *a* "religion," therefore, must in large part, look like the "tradition of group worship" of Carter's definition of "religion."

But this sort of majoritarianism was something the founders clearly sought to avoid. The founders understood that unless most power is left in the hands of individuals, and the sacred civil individual rights are preserved against those who hold the power that is granted to the state, power is likely to be misused. And this is no less so when the majority holds power. As James Madison warned in his speech to the First Congress wherein he proposed the Bill of Rights (June 8, 1789):

> The prescriptions in favor of liberty ought to be levelled
> against that quarter where the greatest danger lies, namely,

---

* Interestingly, Carter acknowledges this problem but then defines "religion" anyway. Carter, *Disbelief,* 17–18, 231. See also Carter, *God's Name,* 166–167, where, on the one hand he acknowledges the problem, and *God's Name,* 25 and 174, where, on the other hand, he defines "religion." Carter ends up with this incongruence because he has failed to realize that a definition of "religion" is unnecessary when we understand that the founders were speaking about freedom of conscience not "the religions" as institutional religion. Accordingly, no such definition is needed.

that which possesses the highest prerogative of power. But it is not found in either the executive or legislative departments of Government, but in the body of the people operating as a majority against the minority.[48]

Madison knew, and we should remember, that democracy is no guarantee against the abuses of power. A Bill of Rights, he told Thomas Jefferson, is no barrier to infringement of the natural rights of individuals when the majority is bent on action that violates its proscriptions.[49] Further, Madison expressed grave concern that a democratic system could be undermined by majoritarian or otherwise powerful "factions" that promote their own interests to the disadvantage of a minority, and he sought ways to ensure against this tendency.[50] Moreover, certain of the founders were concerned that religious institutions were especially prone to override the free consciences of individuals. In this regard James Madison, discussing the pending Bill of Rights, wrote to Thomas Jefferson in 1787:

> The conduct of every popular Assembly, acting on oath, the strongest of religious ties, shews that individuals join without remorse in acts agst. which their consciences would revolt, if proposed to them separately in their closets. When Indeed Religion is kindled into enthusiasm, its force like that of other passions is increased by the sympathy of a multitude.[51]

Therefore, while freedom of conscience is an inalienable right of all, it is clear that the founders' main concern was that the majority could override—tyrannize—the minority. That is why the inalienable rights were included in a written constitution—to remind the state that it is not to infringe those rights even in the face of a powerful majority who wants the state to stand together with it in opposition to a minority.

In this regard, let us not forget that the reason for much of the religious persecution of Locke's day was the fact that the persecuted held to practices that were entirely outside the norm of the day. What was important to Locke was whether one is a good citizen who does not pose a direct risk to public safety (except, of course, to resist the infringement of one's inalienable rights). Everything else, he contended, is "indifferent."[52]

To bring home this point, Jefferson, when he was president, held religious services in the hall of the House of Representatives that were led at times by a Unitarian minister and at other times by a Catholic priest, as well as others. This was so scandalous for the time that many complained[53]—perhaps more "scandalous" from the perspective of the majority at the time, I would offer, than it would be for the chaplain of the United States Senate to be a Buddhist today. Therefore, we must keep in mind that to limit freedom of religion only to groups who fit the mold of the current norm that is accepted by the majority, under their accepted definition of religion, is to run counter to all that the Religion Clauses were meant to address.

We can see, then, that at one end of the secular/religion continuum is dominance by an atheistic secular humanist overarching worldview. At the other extreme is dominance of someone's particular Christian (or Judeo-Christian) overarching worldview. Under Rawls's more moderate secular liberal view it is an "overlapping consensus of reasonable comprehensive doctrines"; and under Carter's right-leaning accommodationist analysis, it is dominance by an overarching "patchwork quilt" made up of all those religious institutions that fulfill the criteria for his majoritarian definition and, I would add, ideology. It is an overarching worldview in its own right, now in the process of being accorded privileged status by the state, and at the same time positioning itself as "mediator" "between the individual and the state."[54] In such a position, it imposes its top-down overarching worldview on those whose freedom of conscience it infringes by virtue of the marginalization that results from a definition that includes some and leaves out others. The consequence for today's America is this: Those who can serve as Carter's "mediating institutions" are those deemed to be members of the *accepted diversity*," whose voices are then heard in public life, while the freedom to express conscience in public life is denied to those who are, in the opinion of whomever constitutes the majoritarian middle at the time, "too" diverse—the "*excepted diversity.*"

This is particularly disturbing from the perspective of America's Sacred Ground when one considers that Carter has adopted the misreading of history often repeated on the religious right, namely, that the "metaphorical separation of church and state originated in an effort to protect religion from the state, not the state from religion."[55] Nothing could be further from fact. The founders were concerned about protecting the state from religion as well, as we have clearly seen. And because Carter has misread history in all of these ways, he concludes that churches should be "mediating institutions" with free reign in influencing the policies of the state through "resistance" and other means.

Of course, Carter would no doubt contend that I have overstated his argument—that he never meant to marginalize the minority "religious traditions." For example, Carter states:

> Yet one who argues, as I do, for a strong public role for the religions as bulwarks against state authority must always be on guard against the possibility—no, let us say the likelihood—that some religions will try to use the privileged societal position that the first amendment grants them as an instrument of oppression. Thus, just as it is important in the abstract to bear witness to the value to society of opening the public square to the religious voice, it is also important, in concrete cases, to bear witness to the dangers that some religious voices present.[56]

Yet Carter never offers any concrete suggestions as to how we can guard against the likelihood that a matrix of majority religious institutions will use their "privileged societal position" "as an instrument of oppression." Rather, the argumentation he proposes actually serves to promote their dominance. This is all the more clear when we recognize that what Carter is advocating is a privileged, majoritarian, overarching worldview "consensus."[57] Because there is nothing to ground Carter's consensus, it is likely to shift from time to time. Consequently, *no one's place is really secure.* Thus, Carter has provided an analysis that is couched as a reasonable compromise, but is really an invitation to domination.

The problem lies in the fact that Carter does not provide any coherent basis for his argument, while, at the same time, Carter's view appears to be a reasonable mediation of the extremes because it points out the concerns of both sides. That is, while he appears to take account of various concerns all around, he never adequately shows the ways in which his analysis addresses those concerns. His more recent work, *God's Name in Vain: The Wrongs and Rights of Religion in Politics,* continues in this vein.[58]* There, too, Carter raises issues and expresses concern about them but then never provides any clear direction as to how he intends to address them. As a result, he confounds the debate even more than do those of the extremes—who *do* have a coherent basis for their views, albeit erroneous ones from the perspective of America's Sacred Ground. For example, on the one hand, in *Disbelief* Carter cites the case of the Donahues who have an apartment to rent over a garage but are confronted with tenant applicants who are unmarried and so are violating the religious moral injunction against the sin of fornication held by the landlords.[59] On the other hand, he acknowledges that religious institutions can become oppressive forces in society and suggests that this is a big concern of his as well.[60] Yet there is no reconciliation of these opposing points.

Meanwhile (and I think I am reasonable in my belief), the majoritarian "middle" who reads Carter's work, in all likelihood, is of the impression that because Carter has been sympathetic to various views all around, he has adequately addressed them when in actuality he has not. Moreover, because Carter provides an "accommodation"

---

* In *God's Name,* Carter points out that religion is in danger of losing its prophetic power when it grasps for coercive power. Nevertheless, even there Carter relies on the same arguments in this later work as he does in the earlier work, which similarly prevent the development of an approach that provides a coherent basis from which to address the various concerns he raises. I offer Carter the foundations of America's Sacred Ground.

that is really a privileged status for those groups *recognized* as "religious traditions," those in the majority *accepted diversity* are coddled into believing that diversity is ensured in a reasonable compromise, and that the Religion Clauses have been well served by Carter's balancing of secular left and religious right along the secular/religion continuum. Yet, in actuality, they have not.

As Carter wades through the ambiguities along the secular/religion continuum, because he has no theoretical framework, his analysis results in numerous logical inconsistencies. By way of example, we can return again to the Donahues. Carter suggests that we can permit them to discriminate on the basis of their religion for some purposes, such as denying an apartment to an unmarried couple, but not on the basis of others, such as racial discrimination. However, he offers no analysis of how these two can be distinguished; and, I suggest, there is no reasonable basis for distinguishing them under Carter's analysis. Rather he resorts to bald assertions such as "[racial] segregation is a constitutional anathema and moral evil"[61]—which really begs the question.

The reason Carter's argument is muddled and inconsistent in this way is because he has failed to grasp what was sacrosanct to the founders. He has failed to stand firmly on America's Sacred Ground, and he has failed to recognize the individual, inalienable right to freedom of conscience and the open forum in which it is to be expressed. While Carter rightly wants to embrace religion in the Public Forum, he wrongly construes its place in it. That is why he cannot conceive of a way to accommodate all religion while, at the same time, comprehending the difference between Dr. Martin Luther King, Jr., and the Christian Coalition under his analysis, nor would he be able to distinguish the Ku Klux Klan, also a "religious" organization that claims an American tradition and that otherwise, as well, would fall within Carter's definition of religion.

Carter has fallen into the erroneous religion/secular dichotomy trap that dominates the contemporary debate on these issues and reasons that if Dr. Martin Luther King, Jr., can use religious arguments in support of his activist causes, then the Christian Coalition (and, it would logically follow, the Ku Klux Klan) should be able to as well.[62] And he is right. However, he is wrong to imply that they are all on the same footing.

Carter arrives at this erroneous conclusion (with results he obviously has not intended) because he has not recognized the difference between argumentation for moral values that promote America's Sacred Ground in the Civic Public Forum and moral argumentation in the Conscientious Public Forum in furtherance of voluntary acceptance of moral principles. That is, certain matters are appropriate for the Civic Public Forum and others for the Conscientious Public Forum *and that is what distinguishes the work of Dr. Martin Luther King, Jr., some activities of the Christian Coalition, and the "resistance" of the Ku Klux Klan.*

On America's Sacred Ground, all are welcome in the Public Forum. However, only those matters that involve preserving, enhancing, or clarifying America's Sacred Ground, or otherwise promoting the safety and general welfare of the people as a whole in service of America's Sacred Ground, are appropriate for the Civic Public Forum and, thus, are legitimately advocated as being the basis of law and regulation enforced by the state. All other matters are properly left to the Conscientious Public Forum of persuasion and voluntary acceptance.

Clearly, King's efforts on behalf of African-Americans involved the Civic Public Forum because his efforts had to do with the Civic Public Forum goals of liberty and equality, which he sought to obtain for African-Americans by changing the law. Whereas prior to his efforts, African-Americans were extremely limited in their ability to express conscience in the Public Forum, after King's work (and the work of others who continued in his quest), their participation was greatly enhanced and the law continues to evolve in this vein.

Similarly, the Christian Coalition's efforts to regain an equal place in the Public Forum for adherents of the evangelical Christian religion involve the Civic Public Forum goals of liberty and equality as well. Thus, both King and the Christian Coalition have revealed the harm to the liberty of their constituents, which was caused by the failure to open the Public Forum to them. Moreover, they have shown how the omission of their admittance to the Public

Forum is a violation of the rule of consistency/no hypocrisy because it is a denial to them of what those in power—the majority—have not denied themselves.

However, when the Christian Coalition (no matter how much many may like what they hear) or the Ku Klux Klan (no matter how much many may abhor what they hear) argue in furtherance of goals inconsistent with America's Sacred Ground, they are making Conscientious Public Forum arguments appropriate only for voluntary compliance—not for law. So, while Carter is correct to defend religious motivation in making political decisions,[63] what is important is whether such motivation is consistent with the goals of the two-tiered Public Forum of America's Sacred Ground, *not whether or not they are religious.*

All of this becomes more clear when we examine Carter's references to the role of religious institutions as "power centers" of "resistance" to the state.[64] Of course, Carter is right that religion can play an important role in this regard, but to imply somehow that by virtue of the fact that they are religious makes them especially good "bulwarks" against the government is to miss the point. Because Carter does not offer a clear basis for "resistance" to the state, he cannot distinguish resistance to the incursions of secularism (which appears to be his primarily concern) from a "resistance" that seeks to impose, for example, racist views in the name of religion.[65]

Of course, Locke and the founders fully recognized the people's right to resist the state—even to rebel. But the right of resistance only arises in one context—infringement of the inalienable rights. *It is not a right to resist the government for any reason.* In other words, if one's religious (or secular for that matter) sensibilities are offended because one is forced to share the Public Forum with someone he or she deems unworthy, but who otherwise functions in accord with the laws of the Public Forum, there is no right of resistance. That is, if the resistance involves an insistence that the state use its coercive power for matters beyond the scope of what is appropriate for the Civic Public Forum, *then resistance is a violation of America's Sacred Ground, which provides for everyone's participation.*

Of course, I agree entirely with Carter that religion should not be trivialized and that the religious can and should play an important role in public life. However, I contend that we cannot merely argue for religious or nonreligious participation without being clear about what the framework for participation is. Otherwise, we end up with arguments that undermine the very thing that grounds everyone's participation. In other words, when Carter argues that "[w]e need conversation not merely about our rights, but about what is right,"[66] he must also recognize that the conversation about "what is right" depends entirely on the context for that conversation, which derives entirely from "our rights."

So, by making a claim along the secular/religion continuum, Carter has fallen into the Hobson's choice between the moral relativity of the secular left and someone's particular dominating moral foundation on the religious right. As a consequence, *alarmingly*, he adopts language implying that freedom and equality are just two of many moral claims by someone (the "liberals") in a morally relative public discourse.[67] The result is that we find him arguing for an open debate, but one with no foundation. He does not recognize what has been established by the founders as the foundation of the Public Forum within which the discussion about values occurs. As a consequence, he leaves all results to the majority without recognizing that *there is a framework for the debate that is the moral foundation of our society*, albeit one that leaves much to individual freedom of conscience to decide and on which to take action. Accordingly, Carter fails to embrace the fact that freedom and equality do not just amount to foundationless moral claims by the "liberals" vying for power. They are *our* moral foundation—central to the American system. *To trivialize these fundamental American principles in this way is more dangerous than any other trivialization Carter may seek to overcome.*

Yet, disturbingly, Carter's argument has a ring of truth for many because they perceive that the pendulum has swung too far to the secular left, resulting in intolerance of religion in America—something clearly not intended by the founders. However, despite his sincere effort to locate a credible and significant role for religion in public life, Carter has failed to grasp the import of America's unique system. Neither he, nor those who embrace his or similar views, realize that the attempt to locate a middle position along the secular/religion continuum serves only to undermine what was sacrosanct to the founders. As a result, such an effort is conceptually deceptive; it is merely a wolf in sheep's clothing thinly disguising a majoritarian ploy for dominance within the language of conciliation. The only thing it "compromises," however, is America's Sacred Ground.

CHAPTER 6

Grounding the Debate

Every man has commission to admonish, exhort,
convince another of error, and by reasoning to
draw him into truth. . . . It is only light and
evidence that can work a change in men's opinions.
—John Locke, *A Letter Concerning Toleration* (1685)

SIFTING THROUGH THE CONFUSION
IN THE CONTEMPORARY DEBATE

Now that we have examined left and right, it becomes easier for us
to see how America's Sacred Ground provides sure footing for the
popular debate about religion and values in public life. The examples in the popular debate about religion and values in public life
that we started with in chapter 1 at pages 11–15 clearly show that
the debate has become confounded and confused. However, when
we reorient the debate by applying what we now understand about
America's Sacred Ground, its values, and its two-tiered Public
Forum, the confusion can be unraveled and placed on a footing that
serves the goals of Locke and the American founders, while at the
same time respecting America's pluralistic society.

In the exchange between Buchanan and Ireland on CNN's
Crossfire, Patricia Ireland (who is generally identified with the secular left) chose to distinguish her efforts to shape values in public life
from those of the Promise Keepers (who are generally identified

with the religious right) based on her lack of religious grounds and their religious grounds. Yet she no doubt would have welcomed Martin Luther King, Jr.'s views, which were obviously religiously grounded. As Pat Buchanan pointed out, this appears to be an inconsistency. But it would not be inconsistent if Patricia Ireland had not distinguished her views from the Promise Keepers by reference to religion and, instead, had acknowledged America's Sacred Ground.

It is America's Sacred Ground that makes her views and King's views consistent. King's religious ideas promoting civil rights were grounded squarely in America's Sacred Ground, and Patricia Ireland's "secular" ideas promoting women's rights are grounded squarely in America's Sacred Ground, because both are arguing for equal freedom in accordance with the underlying political theology of the nation. Consequently, it is not the "religious" or "nonreligious" character of the argument that distinguishes Patricia Ireland and King from the Promise Keepers. What distinguishes them is that Patricia Ireland's and King's arguments are Civic Public Forum arguments. They are arguing, on the basis of the fundamentals of America's Sacred Ground, about the appropriate extent and limit of the use of governmental coercion.

On the other hand, the Promise Keepers are undermining the values of the Civic Public Forum when they attempt to impose their views about the leadership of the husband in the family, among other things, on the public at large through instrumentalities of the state, for example, the public schools and local government. It is very important to understand, however, that to the degree that the Promise Keepers are a community defining themselves or presenting values that they want to encourage the public to adopt voluntarily, they are expressing their freedom to pursue the good in the Conscientious Public Forum of persuasion and voluntary compliance. It is also very important for the left to understand, as well, that to the degree that Patricia Ireland seeks, through the instrumentalities of the state, to rob the Promise Keepers or anyone else of the ability to achieve their Conscientious Public Forum goals, she is in clear violation of the fundamentals of America's Sacred Ground, as well.

But it is not, as Pat Buchanan implied, that all values are relative in the public square, and so all values are just as rightly pursued as a basis for law as are any others. If this were so, then it would follow that legitimate law is whatever a majority of the people, the legislature, or the Justices on the United States Supreme Court say it is. In other words, there would be no basis on which to criticize or discredit their decisions. Moreover, there would be no basis on which to challenge an election or appointment of a judge to the courts, other than competency. Then, whoever gains the power to pack the courts with judges sympathetic to his or her cause, could do so—even when that cause is in violation of America's Sacred Ground.

Government's limited purpose is to preserve the inalienable rights and to promote the safety and welfare of the people in a manner consistent with America's Sacred Ground. The inalienable rights are not subject to majority rule. In fact, they are to be preserved in the face of a majority with a contrary view. Similarly, while the Supreme Court is, for all practical purposes, the arbiter of constitutional disputes, it is not the final authority. Contrary to the view of many, including certain Supreme Court Justices, there *is* a basis on which to criticize their decisions. That basis is an appeal to the principles of America's Sacred Ground. Without this, we are left only with public moral relativity, leaving us with no ground to stand on, risking the gradual undermining of the very foundations of the American system.

Turning now to George W. Bush's presidential debate response that Jesus Christ is the political philosopher that has most influenced him: One can only guess why then-Governor Bush thought it was important for voters to know this about him. One thing we know for certain, however, is that this proclamation told us nothing about whether or not he would make a good president. An assertion of a religious conviction certainly is permitted in the Conscientious Public Forum, but it serves no purpose in the Civic Public Forum with regard to the public policies a president would pursue, unless it is accompanied by an explanation of the values that the religious conviction has instilled in the speaker. Governor Bush's statement, as well as the statement that followed wherein he asserted only that Jesus had changed his heart, left one wondering about all of the things one would be most concerned about in voting for an American president: Does his Christianity promote a top-down overarching worldview approach to government? Would his Christianity preserve the two-tiered Public Forum for debate and action, which promotes the participation of all religious voices? We would not know from his bare statement.

George Bush certainly promoted various values in the programs he proposed during the months leading up to the presidential election and since. But he has never explained how his faith influenced his adoption of any of those values or programs. Rather, he seems to be promoting the idea (as have many politicians of late) that merely being "religious"—in particular, accepting Jesus as Lord—makes a person an especially good leader. Nothing could be further from the truth, as history has amply shown. And even Jesus, himself, put little store in merely calling on his name.[1]

The *Time* article on Senator Lieberman directly called into question what the writer appeared to view as contradictory positions taken by Lieberman. However, when we analyze the apparent inconsistencies presented in the article in light of America's Sacred Ground, we see that Lieberman is, in effect, able to function well within the Public Forum in his exercise of freedom of expression. He recognizes (without my terminology of course) that there is a two-tiered Public Forum for debate and action and that religion plays an important role in public life at both levels of the Public Forum. Accordingly, he is against coerced prayer in public schools as a misuse of governmental power in the Civic Public Forum, while at the same time he recognizes a place for religion in public life that is constitutionally sound. Similarly, he is against abortion when he argues from his Orthodox Jewish perspective in the Conscientious Public Forum, but finds that this "personal judgment" about abortion is not appropriate for the Civic Public Forum where he functions as a lawmaker. Thus Senator Lieberman is not "dodging" the implications of his beliefs. In fact, he is honoring the consistency/no hypocrisy principle of the Civic Public Forum.

Nevertheless, many may disagree with Lieberman's division of the abortion issue between the Civic Public Forum and the Conscientious Public Forum in this way. After all, it can be argued, as it was by Alan Keyes (in effect if not by name) during the 2000 presidential primaries, and by others elsewhere, that abortion is a Civic Public Forum issue because it involves the freedom and equality of "individuals." However, this argument does not work against the fact that Lieberman is making a distinction between two forums and that many others do not recognize the difference. Most important, as I have shown, it is a crucial distinction to make if one wants to avoid undermining America's Sacred Ground.

The ABC *Politically Incorrect* exchange is a paradigmatic example of the great error made by "liberals" on the left regarding the nature of the Public Forum established by the founders. Recall that one guest stated that she had a lot of respect for Marilyn Manson (who performs lewd sex acts on stage during live performances), although she also stated that she did not like what Manson was doing. The guest is typical of those on the secular left who hold the mistaken belief that to be a good American who upholds liberty, one cannot criticize anyone who exercises freedom within the narrow limits of the law. Many, like her, assume that to do so is hypocrisy. In fact, to take a "moral position" on a show like *Politically Incorrect* is to risk ridicule by its host. But it is a mistake to think that this is valuing freedom, as those who ridicule seem to think. Rather, this is a failure to recognize the difference between the purposes of the Civic Public Forum and the Conscientious Public Forum—and, specifically, it is an undermining of the Conscientious Public Forum where debate and action about matters of morality beyond that of the Civic Public Forum should take place.

If the guest was offended by the actions of Marilyn Manson, she certainly was entitled to express her condemnation of his use of freedom, while at the same time recognizing his right to it, and still be a good citizen upholding America's Sacred Ground. Of course,

Marilyn Manson is free to pursue his endeavors under the Civic Public Forum, but that does not require silence when a strong rebuke is felt to be in order. It is not hypocrisy to uphold the Civic Public Forum while exercising one's freedom of participation to condemn those one deems to be immoral from the perspective of one's Conscientious Public Forum views. Rather, to fail to condemn, when condemnation is in order, *is a failure to exercise the full force of one's freedom*; in other words, that failure thwarts the whole purpose of freedom. When we do not exercise our freedom in this way, we contribute to the creation of a society that does not reflect the vision of the true and the good of our consciences.

By failing to exercise freedom, the left, in effect, keeps the Conscientious Public Forum "value-free" by failing to argue against those whose contribution to society it despises. Consequently, the left glorifies freedom for its own sake. Making a virtue of freedom, those on the left proclaim people like Marilyn Manson today, or Larry Flynt a few decades ago, as heroes just for "pushing the envelope" of freedom, while they do not question the value of Manson's or Flynt's contributions to society. Marilyn Manson is not to be respected merely because he has exercised his freedom. He is to be respected *only* if the contribution he makes by his free participation in society is truly believed by the one giving respect to be derived from conscience and to be contributing to the building of a good society.

It is important to point out one more thing in this regard—many Americans have skewed the real meaning and place of the American resistance hero. It is not the mere standing against the tide of public opinion or law alone that makes one a resistance hero, as many have come to think; it is not being a rebel for rebellion's sake alone. An American resistance hero is one who upholds America's Sacred Ground in the face of tremendous odds against him or her. That is why Martin Luther King, Jr., is an American hero, a civically virtuous person, and Larry Flynt, no matter how much of a rebel he has been, is not—unless, of course, the one proclaiming Flynt to be a hero believes that Flynt's actions have been based on conscience for the purpose of promoting truth and goodness in society, and believes, therefore, that Flynt's actions, in fact, have contributed to truth and goodness, and not merely the bald expression of freedom.

Now one example remains: the Nancy Gibbs's reference to "America's true God" and "our faith." In chapter 1, I asked in response to Gibbs's references: "Does America have a faith? a God?" And we can see now that, while America may not have *a* faith or *a* God, it does have *faith* and *God*—the faith of all people who seek truth and goodness under a system of government that preserves to *all* the equal freedom to answer when God, however known or understood, calls.

REORIENTING THE DEBATE TO AIM FOR THE GOOD

As we have seen, the participants in the debate about religion in public life, and religion's role in the pursuit of the good society, be they left, right, or accommodationist, use misplaced rhetoric involving the misuse of terminology (religion, secular), dichotomies (public/private), and concepts (separation of church and state) that are understood today in ways that were not intended by the founders of the nation. This has been exacerbated by all sides because they have drawn from fragments of original intent to support the views of the factions they represent, instead of considering the original *intentions* of the founders underlying the American system as a whole, and appreciating their significance for our time. Further, the extremes have allowed the fear of, or desire for, a "secular" society (depending on their ideological bent) to confound the real meaning of the word. And, they have embraced "moral relativity" as a political reality—accepting that the privilege of defining America's moral and political foundation according one's own worldview is the privilege of the winner of the debate.

No wonder the discourse is muddled and confused. The debate itself has lost its footing in the etymological shifting of the meanings of words and in the fragmented and polarized debate about American history and original intent. Consequently, the debaters are using nineteenth-century conceptions of "religion" and "secular" in a twenty-first-century debate occurring in a legal/political context that arises out of an eighteenth-century idea embodied in the United States Constitution and its Religion Clauses. The result is not only confusion about potential answers to questions, but a confounding of the actual questions themselves. As a result, we find the debate centering around competing overarching worldviews rather than embracing what should be the common ground—what it is that grounds the American system in the first place.

But America's Sacred Ground does not permit anyone to impose an overarching worldview about the true and the good on the populace as a whole through the instrumentalities of the state. Rather, America's Sacred Ground provides for maximum freedom to pursue truth and goodness according to conscience within the framework of the two-tiered Public Forum. Through debate and action in the Civic Public Forum, we can work toward the goals of maximizing the equal freedom of everyone by continually working toward modifications to American law and politics so as to preserve, endorse, reveal, and clarify America's Sacred Ground. And through debate and action in the Conscientious Public Forum, which involves persuasion and voluntary acceptance, we can promote truth and goodness in society from the ground up and in so doing we can take the opportunity freedom has given us to make a better world.

CONCLUSION

America's Sacred Ground: Our Civic Faith

> No people can be bound to acknowledge and adore
> the Invisible Hand which conducts the affairs of
> men more than the people of the United States.
> Every step by which they have advanced to the
> character of an independent nation seems to have
> been distinguished by some token of providential
> agency; and in the important revolution just
> accomplished in the system of their united
> government the tranquil deliberations and
> voluntary consent of so many distinct communities
> from which the event has resulted cannot be
> compared with the means by which most
> Governments have been established without some
> return of pious gratitude, along with an humble
> anticipation of the future blessings which the past
> seems to presage.
> —George Washington *"First Inaugural Address"* (1789)

As we Americans have expanded our understanding of freedom and
equality, we have made it possible to entertain any number of philosophical and theological systems of thought, including their moral
or amoral implications. And as the ongoing discourse has unfolded,
some of us personally adhere to one moral view and others to another, resulting in an often disjointed debate. It is no wonder that
many, like Alasdair MacIntyre in *After Virtue*, lament the contentious
discourse of competing worldviews and metanarratives as various factions vie for dominance in the great debate about American values. In

this disruptive climate, they long for a common community with a unified vision and tradition from which a coherent moral language can be spoken.[1] But this longing is as misplaced as is the degree to which the discourse has been unhinged. It is reflective of the fact that most of us have lost our footing on America's Sacred Ground.

Americans have forgotten their roots, which has resulted in a sense that we have no moral foundation at all. Faced with the abyss of a morally relative freedom, which functions as an excuse for a licentious society and ultimately chaos, many feel an urgent need to fill the gap with *something*. But American society is not without a foundation and common ground. We have merely lost track of it because we have been so fortunate in our freedom that we (the privileged who are having this conversation) have forgotten what it is to be without it. We have forgotten all that the founders knew when, at that most auspicious moment in history, they accomplished what had theretofore been only a dream of the downtrodden and the oppressed. It is incumbent on us today to reclaim that knowledge and that history and, by so doing, rediscover America's Sacred Ground— or risk losing what has made freedom possible in the first place.

The founders' immediate history had provided them with an understanding of one central thing: unchecked power in any hands leads to oppressive power. They and their immediate predecessors, among them in particular John Locke, had witnessed the horrors of the exercise of that power by the two "governors" of the people— ecclesiastical authority and governmental authority. The founders knew that all attempts to establish religious or moral uniformity through the instrumentalities of the state lead to oppressive enforcements and untold harms to the people. Rather than effecting peace, such attempts result in civil unrest as the people rise up to oppose their oppressors, and the authorities rush to quell the dissidents to restore the imposed unity, leading again to more civil uprisings until there is either revolution—or complete totalitarian suppression. This cycle is no less so, the founders knew, when religion serves as the primary governing power. History had revealed that, despite the good intentions of any religion, power in the hands of religious authorities can also result in grave abuses. There, however, religious authorities, corrupted by power, use supernatural justifications for harm in this world for the sake of the next. There, uniformity is not only an outward goal to maintain peace, but an attempt to govern the inward beliefs of individuals so that their minds and hearts, as well as their bodies, are restrained.

And so the founders, in an effort to check the power of the state and the churches, decided to try something entirely new: To place the governing power in the people through a system of representative government that checks power, including the power of the majority, and preserves the rights of minorities. Of course, this idea did not come to light out of nowhere. The struggle of the people of England with inextricably intertwined state and ecclesiastical authorities had a long history in which concessions were made: the Magna Carta, the 1628 Petition of Right, the 1689 Bill of Rights, to name a few. However, none before had placed the power in the people, so that such advancements in rights were no longer concessions of a king to the people.

Significantly, the legal/political system that was designed by the founders to give effect to all of this was based on a theological ground. The concepts of the "state of nature," the inherent freedom and equality of all human beings, and therefore their "natural rights," the "social contract," the "inalienable rights," and the right to rebel when these are infringed, are all derived from John Locke's fundamentals, which were based on this initial theological premise: There is God who created human beings free and equal. And there is a fundamental assumption about God that is inherent to the American system: God communicates to individuals the "natural law" through revelation, reason, and insight—instilling us with conscience. While God is not coercive, nevertheless, we owe a duty to our Creator (however understood) to be and do good in accordance with conscience. The only legitimate judge, other than God, as to what constitutes that duty is each individual for himself according to his own conscience. That is why freedom of conscience and its expression in speech and action are inalienable rights. That is why we are not free to infringe the rights of conscience of others—the ultimate harm.

But freedom was never intended to be an end in itself, as many mistakenly believe. Freedom has a context and a purpose. Freedom's *context* is the Public Forum for speech and action in which individuals are as politically free to be and do in accordance with conscience as they are naturally free under God. That Public Forum has two tiers: the Civic Public Forum and the Conscientious Public Forum. And understanding the function of each is essential to the preservation of the American system and, therefore, ultimately, all of the sacred civil rights.

Furthermore, it is important to remember that the Public Forum involves a particular conception of civic morality and immorality. Our civic moral duty is clear: We must preserve, enhance, and clarify what we now know are the sacred foundations of the American system—America's Sacred Ground, which includes the Public Forum itself. And we are to avoid civic immorality—that which tears down America's Sacred Ground—in particular, attempts to dominate, whether through religious or nonreligious modes of action. Moreover, it is essential to the intended working of the American system that we adhere to the civic and conscientious moral principles of America's Sacred Ground, which direct us to the ultimate *purpose* of freedom—the pursuit of the good.

Religious voices, such as Dr. Martin Luther King, Jr.'s, are extremely important in the Civic Public Forum—the forum for debate and action about the extent and limit of the coercive power of the state through law and public policy, where the preservation, enhancement, and clarification of America's Sacred Ground takes place. Religious voices are also essential to the Conscientious Public Forum—the forum for persuasion and voluntary action with regard to those matters left solely to individual conscience.

But while religious voices are important, even central, to debate and action at both levels of the Public Forum, we must always remember that "the religions" were never intended to hold a privileged place in the discourse by sanction of the state. In this regard, it is critical that we recognize that the metaphor of the "wall of separation of church and state" has been misconstrued in the discourse to imply two things that the founders never intended, both of which obscure what are to be the "just bounds" between religion and the state. First, as has already been acknowledged and as the right vociferously claims, the founders never intended to suppress religious voices or discourse on moral values in the Public Forum. Second, the metaphor implies that the "just bounds" are between church and state. As we have clearly seen, the "just bounds" are between the two recognized "governors"—the state and individual conscience. Churches are to have *no authority*, except to the extent voluntarily chosen by the individual.

Somehow this original concept of the "just bounds" between the state and conscience has gotten lost in the evolution of the law and the discourse. Because of this, as religion claims its rightful place in the Public Forum, it mistakenly claims a privileged place for churches, something entirely contrary to the intentions of the founders. The legacy of this is a confounded debate on a continuum between two extremes—secular and religious—where the only outcome is dominance by one overarching worldview or another. Rather, the focus was always meant to be individual liberty so that individuals alone, or through the spontaneous, voluntary associations they create, can participate according to conscience in the free and open Public Forum for debate and action.

In this regard, perhaps it now is clear that when we are to determine what is the proper role of "religion" in the public discourse about American moral values, the question is not: "Is this a legitimate enough religion to merit recognition and, therefore, freedom?" Neither does the question involve the distinction between "religion" and "secular," any more than it involves a determination of just what constitutes an "establishment." The issue is: Does the law or governmental action in question preserve and enhance or undermine and diminish the individual, inalienable right to freedom of conscience and its expression and/or the Public Forum for debate and action? And, if the law or governmental action does undermine this freedom or the Public Forum, is it justified because it directly involves what Locke referred to as a "political matter,"[2] that is, does it preserve America's Sacred Ground in another way? This is the only "compelling state interest." In difficult cases, as Locke held, the weight should be given to individual freedom of conscience and its expression. That is, in such cases, it is not the legitimacy of a particular religion that is in question; it is the legitimacy of the law that should be reconsidered—in light of the fundamentals of America's Sacred Ground. Only when we examine the issue in this way can we be protected against the dominance of someone's particular majoritarian interest.

It now becomes clear that, essentially, America's Sacred Ground is the common good, which is the foundation for pursuit of the good as each individual perceives it to be. This is what makes authentic, uncoerced community action possible. Accordingly, while America is not without a moral foundation, its moral foundation does not dictate all that is true and good. Rather, most is left for conscience to decide.

It is only natural, then, that we wish to rush to fill the space left to conscience with our visions for the good. MacIntyre advocates a return to Aristotle's virtues; the Christian Coalition and others argue in favor of what they hold are basic Christian moral precepts; Jeffrey Stout, in *Ethics after Babel*, recommends a moral bricolage leading to "certain truths."[3] *And this is what we are supposed to do*—not leave the space empty as a nihilistic void (although we are also free to call it that). It is to be teaming with ideas, feelings, and actions in an ebullient exchange, sometimes heated, sometimes calm, where revelation and spiritual insight, and reason—the means by which God transmits the natural law—all converge. This is how, as John Locke said, truth can shift for herself—the only hope for the true and the good, and the beautiful as well, to be realized.

This does not leave us with no moral language at all, as MacIntyre contends. Nor does it leave us in an entirely free-floating foundationlessness where we are merely "drawing the line here or there in countless particular cases."[4] Rather, we have as our moral ground the framework for the debate about moral values—all that entails America's Sacred Ground. And its moral language is Locke's language of nature and rights, which was adopted and expanded by the founders. One may argue that America's Sacred Ground is a moral foundation with no "teeth." Its moral language is not complete; it leaves too much to choice. How can we realize the true and the good this way? The answer is: We have no other alternative. Imposed overarching worldviews that attempt to create some sort of religious and/or moral uniformity always degenerate into oppressive systems—ultimately immoral from the perspective of our founders. Consequently, such goals, however laudable in theory, in practice never lead to a good society. As Locke said, "[I]f truth makes not her way into the understanding by her own light, she will be but the weaker for any borrowed force violence can add to her."[5]

Moreover, it is important to remember that we have been living recently during a period when the public moral discourse has been stifled—a grave mistake. I, for one, am optimistic that opening the Conscientious Public Forum fully to moral discourse will bring some consensus to that forum of persuasion and voluntary compliance that embraces the diversity of our culture and the plurality of our views. However, while we may voluntarily come to some fragile consensus about Conscientious Public Forum issues, we must *not* *ever* permit any one voice or group of voices to convince us to undermine, in the name of a "specious, and popular pretence of justice, consolidation, and dignity,"[6] the foundation that makes the discourse possible in the first place. If we do, we will unravel our freedom, trading it for a unifying dominance that can only lead eventually to a return to the state of nature where power is wielded by the few against the many, and the freedom to strive for moral virtue is lost.

And, it is critical that, at the forefront of all debate and action in public life, we hold to our highest moral duty, our American civic and conscientious moral duty, above all else. We must always preserve our sacred ground in the face of opposing worldviews, meta-narratives, and comprehensive doctrines, while at the same time, using, as Locke envisioned, all "exhortations and arguments as . . . [one] pleases toward the promoting of another man's salvation . . . [absent] all force and compulsion . . . ."[7]

But this does not mean that there are no tough issues along the line between the Civic Public Forum, ensured by the coercive force of law, and the Conscientious Public Forum, where one pursues the true and the good as individual conscience directs. And certainly I have left many questions about this open in this work. But it has not been my goal to answer the difficult questions along the lines and at the margins. Rather, I have set out to reframe the debate itself by setting it on its proper ground—America's Sacred Ground—because much is at stake.

Without America's Sacred Ground, the whole context and purpose of the American system, the reason for freedom in the first place, is forgotten. We, then, undermine the functioning of the Civic and Conscientious Public Forums, thwarting freedom's purpose—the pursuit of the good. We disrespect and limit the important role of religion in public life. We privilege institutionalized religion over individual conscience. We uproot America's plurality, swinging back and forth from disparaging it to exulting it, with neither approach recognizing the ground that makes it possible in the first place. In an effort to accommodate all views regarding American values, we adopt a public moral relativity, which makes the majority of the people, the legislature, or the United States Supreme Court the final authority with nothing on which to ground their decisions and which, in turn, leaves no basis on which to criticize or discredit their decisions. This is so even if they violate the fundamentals that underlie the American system. And, because of *all* of these things, we risk moving toward an overarching worldview that will take the place of America's Sacred Ground, sapping the sacred civil rights of their force and effect. *We must not allow this to happen.*

As we Americans develop our society at home and spread our influence around the world, we must remember who we are. We must see that those who proclaim that America has a "civil religion" are right—although often wrong about what it entails. Our civil religion—or what is more properly called our "civic faith"—is America's Sacred Ground, our beacon, unique in all history. It is the common good for America's pluralistic society, and it is the means to a good society. In 1988, Jeffrey Stout warned that "we had better strive to maintain and strengthen whatever *it* is about our society that makes [the virtue of practical wisdom] and other virtues possible."[8] What everyone in the debate needs to recognize is: *This is it.*

There is still time to reclaim the foundation that is our heritage, together with its moral language of God-given natural, inalienable rights. In particular, we must reclaim the roots of our freedom in the state of nature where we are free and equal because we are God's creations and, therefore, are called to mutual love; where we form a government by mutual consent for the limited purpose of preserving the natural rights of the people, providing an impartial judge of disputes, and ensuring the safety and general welfare of the people in a way that is consistent with those natural rights. We must remember that it is only when government infringes the natural rights of individuals that the people have a right of resistance; they do not have a right to resist the enforcement of the inalienable rights, themselves. And we must recall that freedom extends to the fullest extent possible without harm to others in life, liberty, and property so that what we have is free for all and not the "free-for-all" of the state of nature. Unless we do reclaim this heritage, we will not grasp what the founders knew: Our political framework is a fragile one; its survival depends wholly on a people who recognize that our enemy is not so much a force from outside our boundaries, but *our own ignorance* about what grounds the American system.

There has always been a tension between those who locate the sacred solely outside the natural world, the realm of the eternal, and therefore hold the natural world to be the realm of the profane, and those who find the sacred in the natural world as well, the realm of the temporal. For the founders, however, it was clear: the temporal world, that is the "secular" world, is sacred too. What is sacred, temporal, and secular is America's Sacred Ground, which has a view to the eternal but is focused on the here and now. In this way, we can say that America's Sacred Ground creates the framework in society—a "secular" framework—for those who wish to listen and hear the voice of God through revelation, spiritual insight, and nature. And, in turn, it makes possible the reflection of God in that secular world through the works of those who use their freedom well.

So, as we Americans dig deeply to find the roots of our identity— what it is that joins all of the multifarious beauty of the diversity of our people and the plurality of our beliefs—we discover that our identity is not found in a vision of the many made one. We are not a people with one appearance, one history, one culture, one religion. Ours is a people that is much more beautiful because we are not defined by ethnicity, national origin, common perspective, appearance, or anything else like that. We are defined by a vision of the many *as* one, all standing on America's Sacred Ground—all striving in a free and open forum, where truth can "shift for herself," for what we believe will make a better world. And if, and only if, the Public Forum is free and open, and conscience is expressed, can it be said, as it was said in 1778, that "[t]he voice of the people is . . . the voice of God."[9]

APPENDIX A

❧ ⟡ ❧

A Few Definitions

"RELIGION" AND "RELIGIOUS"

It is easy to see that something crucial is missing in the debate: There is no clear understanding of what everyone is talking about when they refer to "religion." Instead, there are covert definitions of, and assumptions regarding, "religion" lurking in the arguments themselves, even when definitions are proffered. Although some commentators note the absence of clear definitions, and the confusion in the discourse that arises because of that deficiency,[1] most, particularly in the legal/political context, do not even acknowledge the definitions implied by the theories and arguments they proffer.

This should be of concern because the battle in the religion-in-public-life debate is waged in large part over definitions, in particular, the definitions of "religion" and "secular," as the battle lines have been drawn with reference to these two opposing concepts. This is not merely semantics. These definitions have real political and legal implications.

This becomes abundantly clear as we recognize that as Establishment Clause jurisprudence has evolved, it has come to require a differentiation between what constitutes "religion" and what constitutes the "secular." For example, the Supreme Court, in *Lemon v. Kurtzman* (1971), set out what has become known as the "*Lemon* Test," which includes a requirement that a law have a "secular purpose" in order to be valid under the Establishment Clause.[2]

We can readily see, then, that the lack of clarity or consistency in defining religion in sociological and historical contexts may be

185

problematic, but in the legal/political context it is disastrous. How we define "religion" determines *who* is entitled to "free exercise of religion" and *what*, if anything, is to be "accommodated" as the Justices of the United States Supreme Court reconsider Establishment Clause jurisprudence.

Wilfred Cantwell Smith's classic work *The Meaning and End of Religion* helps to shed light on the problem.[3] Cantwell Smith tells us that the word "religion" derives from the Latin *religio*, which itself is an imprecise word, the meaning of which has been difficult to pin down.[4] For the most part, however, it originally seems to describe those things in the world that pertain to the gods, for example, religious rites, taboos, superstitions, duties, oaths, sacred places, and the like.[5] Through Christian history up to modern times, however, "*religio*" connoted a personal relationship with God, meaning something more akin to our words "piety" and "faith" than what we generally mean by "religion" today. This was so for the prominent theologians of Christianity—Augustine, Thomas Aquinas, Calvin, and Luther.[6] In the seventeenth and eighteenth centuries, however, the words "*religio*" and "religion" began to shift and take on an additional meaning as a system of beliefs.[7]

But it was not until the nineteenth century that the term came to be used commonly to denote a reified concept of "religion" "as an objective systematic entity."[8] The reason for this development is that nineteenth-century scholars began to study such things as the "history of the religions" of the world. Consequently, it was necessary to identify what was to be the object of such a study. We see during this period, then, that the word "religion" develops a use in the plural. Thus, we have scholars studying "the religions" of the world, rather than the religious nature of human activity within a particular culture, for example.* Hence, the "idea was widely accepted

---

* Interestingly, during this same period, there also developed an interest in identifying the "true" religion or the "essence" of religion. Wilfred Cantwell Smith, *The Meaning and End of Religion* (1962; Minneapolis: Fortress Press, 1991), 47. Consequently, not only was there interest in studying an entity called "religion," but there was also an interest in abstracting from that "entity" what should be or is the core of any particular religion. This generally involved the idealization of one's own religion, which countered the objectification of everyone else's.

that religion is something with a definite fixed form, if only one could find it." "Ever since then," Cantwell Smith tells us, "the hunt has been on."[9] And along with the hunt for the "fixed form" of "the religions," there has been a related search for the definition of what they were hunting for. As a consequence, there has been a continual dialectic between the two, resulting in an ever-unattainable certainty about either.

Cantwell Smith tells us that we have inherited all of the usages from the etymological development of the word "religion" and today we use it in four distinct ways:[10]

1. Personal piety or relationship with God
2. The ideal of a system of beliefs, practices, and values (i.e., the subject of theologians)
3. The "empirical phenomenon" of a system of beliefs, practices, institutions, and values (i.e., the subject of historians and sociologists)
4. a "generic summation, 'religion in general.' "

The word "religion" is used throughout this work in all of these ways depending on the context and the person whose position is being represented. It is important for the reader to be aware of the word's multiple meanings, however, because arguments about the founders' original intentions often rely on a particular assumed meaning, for example, the third of Cantwell's list, when, as we will see, what was understood by the word at the time was entirely different—most likely, the first or at most the second of Cantwell's list.

"Secular" and "Secularism"

In popular usage, the word "secular" and its derivatives are generally defined in the negative. It is everything that is not "religion." However, the word, of course, has its own etymology, which is important to note here, and this work makes it clear that defining it only in terms of the negative in this way contributes to the confusion in the debate about the role of religion in public life and in the pursuit of the good.

The word "secular" derives from the Latin word "*saeculum.*" It means literally "time" or "age." Consequently, "secular" means "of this time," in other words, of this world. That is, a secular person is a "this-worldly" directed human being.[11]

Although the word "secular" was used intermittently prior to modern times, the concept of "secularism," like "religion," arose in the nineteenth century.[12] Perhaps, as scholars began to feel a need to identify what they were studying as "religion," they also needed a term for what is not "religion." Whatever the reason, they began to use the word "secular" in order to distinguish "religion" from other aspects of human life.

However, the word "secularism" actually was coined by Jacob Holyoake in Europe in 1851 after he was imprisoned for blasphemy.[13] By "secularism" he was referring to "the doctrine that morality should be based on regard to the well-being of mankind in the present life" and not to overriding those concerns for the sake of one's eternal salvation. "Secularism" was not meant to imply the eventual eradication of all such beliefs, but merely to keep the focus of government on the here and now.[14]

We can see at the outset, therefore, that what was once deemed to be "secular" was not necessarily exclusive of what was deemed to be "religion." Rather, the "secular" could be this-worldly directed religion, in the sense of acting in accordance with one's personal piety or relationship with God *in the world.* Its emphasis was the here and now in the hope that government would not use supernatural justifications for worldly harms. Nevertheless, this is not how "secular" and "secularism" are used today.

The word "secular" and its derivatives are used throughout this work primarily as understood in common usage as "that which is not religion." However, this work shows how this understanding of the word obscures the original intentions of the founders.

"GOD"

Intentionally, "God" is left undefined and understood in very general and simplistic terms. The reason is that none of those cited from the founding era specifically identified the attributes of "God," or what was meant by the word "God," in their political writings. One may say that they must have meant the biblical God, since they were Christians; however, interpretations abound throughout the history of Judaism and Christianity as to what or who is the biblical God. Consequently, reference to the Bible does not provide us with a very useful identifier.

The most that can be said is that whomever or whatever the founders meant by use of the word "God" or "Supreme Governor of the Universe" or "Divine Providence" or any number of other similar terms used to reference God, for them God is what or who created human beings and the world. Moreover, for them, God is someone or something that is capable of communicating knowledge and truth to individual human beings that provides them with consciousness of the ultimately good. In other words, God is someone or something that human beings are able to touch, feel, or sense, literally or figuratively, in some way that provides them with a conscience, that is, a conscience imbued with God

Accordingly, God is referenced throughout this work in personal theological terms, for example, "the voice" of God and the like. This may be taken literally or figuratively depending on the reader's understanding of God within the parameters of the definition of God above. However, as the argument set out in the work shows, belief in a personal God, or any particular conception of God, is not required in order to stand firmly on America's Sacred Ground.

"SACRED"

The "sacred" denotes that which especially pertains to God. In some sense, this means everything, if God created the universe. However, here what is meant by "sacred" is not everything. Rather it is God, contact with or relationship with God, all that people do in response to God, and anywhere God is especially present. It is important to note that the word "sacred" is not used herein in the "Durkheimian" sense, that is, as what society or any person holds most dear or reveres, unless what society or any person holds most dear or reveres is God as described above.[15]

"THE GOOD"

"The Good" is what is "morally excellent; virtuous; righteous"[16] as projected by God. Therefore, it is, as the American founders believed, ultimate, absolute, and universal. The "good" is determined by human beings by reference to conscience informed by revelation and reason, which come from God. Significantly, "the good" is not "good" in the sense of being attractive, advantageous, enjoyable, and the like,[17] although it incidentally may be these things as well.

"MORAL RELATIVITY"

The moral relativity argument arises out of the postmodern view that morality has *no absolute foundation*, and therefore morality is neither ultimate or universal. For those in America for whom this is the prevailing view of morality (and there appear to be many), there is no legitimate moral basis for law or American political institutions. The moral relativists tell us that there is no valid foundational principle on which to construct society.[18] They reject all "overarching worldviews" (see definition below) as illegitimate efforts to formulate assumptions on which to ground knowledge and morality. And such assumptions are without validity, they contend, because they are "logocentric, transcendental totalizing metanarratives that anticipate all questions and provide predetermined answers."[19]

According to moral relativists, everyone's proposed moral foundation or narrative is merely based on a play for power by one group over another, or is, at best, useless. The shifting theories and metanarratives reflect only a vying for power among the elites that will forever oppress somebody somewhere at all times.[20] Hence, there is no solution to the moral dilemma that plurality poses, except, perhaps, a claim to what can be found in a "collective understanding" of "lived values,"[21] which could be anything.

Many view the religion-in-public-life debate as a clash of competing worldviews, each with no more legitimate claim to absolute authority than another, but all vying for dominance.

"OVERARCHING WORLDVIEWS"

As noted earlier, the debate about the role of religion in public life, and religion's role in the pursuit of the good, appears to lack a common point of reference. The result is a disjointed and incoherent discourse where mutual understanding remains a remote possibility. Many commentators have concluded that the reason this is occurring is that the various factions in the debate are operating out of completely different "systems of moral understanding."[22] In other words, they each hold to different "worldviews," "metanarratives," "sacred canopies,"* or "comprehensive doctrines"† that form the overriding moral context for each of their various perspectives. Each faction promotes its own moral context, and the perspective derived therefrom, as the candidate for remaining, becoming, or being reinstated as the most appropriate or best moral context, that is, worldview, that will serve to unify the moral understanding of American culture and law. Some in the debate claim that a moral understanding similar to their own was what once unified Western culture. The demise of this previously stable overall moral context has resulted in America's moral decline, they claim.

I refer to all such candidates in the debate, as well as all theoretical or actual overriding and culturally unifying moral understandings, both past and present, as "overarching worldviews," or in the singular as an "over-arching worldview."

"SECULARIZATION"

The term "secularization" arose out of "secularization theory," which, under most versions of the theory, holds that institutionalized religion or its influence on society is in a process of decline and

---

* Peter L. Berger once argued that religion is a social construct—a "sacred canopy"—that is produced by the objectification of what is perceived as being reality, but it is merely a world of meanings produced by human beings and projected onto God. Peter L. Berger, *The Sacred Canopy: Elements of a Sociological Theory of Religion* (New York: Doubleday, 1967).

† This is John Rawls's term. See chapter 4 pages 128–136.

that the eventual end of this trend is the demise of institutionalized religion as anything but a trivial force in society. Secularization theory has roots in the nineteenth century[23] and continues in the work of contemporary scholars in the sociology and history of religion.[24]

There is considerable debate among historians and sociologists of religion as to the viability of the theory.[25] However, what is important about it for this project is that it has captured the popular political imagination of a great number of people in the debate about the role of religion in public life and religion's role in the pursuit of the good. Consequently, it provides a background motivation and support for their views.

Some (generally those of the secular left) view secularization as a positive trend in American society. They see it as a move away from unreliable and potentially oppressive supernatural moral justifications for actions taken, and as a move toward the more rational approach of science and nonreligious philosophy. Others (generally those of the religious right) view secularization as a negative trend because it divorces society from the moral context out of which it arose—the moral perspective of the Judeo-Christian tradition.

Although the secularization theses of contemporary writers vary,[26] a general statement of it goes something like this: Modernity, with the development of science, the rationalization of reality, the liberalization of scholarship and politics, and the social differentiation brought on by urbanization and industrialization, has set in motion an inevitable pluralism, resulting in the relativization of all religious overarching worldviews, and therefore the decline of institutionalized religion.[27]

"Freedom"

"Freedom" or "liberty" is, as M. Stanton Evans says in *The Theme Is Freedom: Religion, Politics, and the American Tradition*, "the absence of coercion."[28] More specifically, it is the absence of coercion from governmental power so as to provide the maximum individual freedom possible up to the point where one's freedom would infringe on other individuals' freedom.

APPENDIX B

Freedom of Conscience in Revolutionary Period State Constitutions and Declarations of Rights

Virginia Declaration of Rights (1776): "Religion, or the duty which we owe to our Creator, and the manner of discharging it, can be directed only by reason and conviction, not by force or violence, and, therefore, all men are equally entitled to the free exercise of religion, according to the dictates of conscience; and that it is the mutual duty of all to practise Christian forbearance, love, and charity, towards each other.

The New Jersey Constitution (1776): "[N]o person shall ever, within this Colony, be deprived of the inestimable privilege of worshipping Almighty God in a manner agreeable to the dictates of his own conscience; nor, under any pretence whatever, be compelled to attend any place of worship, contrary to his own faith and judgment; nor shall any person, within this Colony, ever be obliged to pay tithes, taxes, or any rates, for the purpose of building or repairing any other church or churches, place or places of worship, or for the maintenance of any minister or ministry, contrary to what he believes to be right, or has deliberately or voluntarily engaged himself to perform."

Source: Bernard Schwartz, ed. *The Bill of Rights: A Documentary History*, 2 vols. (New York: Chelsea House Publishers, 1971).

Pennsylvania Declaration of Rights (1776): "[A]ll men have a natural and unalienable right to worship Almighty God according to the dictates of their own consciences and understanding: And that no man ought or of right can be compelled to attend any religious worship, or erect or support any place of worship, or maintain any ministry contrary to, or against, his own free will and consent: Nor can any man, who acknowledges the being of God, be justly deprived or abridged of any civil right as a citizen, on account of his religious sentiments or peculiar mode of religious worship: And that no authority can or ought to be vested in, or assumed by any power whatever, that shall in any case interfere with, or in any manner controul, the right of conscience in the free exercise of religious worship."

Delaware Declaration of Rights (1776): "[A]ll men have a natural and unalienable right to worship Almighty God according to the dictates of their own consciences and understandings; and that no man ought or of right can be compelled to attend any religious worship or maintain any ministry contrary to or against his own free will and consent, and that no authority can or ought to be vested in, or assumed by any power whatever that shall in any case interfere with, or in any manner controul the right of conscience in the free exercise of religious worship. . . . "[A]ll persons professing the Christian religion ought forever to enjoy equal rights and privileges in this state, unless under colour of religion, any man disturb the peace, the happiness or safety of society."

Maryland Declaration of Rights (1776): "[A]s it is the duty of every man to worship God in such manner as he thinks most acceptable to him; all persons, professing the Christian religion, are equally entitled to protection in their religious liberty; wherefore no person ought by any law to be molested in his person or estate on account of his religious persuasion or profession, or for his religious practice; unless under colour of religion, any man shall disturb the good order, peace or safety of the State, or shall infringe the laws of morality, or injure others, in their natural, civil, or religious rights;

nor ought any person to be compelled to frequent or maintain, or contribute, unless on contract, to maintain any particular place of worship, or any particular ministry: yet the Legislature may, in their discretion, lay a general and equal tax, for the support of the Christian religion; leaving to each individual the power of appointing the payment over of the money, collected from him, to the support of any particular place of worship or minister, or for the benefit of the poor of his own denomination, or the poor in general of any particular county: but the churches, chapels, glebes, and all other property now belonging to the church of England, ought to remain to the church of England forever." "[T]he manner of administering an oath to any person, ought to be such, as those of the religious persuasion, profession, or denomination, of which such person is one, generally esteem the most effectual confirmation, by the attestation of the Divine Being. And that the people called Quakers, those called Dunkers, and those called Menonists, holding it unlawful to take an oath on any occasion, ought to be allowed to make their solemn affirmation, in the manner that Quakers have been heretofore allowed to affirm. . . ."

North Carolina Declaration of Rights (1776): "[A]ll men have a natural and unalienable right to worship Almighty God according to the dictates of their own consciences."

Georgia Constitution (1777): "All persons whatever shall have the free exercise of their religion; provided it be not repugnant to the peace and safety of the State: and shall not, unless by consent, support any teacher or teachers except those of their own profession."

New York Constitution (1777): "And whereas we are required, by the benevolent principles of rational liberty, not only to expel civil tyranny, but also to guard against that spiritual oppression and intolerance wherewith the bigotry and ambition of weak and wicked priests and princes have scourged mankind, this convention doth further, in the name and by the authority of the good people of this State, ordain, determine, and declare, that the free exercise and enjoyment of religious profession and worship, without discrimination or preference, shall forever hereafter be allowed, within this State, to all mankind: Provided, That the liberty of conscience, hereby granted, shall not be so construed as to excuse acts of licentiousness, or justify practices inconsistent with the peace or safety of this State." "That all such parts of the said common law, and all such of the said statutes and acts aforesaid, or parts thereof, as may be construed to establish or maintain any particular denomination of Christians or their ministers, . . . or are repugnant to this constitution, be, and they hereby are, abrogated and rejected."

Vermont Declaration of Rights (1777): "[A]ll men have a natural and unalienable right to worship Almighty God, according to the dictates of their own consciences and understanding, regulated by the word of God; and that no man ought, or of right can be compelled to attend any religious worship, or erect, or support any place of worship, or maintain any minister, contrary to the dictates of his conscience; nor can any man who professes the protestant religion, be justly deprived or abridged of any civil right, as a citizen, on account of his religious sentiment, or peculiar mode of religious worship, and that no authority can, or ought to be vested in, or assumed by, any power whatsoever, that shall, in any case, interfere with, or in any manner controul, the rights of conscience, in the free exercise of religious worship: nevertheless, every sect or denomination of people ought to observe the Sabbath, or the Lord's day, and keep up, and support, some sort of religious worship, which to them shall seem most agreeable to the revealed will of God."

South Carolina Constitution (1778): "[A]ll persons and religious societies who acknowledge that there is one God, and a future state of rewards and punishments, and that God is publicly to be worshipped, shall be freely tolerated. The Christian Protestant religion shall be deemed, and is hereby constituted and declared to be, the established religion of this State. That all denominations of Christian Protestants in this State, demeaning themselves peaceably and faithfully, shall enjoy equal religious and civil privileges." "No person shall, by law, be obliged to pay toward the maintenance and support of a religious worship that he does not freely join in, or has not voluntarily engaged to support. But the churches, chapels, parsonages, glebes, and all other property now belonging to any societies of the Church of England, or any other religious societies, shall remain and be secured to them forever."

Massachusetts Declaration of Rights (1780): "It is the right as well as the duty of all men in society, publicly, and at stated seasons, to worship the Supreme Being, the great creator and preserver of the universe. And no subject shall be hurt, molested, or restrained, in his person, liberty, or estate, for worshipping God in the manner and season most agreeable to the dictates of his own conscience; or for his religious profession or sentiments; provided he doth not disturb the public peace, or obstruct others in their religious worship." "As the happiness of a people, and the good order and preservation of civil government, essentially depend upon piety, religion and morality; and as these cannot be generally diffused through a community, but by the institution of the public worship of God, and of public instructions in piety, religion and morality: Therefore, to promote their happiness and to secure the good order and preservation of their government, the people of this Commonwealth have a right to invest their legislature with power to authorize and require, and the legislature shall, from time to time, authorize and require, the several towns, parishes, precincts, and other bodies-politic, or religious societies, to make suitable provision, at their own expense, for the institution of the public worship of God, and for the support and maintenance of public protestant teachers of piety, religion and morality, in all cases where such provision shall not be made voluntarily. And the people of the Commonwealth have also a right to, and do, invest their legislature with authority to enjoin upon all the subjects an attendance upon the instructions of the public teachers aforesaid, at stated times and seasons, if there be any on whose instructions they can conscientiously and conveniently attend." It goes on to say that people shall have the right to direct such funds as are paid for public worship, and for the support of public teachers, to "his own religious sect or denomination." "[E]very denomination of christians, demeaning themselves peaceably, and as good subjects of the Commonwealth, shall be equally under the protection of the law; And no subordination of any one sect or denomination to another shall ever be established by law."

New Hampshire Bill of Rights (1783): "Every individual has a natural and unalienable right to worship God according to the dictates of his own conscience, and reason; and no subject shall be hurt, molested, or restrained in his person, liberty or estate for worshipping God, in the manner and season most agreeable to the dictates of his own conscience, or for his religious profession, sentiments or persuasion; provided he doth not disturb the public peace, or disturb others, in the religious worship." "As morality and piety, rightly grounded on evangelical principles, will give the best and greatest security to government, and will lay in the hearts of men the strongest obligations to due subjection: and as the knowledge of these, is most likely to be propagated through a society by the institution of the public worship of the Deity, and of public instruction in morality and religion; therefore, to promote those important purposes, the people of this state have a right to impower, and do hereby fully impower the legislature to authorize from time to time, the several towns, parishes, bodies-corporate, or religious societies within this state, to make adequate provision at their own expense, for the support and maintenance of public protestant teachers of piety, religion and morality." "And no portion of any one particular religious sect or denomination, shall ever be compelled to pay towards the support of the teacher or teachers of another persuasion, sect or denomination. And every denomination of christians demeaning themselves quietly, and as good subjects of the state, shall be equally under the protection of the law: and no subordination of any one sect or denomination to another, shall ever be established by law. And nothing herein shall be understood to affect any former contracts made for the support of the ministry; but all such contracts shall remain, and be in the same state as if this constitution had not been made."

APPENDIX C

Drafts of the Religion Clauses Proposed in the Debates of the First Congress

1. Proposal by Madison in the House, June 8, 1789: "The civil rights of none shall be abridged on account of religious belief or worship, nor shall any national religion be established, nor shall the full and equal rights of conscience be in any manner, or on any pretext infringed.

The people shall not be deprived or abridged of their right to speak, to write, or to publish their sentiments; and the freedom of the press, as one of the great bulwarks of liberty, shall be inviolable.

The people shall not be restrained from peaceably assembling and consulting for their common good; nor from applying to the Legislature by petitions, or remonstrances, for redress of their grievances." Thomas Lloyd, ed. *The Congressional Register*. 2 vols. New York, June 8, 1789, vol. 1, 427. (Hereafter *Congressional Register*.)

2. Proposal by Sherman to the House Committee of Eleven, July 21–28, 1789: The people have certain natural rights which are retained by them when they enter into society, Such are the rights of conscience in matters of religion; of acquiring property, and of pursuing happiness & safety; of Speaking, writing and publishing their Sentiments with decency and freedom; of peaceably Assembling to

Source: Neil H. Cogan, ed. *The Complete Bill of Rights: The Drafts, Debates, Sources, and Origins* (New York, Oxford: Oxford University Press, 1997).

consult their common good, and of applying to the Government by petition or remonstrance for redress of grievances. Of these rights therefore they Shall not be deprived by the government of the United States. Madison Papers, Library of Congress, Washington, D.C.

3. Report of House Committee of Eleven, July 28, 1789: "No religion shall be established by law, nor shall the equal rights of conscience be infringed." Broadside Collection, Library of Congress, Washington, D.C.

4. Motion by Livermore in the House, August 15, 1789: "[C]ongress shall make no laws touching religion, or infringing the rights of conscience." *Congressional Register*, August 15, 1789, vol. 2, 196.

5. Motion by Ames in the House, August 20, 1789: "[C]ongress shall make no law establishing religion, or to prevent the free exercise thereof, or to infringe the rights of conscience." *Congressional Register*, August 20, 1789, vol. 2, 242.

6. Further House Consideration, August 21, 1789: "Congress shall make no law establishing religion, or prohibiting the free exercise thereof, nor shall the rights of conscience by infringed." *Journal of the House of Representatives*. New York, 1789, 107. (Hereafter *House Journal*.)

7. House Resolution, August 24, 1789: "Congress shall make no law establishing religion, or prohibiting the free exercise thereof, nor shall the rights of Conscience be infringed." House Pamphlet, Rough Copy of the Legislative Journal, Part of the First Session (March 4–September 10, 1789), and Transcribed and Corrected Copy of the Legislative Journal, First Session and Part of the Second Session (March 4, 1789–June 11, 1790). Record Group 46, General Records of the United States Government, National Archives, Washington, D.C. (Hereafter *Legislative Journal*.)

8. Senate Consideration, August 25, 1789: "Congress shall make no law establishing Religion, or prohibiting the free exercise

thereof, nor shall the rights of conscience be infringed." Journal of the First Session of the Senate of the United States of America. New York, 1789, 104. (Hereafter *Senate Journal.*)

9. Further Senate Consideration, September 3, 1789: On motion, To amend Article third, and to strike out these words, "Religion or prohibiting the free Exercise thereof," and insert, "One Religious Sect or Society in preference to others," *Senate Journal* 116.

10. Further Senate Consideration, September 3, 1789: On motion, To adopt the following, in lieu of the third Article, "Congress shall not make any law, infringing the rights of conscience, or establishing any Religious Sect or Society," *Senate Journal* 116.

11. Further Senate Consideration, September 3, 1789: On motion, To amend the third Article, to read thus—"Congress shall make no law establishing any particular denomination of religion in preference to another, or prohibiting the free exercise thereof, nor shall the rights of conscience by infringed" *Senate Journal* 117.

12. Further Senate Consideration, September 3, 1789: On motion, To adopt the third Article proposed in the Resolve of the House of Representatives, amended by striking out these words—"Nor shall the rights of conscience be infringed"—*Senate Journal* 117.

13. Further Senate Consideration, September 9, 1789: "To erase from the 3d. Article the word "Religion" & insert—<u>Articles of faith or a mode of Worship.</u>—And to erase from the same article the words "<u>thereof, nor shall the rights of Conscience be infringed</u>" insert—<u>of Religion; or abridging the freedom of speech, or of the press, or of the right of the people peaceably to assemble, & to petition to the government for a redress of grievances</u>" Senator Oliver Ellsworth's Handwritten Notes of the Senate Amendments to the Proposed Bill of Rights, 1–2. *Legislative Journal.*

14. Senate Resolution, September 9, 1789: "Congress shall make no law establishing articles of faith or a mode of worship, or

prohibiting the free exercise of religion, or abridging the freedom of speech, or of the press, or the right of the people peaceably to assemble, and to petition to the government for a redress of grievances." Senate Pamphlet, *Legislative Journal.*

15. Conference Committee Report (Conference Among Representatives from the Senate and Representatives from the House), September 24, 1789: "Congress shall make no Law <u>respecting an</u> <u>establishment of Religion</u>, or prohibiting the free exercise thereof; or abridging the freedom of Speech, or of the Press; or the right of the people peaceably to assemble and to Petition the Government for a redress of grievances;" Conference Notes, *Legislative Journal.*

16. House Consideration of the Conference Committee Report, September 24 [25], 1789: "Congress shall make no law respecting an establishment of religion, or prohibiting the free exercise thereof; or abridging the freedom of speech, or of the press; or the right of the people peaceably to assemble, and to petition the government for a redress of grievances." *House Journal* 152.

17. Senate Consideration of Conference Committee Report, September 24, 1789: "Congress shall make no Law respecting an establishment of Religion, or prohibiting the free exercise thereof; or abridging the freedom of Speech, or of the Press; or the right of the people peaceably to assemble and petition the Government for a redress of Grievances;" *Senate Journal* 117.

18. Enrolled Resolution, September 28, 1789: "Congress shall make no law respecting an establishment of religion, or prohibiting the free exercise thereof; or abridging the freedom of speech, or of the press, or the right of the people peaceably to assemble, and to petition the Government for a redress of grievances." Enrolled Resolutions, Certificates of Ratification of the Constitution and Bill of Rights and Related Correspondence and Rejections of Proposed Amendments. Record Group 11, General Records of the United States Government, National Archives, Washington, D.C.

Notes

Chapter 1: Toward a Debate on Common Ground

1. *Everson v. Board of Education*, 330 U.S. 1, 76 S.Ct. 504, 91 L.Ed. 711 (1947).

2. Richard John Neuhaus, *The Naked Public Square: Religion and Democracy in America* (Grand Rapids, MI: William B. Eerdmans Publishing, 1984).

3. John Eidsmore, *Christianity and the Constitution: The Faith of Our Founding Fathers* (Grand Rapids, MI: Baker Books, 1987).

4. John Adams, "To the Officers of the First Brigade of the Third Division of the Militia of Massachusetts," 11 October 1798, *The Works of John Adams, Second President of the United States with a life of the author, notes, and illustrations*, compiled Charles Francis Adams, 10 vols., vol. 9 (Boston: Charles C. Little & James Brown, 1850–1856), 228–229. [Hereafter *Adams Works.*]

5. George Washington, "First Inaugural Address," 30 April 1789, *A Compilation of the Messages and Papers of the Presidents* (Prepared Under the Direction of the Joint Committee on Printing, of the House and Senate, Pursuant to an Act of the Fifty-Second Congress of the United States)(with Additions and Encyclopedia Index by Private Enterprise), ed. James D. Richardson, 20 vols., vol. 1 (New York: Bureau of National Literature, 1911–1922), 44.

6. Stephen L. Carter, *The Culture of Disbelief: How American Law and Politics Trivialize Religious Devotion* (New York, London, Toronto, Sydney, Auckland: Anchor Books, 1993).

7. http://usinfo.state.gov/usa/faith/pr070102.htm.

8. Nancy Gibbs, "If You Want to Humble an Empire," *Time* September 11, 2001.

9. Nancy Gibbs, "Whose Bully Pulpit Now?" *Time* September 11, 2000.

10. Alasdair MacIntyre, *After Virtue: A Study in Moral Theory* (Notre Dame, IN: University of Notre Dame Press, 1981).

Chapter 2—Rediscovering the Roots of America's Sacred Ground in John Locke

1. Nathan Tarcov, *Locke's Education for Liberty* (Chicago: University of Chicago Press, 1953), 1.

2. George W. Ewing, Introduction, *The Reasonableness of Christianity*, by John Locke, ed. George W. Ewing (Washington, DC: Regnery Gateway, 1965), viii.

3. Carl L. Becker, *The Declaration of Independence: A Study in the History of Political Ideas* (1922; New York: Vintage, 1942), 27; Ewing xv. There have been those who have disputed this, but a reading of the writings of those in the founding generation leave little doubt of Locke's pervasive influence, as has been clearly argued in Jerome Huyler, *Locke in America: The Moral Philosophy of the Founding Era* (Lawrence: University of Kansas Press, 1995), an in-depth analysis of the subject.

4. See, for example, John Marshall, *Resistance, Religion and Responsibility* (Cambridge: Cambridge University Press, 1994). See also references to the essential theological tendencies of Locke's philosophy in A. James Reichley, *The Values Connection* (Lanham: Rowman & Littlefield Publishers, 2001); David Wootton, Introduction, *Political Writings*; Mark Goldie, Introduction, *Political Essays*, ed. Mark Goldie (Cambridge: Cambridge University Press, 1997), xxv; and Ewing, xvi; John Dunn, *The Political Thought of John Locke* (Cambridge: Cambridge University Press, 1969).

5. Wootton, 11.

6. Ewing, xvi.

7. John Dunn, *The Political Thought of John Locke* (Cambridge: Cambridge University Press, 1969).

8. Wootton, 33.

9. Wootton 31–36; Goldie, xv. The *Two Tracts on Government*, written by Locke in 1660, supported authoritarian power based on traditional Christian political theory derived from the works of Augustine, which held that government is necessary to restrain the sinful nature of human beings.

10. Wootton, 36–41.

11. Wootton, 13.

12. Goldie, xxi.

13. John Locke, *A Second Vindication of the Reasonableness of Christianity, The Works of John Locke*, 9 vols., vol. VI (London, 1824), 357. [Hereafter *Works*.]

14. John Locke, *The Reasonableness of Christianity*, ed. George W. Ewing (Washington, DC: Regnery Gateway, 1965), ¶ 155, p. 114.

15. John Locke, *Essay on Human Understanding*, Book IV, Ch. XIX, ¶ 4, vol. II, *Works* 273.

16. John Locke, *Of Government, Two Treatises of Government, Works*, vol. IV, Ch. IX, ¶ 86, p. 279. [Hereafter *First Treatise*.]

17. Locke, *The Reasonableness of Christianity*, ¶¶ 39–40, pp. 24–26; see Ewing, xviii.

18. Locke, *Essay on Human Understanding*, Book IV, Ch. XIX, ¶ 4, vol. II, *Works*, 273.

19. John Locke, *A Letter Concerning Toleration*, trans. William Popple (1685, published 1689), *Political Writings of John Locke*, ed. David Wootton (London: Mentor, 1993), 397. [Hereafter *Political Writings*.]

20. Locke, *Letter Concerning Toleration, Political Writings*, 407.

21. Locke, *Letter Concerning Toleration, Political Writings*, 397.

22. Wootton, 67; Dunn, 213, 222–228, 250–254,

23. This was fundamental to Locke's view of Christianity: "Praises and prayer, humbly offered up to the Deity, were the worship he now demanded, and in these everyone was to look after his own heart, and to know that it was that alone which God had regard to and accepted." "To be worshiped in spirit and truth, with application of mind and sincerity of heart, was what God henceforth only required. Magnificent temples, and confinement to certain places, were now no longer necessary to his worship, which by a pure heart might be performed anywhere." Locke, *The Reasonableness of Christianity*, ¶ 244, pp. 181–182. And it is works that are central for Locke. Locke, *The Reasonableness of Christianity*, ¶ 227, pp. 155–156. Although one may be forgiven by the law of faith for a failure to do good, that forgiveness will not be forthcoming without a sincere commitment to do good works.

24. Wootton, 39.

25. Locke, *Letter Concerning Toleration, Political Writings*, 390.

26. Locke, *Letter Concerning Toleration, Political Writings*, 431.

27. Locke, *Letter Concerning Toleration, Political Writings*, 420.

28. Locke, *Letter Concerning Toleration, Political Writings*, 412, 420, 431.

29. Locke, *Letter Concerning Toleration, Political Writings*, 431.

30. Locke, *Letter Concerning Toleration, Political Writings*, 416.

31. Locke, *Letter Concerning Toleration, Political Writings*, 400, 417, 431.

32. Locke, *Letter Concerning Toleration, Political Writings*, 431.

33. Locke, *Letter Concerning Toleration, Political Writings*, 402, 420. Locke makes a negative reference to superstition in the *Letter Concerning Toleration*, where he says that "indifferent" things should not be the source of conflicts in religion, but implies that "superstition" is not one of these. But this is inconsistent with the statement cited above in the text. To reconcile this discrepancy, one must reach the conclusion that Locke means one may not think such things "indifferent," but nevertheless they are to be tolerated by the magistrate.

34. Locke, *Letter Concerning Toleration, Political Writings*, 390.

35. Locke, *Letter Concerning Toleration, Political Writings*, 392.

36. Locke, *Letter Concerning Toleration, Political Writings*, 391.

37. Locke, *Letter Concerning Toleration, Political Writings*, 392.

38. Locke, *Letter Concerning Toleration, Political Writings*, 394.

39. Locke, *Letter Concerning Toleration, Political Writings*, 394.

40. Locke, *Letter Concerning Toleration, Political Writings*, 399.

41. Locke, *Letter Concerning Toleration, Political Writings*, 397.

42. Locke, *Letter Concerning Toleration, Political Writings*, 394–395.

43. Locke, *Letter Concerning Toleration, Political Writings*, 417.

44. Locke, *Letter Concerning Toleration, Political Writings*, 409.

45. Locke, *Letter Concerning Toleration, Political Writings*, 409.

46. Locke, *Letter Concerning Toleration, Political Writings*, 398.

47. Locke, *Letter Concerning Toleration, Political Writings*, 396. Wootton refers to Locke's reasoning method here as "probability" decision-making, which he sees as running throughout much of Locke's work. Wootton, 103–104.

48. Locke, *Letter Concerning Toleration, Political Writings*, 409.

49. Locke, *Letter Concerning Toleration, Political Writings*, 410.

50. Wootton, 97.

51. Locke, *Letter Concerning Toleration, Political Writings*, 406–407.

52. Locke, *A Second Vindication of the Reasonableness of Christianity, Works*, vol. VI, 351–354.

53. Locke, *Letter Concerning Toleration, Political Writings*, 406.

54. Locke, *Letter Concerning Toleration, Political Writings*, 410.

55. Locke, *Letter Concerning Toleration, Political Writings*, 407.

56. Locke, *Letter Concerning Toleration, Political Writings*, 411.

57. Ewing, xii.

58. Alasdair MacIntyre, *After Virtue: A Study in Moral Theory* (Notre Dame, IN: University of Notre Dame Press), 1981.

59. John Locke, *Of Civil Government, Two Treatises of Government, Works*, vol. IV, 338–485. [Hereafter *Second Treatise.*]

60. Obviously the concept of a "state of nature" was not Locke's alone. Hobbes and Pufendorf, among others, had developed theories on this basis as well. It is interesting to note that Locke's view of the social contract differed from that of his contemporaries who espoused social contract theory. For Locke, the contract was made among the people— the rulers being the servants of the people. For others it was made between the people and the king. Locke, *Second Treatise*, Ch. XIII, ¶¶ 151–152, pp. 427–428.

61. "God, out of the infiniteness of his mercy, has dealt with man as a compassionate and tender Father. He gave him reason and with it a law, that cannot be otherwise than what reason should dictate, unless we should think that a reasonable creature should have an unreasonable law." Locke, The *Reasonableness of Christianity*, ¶ 252, pp. 192–193.

62. Locke, *Second Treatise*, Ch. II, ¶ 5, p. 340. Reason "directs" "charity, bounty, and liberality." Locke, *Letter Concerning Toleration, Political Writings*, 400.

63. Locke, *Second Treatise*, Ch. II, ¶ 6, p. 341.

64. Locke, *Second Treatise*, Ch. III, ¶ 16, p. 347.

65. Locke, *Second Treatise*, Ch. II, ¶ 8, p. 342.

66. Locke, *Second Treatise*, Ch. II, ¶ 13, pp. 345–346; Ch. III, ¶¶ 20–21, pp. 349–350.

67. Goldie, xl.

68. Feminists have disagreed on Locke's record as regards women's natural rights to liberty and equality. Some have pointed out that Locke argued against the traditional view of society where religious doctrine justifies the king's authority over the subjects, as well as the husband's authority over the wife who is the subject not of the king, but of the husband. Furthermore, Locke rejected the conventional position that Eve was more culpable than Adam for the Fall and, therefore, she was rightfully subjected to Adam's authority. Contrary to these views, Locke suggested that women were not necessarily to be subject to their husbands and he advocated greater rights for women than were generally allowed at the time, for example, property and divorce rights. See *First Treatise*, Ch. V, ¶¶ 44–49, pp. 244–249; Ch. VI, ¶ 55, p. 253; ¶ 62, pp. 258–259; ¶ 66, pp. 261–262; and *Second Treatise*, Ch. VI, ¶¶ 52–53, pp. 367–368; Ch. IX, ¶¶ 81–83, pp. 275–277. Instead of the conventional view, Locke held that the marriage is a contract under which the woman, theoretically at least, could assert superior rights to the husband, *First Treatise*, ¶ 47, pp. 246–247, although Locke allowed that because the husband is "the abler and the stronger," it follows that the "last determination" "naturally falls to the man's share." But still the wife is "in full and free possession of what by contract is her peculiar right, and give the husband no more power over her life than she has over his . . . ." Locke, *Second Treatise*, Ch.VII, ¶¶ 81–83, pp. 385–386. See also Carol Pateman, *The Sexual Contract* (Stanford, CA: Stanford University Press, 1988), generally; Wootton 65; Goldie, xxiii. As David Wootton points out, "[w]e learn from a journal note of 1681 that Locke thought that according to nature women were 'at their own disposal,' as free as the men with whom they had relations." Wootton 65, quoting "Virtus" (1681) from the 1661 Commonplace, *Political Writings*, 241.

69. Locke, *First Treatise*, Ch. IX, ¶ 86, p. 279.

70. Locke, *Second Treatise*, Ch. VIII, ¶¶ 95–122, pp. 394–411.

71. Locke, *Letter Concerning Toleration, Political Writings*, 405.

72. Locke, *Letter Concerning Toleration, Political Writings*, 392–393.

73. Locke, *Letter Concerning Toleration, Political Writings*, 421.

74. Locke, *Letter Concerning Toleration, Political Writings*, 420–421.

75. Locke, *Second Treatise*, Ch. XIV, ¶ 168, pp. 438–439. "The law is the eternal, immutable standard of right," Locke, *The Reasonableness of Christianity*, ¶ 232, p. 162, which is knowable through reason and revelation, although reason often needs the light of truth for direction. Locke, *The Reasonableness of Christianity*, ¶ 243, pp. 176–177, 179.

76. Locke, *Second Treatise*, Ch. III, ¶ 19, p. 318.

77. Locke, *Letter Concerning Toleration, Political Writings*, 401, 404, 431.

78. Locke, *Letter Concerning Toleration, Political Writings*, 426.

79. Clearly this was not always the case in practice. As kings and bishops vied for power, the relations between them shifted back and forth.

80. Locke, *The Reasonableness of Christianity*, ¶¶ 4–6, p. 3–6; Locke, *Second Treatise*, generally.

81. In *The Sacred Canopy: Elements of a Sociological Theory of Religion* (New York: Doubleday, 1967), Peter L. Berger argued that human beings collectively objectify their own world of meanings onto a socially constructed concept of God. Locke's view is that there is a God that provides the "meanings" and that human beings confronted with those meanings construct a world in accordance with them. Unfortunately, people ignore those "meanings" when they hold power and are motivated by self-interest. Consequently, those so motivated construct an overarching worldview or "sacred canopy" in order to subdue the masses, while they pursue their own interests. To avoid this, Locke places world construction back into the hands of individuals by providing a context in which conscience can be swayed to God. The hope is that this context—this "sacred ground"— will be fertile enough for world construction based on the "meanings" of God to take root.

82. Locke, *Letter Concerning Toleration, Political Writings*, 420.

83. Although not articulated in precisely this way, this is what Locke, a committed Christian, was after, as is clear from the things he wrote about others. He admonished the intolerant that their methods do not lead to the kingdom of God. Significantly, Locke was offering another program for that goal. For example, he argued: "[W]hilst he is cruel and implacable towards those that differ from him in opinion, he be indulgent to such iniquities and immoralities as are unbecoming the name of a Christian, let such a one talk never so much of the Church, he plainly demonstrates by his actions that 'tis another kingdom he aims at, and not the advancement of the kingdom of God." Locke, *Letter Concerning Toleration, Political Writings*, 392.

84. Locke, *Letter Concerning Toleration, Political Writings*, 393.

85. Locke, *Letter Concerning Toleration, Political Writings*, 423.

86. Locke, *Letter Concerning Toleration, Political Writings*, 420.

87. Locke, *Letter Concerning Toleration, Political Writings*, 411.

88. Locke, *Letter Concerning Toleration, Political Writings*, 415, 417, 420, 424.

89. Locke, *Letter Concerning Toleration, Political Writings*, 415 (emphasis added).

90. Locke, *Letter Concerning Toleration, Political Writings*, 415. This foreshadows the United States Supreme Court holding in *Lemon v. Kurtzman*, 403 U.S. 602, 91 S.Ct. 2105, 29 L.Ed. 745 (1971), that there must be a compelling state interest in order for a law that impacts religious freedom to be valid under the Religion Clauses of the First Amendment to the Constitution.

91. Locke, *Letter Concerning Toleration, Political Writings*, 425.

92. Locke, *Letter Concerning Toleration, Political Writings*, 410–411.

93. Locke, *Letter Concerning Toleration, Political Writings*, 431.

94. Locke, *Letter Concerning Toleration, Political Writings*, 432.

95. Locke, *Letter Concerning Toleration, Political Writings*, 425 (emphasis added).

96. Locke, *Letter Concerning Toleration, Political Writings*, 391.

97. Locke, *Letter Concerning Toleration, Political Writings*, 403.

98. Locke, *Letter Concerning Toleration, Political Writings*, 403.

99. Locke, *Letter Concerning Toleration, Political Writings*, 399–400.

100. Locke, *Letter Concerning Toleration, Political Writings*, 433.

101. Locke, *Letter Concerning Toleration, Political Writings*, 409.

102. Locke, *Letter Concerning Toleration, Political Writings*, 409.

103. Locke, *Letter Concerning Toleration, Political Writings*, 401.

104. Locke, *Letter Concerning Toleration, Political Writings*, 421.

105. Locke, *Letter Concerning Toleration, Political Writings*, 421.

106. Locke, *Letter Concerning Toleration, Political Writings*, 423.

107. Locke, *Letter Concerning Toleration, Political Writings*, 421.

108. Locke, *Letter Concerning Toleration, Political Writings*, 422–423.

109. Locke, *Letter Concerning Toleration, Political Writings*, 422.

110. Locke, *Letter Concerning Toleration, Political Writings*, 415, 423–424. The nuances of these arguments are beyond the scope of this work, which is to clarify the boundaries for discussion, not to solve every moral dilemma in the "gray area." In other words, my goal here is to locate the sacred roots of the discourse, but not to apply it (in this work at least) to moral issues of the day. However, the mere fact that there is a "gray area" in which questions are difficult to settle does not undermine the framework of the theory.

111. See, for example, Wootton, 105.

112. Goldie, xxviii.

113. Locke, *Second Treatise,* Ch. XIX, ¶ 224, p. 471.

114. Locke, *Second Treatise,* Ch. XIX, ¶¶ 226–227, pp. 472–473.

115. Locke, *Letter Concerning Toleration, Political Writings*, 428.

116. Locke, *Letter Concerning Toleration, Political Writings*, 428–429.

117. Locke, *Letter Concerning Toleration, Political Writings*, 410–411.

118. Locke, *Letter Concerning Toleration, Political Writings*, 424.

119. Locke, *Second Treatise* Ch. I, ¶ 6, p. 341.

120. Locke, *Letter Concerning Toleration, Political Writings*, 415, 417, 420, 424.

121. Locke, *Letter Concerning Toleration,* Political Writings, 417.

122. Locke, *Letter Concerning Toleration, Political Writings*, 416.

123. Locke, *Letter Concerning Toleration, Political Writings*, 429.

124. Locke, *Letter Concerning Toleration, Political Writings*, 429–430.

125. Locke, *Letter Concerning Toleration, Political Writings*, 430.

126. Ewing xi, quoting Locke, *A second Vindication of the Reasonableness of Christianity, Works,* vol. VI, 359.

127. Wootton, 67.

128. Locke, preface, *The Reasonableness of Christianity*, xxvii.

129. Locke, *The Reasonableness of Christianity*, ¶ 244, pp. 181–182.

130. Locke, *The Reasonableness of Christianity*, ¶ 4, p. 4.

131. Locke, *The Reasonableness of Christianity*, ¶ 238, pp. 165–166; ¶ 241, pp. 169–172; ¶ 243, pp. 178, 180.

132. Locke, *The Reasonableness of Christianity*, ¶ 252, p. 193.

133. Locke, *The Reasonableness of Christianity*, ¶¶ 238, pp. 165–167; ¶ 243, pp. 176–181.

134. Locke, *Letter Concerning Toleration, Political Writings*, 402; cf. 431.

135. Locke, *A Second Vindication of the Reasonableness of Christianity, Works*, vol. VI, 188–189.

136. Locke, *Second Treatise* and *Letter Concerning Toleration*, generally.

137. Locke, The Reasonableness of Christianity, ¶¶ 9–22, pp. 7–14.

138. Locke, *Letter Concerning Toleration, Political Writings*, 420.

139. Locke, *The Reasonableness of Christianity*, ¶ 155, p. 144, quoting John 16:13.

CHAPTER 3—THE UNITED STATES CONSTITUTION: ESTABLISHING AMERICA'S SACRED GROUND

1. Bernard Schwartz, commentary, *The Bill of Rights: A Documentary History*, ed. Bernard Schwartz (New York, Toronto, London, Sydney: Chelsea House Publishers, 1971), 179.

2. James H. Hutson, Religion and the Founding of the American Republic (Washington, DC: Library of Congress, 1998), 16. Regarding the founding of the colonies by those who fled religious persecution, see Sydney Ahlstrom, *A Religious History of the American People* (New Haven: Yale University Press, 1972), 167; Patricia Bonomi, Under the Cope of Heaven (New York: Oxford University Press, 1986), 20, 35; Sally Schwartz, A Mixed Multitude (New York: New York University Press, 1987), 85.

3. Bernard Schwartz, ed., *The Bill of Rights: A Documentary History* (New York, Toronto, London, Sydney: Chelsea House Publishers, 1971), 200–211. [Hereafter *Documentary History*.]

4. See, for example, references to "life, liberty, property" as fundamental rights in the following documents: (1) Maryland Declaration of Rights, 1776 (*Documentary History*, 279, 282); (2) Delaware Declaration of Rights, 1776 (*Documentary History*, 277); (3) North Carolina Declaration of Rights, 1776 (*Documentary History*, 286); (4) Vermont Declaration of Rights, 1777 (*Documentary History*, 323); (5) Massachusetts Declaration of Rights, 1780: "Government is instituted for the common good; for the protection, safety, prosperity and happiness of the people; and not for the profit, honor or private interest of any one man, family, or class of men: Therefore the people alone have an incontestable, unalienable, and indefeasible right to institute government; and to reform, alter, or totally change the same, when their protection, safety, prosperity and happiness require it. Each individual of the society has a right to be protected by it in the enjoyment of his life, liberty and property, according to the standing laws" (*Documentary History*, 341); (6) New Hampshire Bill of Rights, 1783: "All men have certain natural, essential, and inherent rights; among which are—the enjoying and defending [of] life and liberty—acquiring, possessing and protecting property—and in a world of seeking and obtaining happiness" (*Documentary History*, 375); (7) New Hampshire Bill of Rights, 1783: "Every member of the community has a right to be protected by it in the enjoyment of his life, liberty and property. . . ." (*Documentary History*, 376).

5. Jon Butler, *A wash in a Sea of Faith: Christianizing the American People* (Cambridge: Harvard University Press, 1990), 188; Hutson 35.

6. Nathan O. Hatch, *The Sacred Cause of Liberty: Republican Thought and the Millennium in Revolutionary New England* (New Haven & London: Yale University Press, 1977), 11–13.

7. Hutson, 38. See also, Alan Heimert, *Religion and the American Mind* (Cambridge: Harvard University Press, 1966), 12–13.

8. Hatch, 16–17.

9. Hutson, 39–42.

10. Stephen A. Marini, "Religion, Politics, and Ratification," *Religion in a Revolutionary Age*, ed. Ronald Hoffman and Peter J. Albert (Charlottesville: University Press of Virginia, 1994), 193–199; Hutson, 33. See also Heimert, 12, 21.

11. In this regard, it is interesting to note that Thomas Jefferson was known to practice regular "private devotions." Charles B. Sanford, *Thomas Jefferson and His Library: A Study of His Literary Interests and of the Religious Attitudes Revealed by Relevant Titles in His Library* (Hamden, CT: Archon Books, 1977), 150, citing Henry Stephens Randall, *The life of Thomas Jefferson*, 3 vols., vol. 3 (New York: Derby & Jackson, 1858), 407–410, quoting Jefferson's grandson.

12. Thomas Jefferson "copied long passages from Locke's *Letter Concerning Toleration* in his commonplace notebook, and used many of Locke's ideas and phrases in his own writing on the need for religious freedom." Sanford, 121. Moreover, Jefferson considered John Locke to be one of the "three greatest men that ever lived, without any exception. . . ," the other two being Bacon and Newton. Thomas Jefferson, "To John Trumpbell," 15 February 1789, *The Papers of Thomas Jefferson*. ed. Julian P. Boyd, 29 vols., vol. 14 (Princeton, NJ: Princeton University Press, 1958), 561.

13. *Documentary History*, 201. The document goes on to say, however, that those religious groups that are subversive of the laws of civil government should be excluded from toleration, as Locke had maintained. But this is Merely to acknowledge that those actions that undermine the social contract cannot be tolerated, if the civil society based on it is to be preserved. That is why, for example, Catholic doctrines "that Princes excommunicated may be deposed, and those they call Hereticks may be destroyed without mercy. . . .," and that the Pope's edicts should be enforced absolutely over the laws of civil government, are practices that were excluded from the framework set out by Locke and embraced by the Americans. *Ibid.*

14. Documentary History, 349.

15. Drawing on the writings of missionaries and preachers of the eighteenth century who claimed that America exhibited a "careless, rimiss, flat, dry, cold dead frame of spirit," generally accepted twentieth-century scholarship held that religion was in decline in the eighteenth century. See, for example, Perry Miller, *The New England Mind: From Colony to Province* (Cambridge: Harvard University Press, 1953), 34–36, quoted in Hutson, 21. Newer scholarship challenges that view, however, arguing that the dire reports of religious decline at the time actually indicate a burgeoning faith among the American people. Apparently, the complaints report a lack of "true" religion on the part of those who are labeled "heathens and heretics," but not a lack of religion per se. Hutson, 19. In other words, these were charges leveled against religious dissenters from the "true church" of those making the complaint. What is being reported, then, is frustration with the increasing denominationalism among the people, rather than a decrease in religion as a whole. Some recent scholarship has reported that there actually was a dramatic increase in Anglican, Baptist, Congregationalist, German and Dutch Reformed, Lutheran, and Presbyterian churches from 1700 to 1780. Hutson, 24. And the mid-century Great Awakening witnessed throngs of people attending the emotional evangelical revivals of the likes of Jonathan Edwards (1703–1758), George Whitefield (1714–1770), and John (1703–1791) and Charles Wesley (1707–1788) and their progeny, who brought religious fervor to a fevered pitch in the eighteenth century. Such scholarship holds that, contrary to prior misconceptions, the American religious landscape was as vital in the decades leading up to the American Revolution as it ever had been before or has been since.

16. *Documentary History*, 321, 264.

17. *Documentary History*, 339.

18. James Madison, "A Memorial and Remonstrance against Religious Assessments," 1785, *The Writings of James Madison*, ed. Gaillard Hunt, 9 vols., vol. 2 (New York, London: G. P. Putnam's Sons, 1900–1903), 184. [*Hereafter Madison Writings.*]

19. *Documentary History* 511. See also "The Letters of Luther Martin," 21 March 1788, Number II, *Documentary History*, 497–498.

20. George Washington, "Circular to the States," 8 June 1783, *Basic Writings of George Washington*, ed. Saxe Commins (New York: Random House, 1948), 489. [Hereafter *Basic Writings.*]

21. George Washington, "First Inaugural Address," 30 April 1789, *A Compilation of the Messages and Papers of the Presidents* (Prepared Under the Direction of the Joint Committee on Printing, of the House and Senate, Pursuant to an Act of the Fifty-Second

Congress of the United States)(with Additions and Encyclopedia Index by Private Enterprise), ed. James D. Richardson, 20 vols., vol. 1 (New York: Bureau of National Literature, 1911–1922), 44. [Hereafter *Papers of the Presidents.*]

22. *Documentary History*, 202.

23. *Documentary History*, 223.

24. *Documentary History*, 524, 511. Also, Richard Henry Lee said, "There are certain rights which we have always held sacred in the United States . . . ." Richard Henry Lee, *Observations Leading to a Fair Examination of the System of Government*, Letter IV, 12 October 1787, *Letters from the Federal Farmer to the Republican*, ed. Walter Hartwell Bennett (Tuscaloosa: University of Alabama Press, 1978), 26. [Hereafter *Letters from the Federal Farmer.*]

25. See, for example, John Toland, *Christianity Not Mysterious* (London, 1696).

26. See, for example, Denise L. and John Carmody, *Exploring American Religion* (Mountain View, CA: Mayfield, 1990), 53.

27. Benjamin Franklin, "To Richard Price," 9 October 1780, *The complete works of Benjamin Franklin*, ed. John Bigelow (New York, London: G. P. Putnam's Sons, 1888), 140.

28. Benjamin Franklin, "Motion for Prayers in the Convention," 28 June 1787, *Benjamin Franklin Writings*, ed. J. A. Leo Lemay (New York: The Library of America, 1987), 1138–1139 (emphasis in original). [Hereafter *Franklin Writings.*]

29. Benjamin Franklin, "To Ezra Stiles," 9 March 1790, *Franklin Writings* 1179. He also said: "Morality or Virtue is the End, Faith only a Means to obtain that End: And if the End be obtained, it is no matter by what means." Benjamin Franklin, "Dialogue Between Two Presbyterians," 10 April 1735, *Franklin Writings*, 257.

30. James Madison, "A Memorial and Remonstrance," 1785, *Madison Writings*, 185.

31. John Adams, "To Benjamin Rush," 28 August 1811, *The Spur of Fame: Dialogues of John Adams and Benjamin Rush, 1805–1813.* eds. John A. Schutz and Douglas Adair (Indianapolis: Liberty Fund, n.d.), 208.

32. Paul H. Smith, et al., eds., Letters of Delegates to Congress 1774–1789, 25 vols. (Washington: Government Printing Offices, 1876–1998), 311–312.

33. Thomas Jefferson, "A Bill for Establishing Religious Freedom," submitted to the Virginia General Assembly 1779, enacted in an edited form in 1786, emphasis added, *The Complete Jefferson: Containing His Major Writings, Published and Unpublished, Except His Letters*, ed. Saul K. Padover (New York: Duell, Sloan & Pearce, 1943), 946. [Hereafter *The Complete Jefferson.*] In some reprints of Jefferson's "Bill," the opening line reads: "Well aware that the opinion and beliefs of men depend on their own will . . . ."

34. Harry S. Stout, "George Whitefield in Three Countries," *Evangelicalism: Comparative Studies of Popular Protestantism . . . . 1700–1900*," eds. Mark A. Noll, et al. (New York, Oxford: Oxford University Press, 1994), 63, 69.

35. John Boles, *The Great Revival, 1787–1805: The Origins of the Southern Evangelical Mind* (Lexington: University Press of Kentucky, 1972), 40.

36. Thomas Jefferson, "A Bill for Establishing Religious Freedom," *The Complete Jefferson*, 946; "Notes on the State of Virginia," QXVII, *The Complete Jefferson*, 675.

37. Hutson 12, citing "Protestant Pluralism," *Encyclopedia of North American Colonies*, ed. Jacob Ernest Cooke (New York: C. Scribner's Sons, 1993), 3, 619.

38. Hutson, 8.

39. As noted in chapter 1, just one of many often cited examples is John Adams's assertion: "Our Constitution was made only for a moral and religious people. It is wholly inadequate to the government of any other." John Adams, "To the Officers of the First Brigade of the Third Division of the Militia of Massachusetts," 11 October 1798, *The Works of John Adams, Second President of the United States*, compiled Charles Francis Adams, 10 vols., vol. 9 (Boston: Charles C. Little & James Brown, 1850–1856), 228–229. [Hereafter *Adams Works*.] See, also, for example, (1) Virginia Independent Chronicle article 1784: "Mankind have, generally speaking, enacted laws to restrain and punish enormities, to countenance virtue and discourage vice: yet the most approved and wisest legislatures in all ages, in order to give efficacy to their civil institutions, have found it necessary to call in the aid of religion; and in no form of government whatever has the influence of religious principles been found so requisite as in that of a republic." Paul A. Rahe, *Republics Ancient and Modern* (Chapel Hill: University of North Carolina Press, 1992), 749, quoted in Hutson 62; (2) The people of Lunenburg County, Virginia (1779): "[Religion is] the best means of promoting Virtue, Peace and Prosperity" (Library of Virginia, Richmond), quoted in Hutson, 64; (3) A Georgia newspaper editor: "I need not prove, for it is evident, that without Religion there can be no virtue; and it is equally incontestible that without virtue, there can be no liberty. At least, it is allowed, on all hands, that a large *Republic*, especially, cannot subsist without virtue." Henry Holcombe, "Address to the Friends of Religion, in the State of Georgia, on their Duties, in reference to Civil Government," *Georgia Analytical Repository*, ed. Henry Holcombe, vol. 1, nos. 3, 4, and 5, January–February, 1803, 203, quoted in Boles, 176; (4) Benjamin Rush (1745–1813): "[Christianity is] the strong ground of republicanism . . . many of its precepts have for their objects republican liberty and equality as well as simplicity, integrity, and economy in government." Benjamin Rush, "To Thomas Jefferson," 22 August 1800, Lyman H. Butterfield, ed., *Letters of Benjamin Rush*, 2 vols., vol. 2 (Princeton: Princeton University Press, 1951), 820–821; (5) Timothy Dwight (1794): "[M]oral and religious instructions, the cogent motives to duty, and the excitements to decent, amiable and useful conduct which it [Christianity] furnishes, establishes, perhaps more than any single thing, good order, good morals and happiness public and private. It makes good men and good men must be good citizens." Charles Keller, *The Second Great Awakening in Connecticut* (Hamden, CT: Anchor Books, 1968), 148; and (6) George Washington, "Farewell Address," 19 September 1796, *Basic Writings* 637: "Of all the dispositions and habits which lead to political prosperity, Religion and morality are indispensible supports. In vain would that man claim the tribute of Patriotism, who should labour to subvert these great Pillars of human happiness, these firm props of the duties of Man and citizens."

40. John Adams, "To Zabdiel Adams," 21 June 1776, Lyman H. Butterfield, ed. *Adams Family Correspondence*, 6 vols., vol. 2 (Cambridge: Belknap Press, 1963–1993), 20–21.

41. Note in this regard that the British government does not have a specifically designated "Bill of Rights." Rather, it has a body of common law that serves this purpose.

The American constitutions were the first to expressly include such rights in written constitutional form. Also, note that in Britain rights are deemed to be derived from the king, not directly from God to the people. "Pennsylvania Convention Debates," 1787, *Documentary History*, 643. Thus, the British government is, essentially, a top-down government, which is evidenced further by its established church—the Church of England. Consequently, the British do not enjoy as broad religious liberty as do Americans.

42. Bernard Schwartz, 374.

43. Bernard Schwartz, 301, 325. Note in this regard that the people of Massachusetts overwhelmingly rejected the first proposed Massachusetts Constitution (1778) on the grounds that it did not include a declaration of rights. They published a pamphlet, known as the *Essex Result* (1778), which gave the reasons for the importance of including a bill of rights in a Constitution and stated what came to be known as the "Essex Theory." The "Essex Theory" held that when a government is formed by mutual consent of the people, and certain rights that the people hold in the state of nature are relinquished, the express reservation of the inalienable rights in a constitution is "the equivalent every man receives, as a consideration for the rights he has surrendered." Bernard Schwartz 337.

44. The Delaware Declaration of Rights (1776) states: "[A]ll government of right originates from the people, is founded in compact only, and instituted solely for the good of the whole." *Documentary History*, 277. See also the same language in the Maryland Declaration of Rights (1776). *Documentary History*, 280. See also, the Georgia Constitution (1777): "We, therefore, the representatives of the people, from whom all power originates, and for whose benefit all government is intended . . . ." *Documentary History*, 292. The Pennsylvania Declaration of Rights (1776) states that God permits the people "by common consent, and without violence, deliberately to form for themselves such just rules as they shall think best, for governing their future society . . . ." *Documentary History*, 264. The New York Constitution (1777) states that government is to "secure the rights, liberties, and happiness of the good people of this colony" and "to secure the rights and liberties of the good people of this State." *Documentary History*, 302–303.

45. It is important to note that it is unclear as to whether the founders of the state and federal constitutions sought self-consciously to exclude women from the inalienable rights of "man." There is evidence that this was not the case, however, and certainly, as we have noted, Locke did not intend to exclude women from the fundamental rights of "man." In this regard, note that, for example, the Vermont Declaration of Rights (1777) states that "all men are born equally free and independent, but when it refers specifically to men and women, it uses the terms "male" and "female." *Documentary History*, 322. The exploration of this topic is, however, beyond the scope of this work and will have to be left to others.

46. Locke also sought to distinguish freedom from license. Locke, *Second Treatise*, ¶ 6.

47. *Documentary History*, 236.

48. The "Pennsylvania Declaration of Rights (1776)" stated:

[A] frequent recurrence to fundamental principles, and a firm adherence to justice, moderation, temperance, industry, and frugality are absolutely necessary to preserve the blessings of liberty, and keep a government free: The people ought therefore to pay particular attention to these points in the choice of officers and representatives, and have a right to exact a due and constant regard to them, from their legislatures and magistrates, in the making and executing such laws as are necessary for the good government of the state. *Documentary History*, 266.

And the "Massachusetts Declaration of Rights" (1780) stated that "[a] frequent re-currence to the fundamental principles of the constitution, and a constant adherence to those of piety, justice, moderation, temperance, industry, and frugality, are absolutely necessary to preserve the advantages of liberty, and to maintain a free government . . . ." *Documentary History*, 343.

49. *Documentary History*, 312.

50. *Documentary History*, 312.

51. *Documentary History*, 277.

52. *Documentary History*, 376.

53. *Documentary History*, 264 (emphasis added).

54. *Documentary History*, 322.

55. *Documentary History*, 273. Similarly, the South Carolina Constitution (1778), which expressly established the Protestant Christian religion, required members of the state senate and house of representatives to be "all of the Protestant religion." *Documentary History*, 326.

56. "Continental Journal," 9 March 1780, quoted in Hutson, 61.

57. Hutson, 65.

58. Hutson, 69–70.

59. The Baptist Anti-assessment Petition in Virginia stated:

Certain it is that the Holy Author of our Religion not only supported and maintained his Gospel in the world for several hundred years without the aid of Civil Power, but against all the Powers of the Earth. The excellent purity of its precepts and the unblamable behavior of its Ministers (with the divine Blessing) made its way through all Opposition. Nor was it the better for the Church when Constantine first established Christianity by human Laws. True, there was rest from persecution, but how soon over Run with Error, Superstition, and Immorality; how unlike were Ministers then, to what they were before, both in orthodoxy of principle and purity of Life.

"To the Virginia General Assembly," 2 November 1785, Westmoreland County, peti-tion, Library of Virginia, quoted in Hutson, 70.

60. In fact, during the Revolutionary period and in the years following, and in some cases even before the adoption of the United State's Bill of Rights, the trend was to-ward delineating more clearly the bounds between religion and state by eliminating state

establishments of religion, and by expanding freedom of conscience. Five states never established a state religion (North Carolina, Delaware, New Jersey, Rhode Island, and Pennsylvania). The remaining states disestablished relatively soon after the Revolution with the exception of Connecticut and Massachusetts, the last remaining holdouts, which disestablished in 1818 and 1833, respectively. Moreover, every state provided for freedom of conscience, although at first this was not construed as broadly as we often see today. (For example, in some places it remained unlawful to commit blasphemy against the Christian religion.) And, while religion tests for holding public office prevailed in a few states, by 1800 more than a mere majority either did not include religion tests or had provisions that expressly forbade them. See John K. Wilson, "Religion Under the State Constitutions, 1776–1800," *Journal of Church and State* 32.4 (1990): 753–763. See also, generally, Edwin S. Gaustad, "Religious Tests, Constitutions, and 'Christian Nation,'" *Religion in a Revolutionary Age*, eds. Ronald Hoffman and Peter J. Albert (Charlottesville: University Press of Virginia, 1994), 218–235. See also, H. Frank Way, "The Death of the Christian Nation: The Judiciary and Church-State Relations," *Journal of Church and State* 29.3 (1987): 509–529.

Further, the United States approach was applied to the states through what has become known as the "incorporation doctrine" in *Cantwell v. Connecticut,* 310 U.S. 296 (1940) and *Everson v. Board of Education,* 330 U.S. 1, 76 S.Ct. 504, 91 L.Ed. 711 (1947), wherein the Religion Clauses of the First Amendment were held to be applicable to the states through the Due Process Clause of the Fourteenth Amendment. For a general discussion of the evolution of the "incorporation doctrine," see Cord, *Separation of Church and State: Historical Fact and Current Fiction* (Grand Rapids, MI: Baker Book House, 1988). See also, Leonard Levy, *The Establishment Clause: Religion and the First Amendment,* 2nd ed. (Chapel Hill and London: The University of North Carolina Press, 1994).

Those involved in the contemporary debate about the propriety of the Supreme Court's adoption of the "incorporation doctrine" may find it disconcerting that I do not take up the issue in full here. However, it is not the goal of this work to argue such points. Rather, I am putting forward what I see as the fundamental ground of the American system in order to reframe such debates. An argument that the United States government may have usurped the authority of the states on this point does not undercut the thesis set out here regarding the fundamental original intentions of the founders. Moreover, arguments in favor of the reversal of the "incorporation doctrine" are no longer relevant as that development is highly unlikely to be realized.

61. Freedom of speech was recognized for the first time in the "Pennsylvania Declaration of Rights, 1776" and was not even recognized in all state constitutions. Freedom of the press had been recognized in the "Virginia Declaration of Rights, 1776" as "one of the greatest bulwarks of liberty. . . .," *Documentary History,* 235, while the right to assemble and to petition the government also were not recognized until the enactment of the "Pennsylvania Declaration of Rights, 1776." *Documentary History,* 266.

62. James Madison, "A Memorial and Remonstrance against Religious Assessments," 1785, *Madison Writings,* vol. 2, 184–185 (emphasis added).

63. Irving Brant, *James Madison: The Virginia Revolutionist* (New York, Indianapolis: The Bobbs-Merrill Company, 1941), 243. "In this thought he followed the aphorisms of

Harrington, who greatly influenced his thinking: ÔWhere civil liberty is entire, it includes liberty of conscience. Where liberty of conscience is entire, it includes civil liberty.'" Brant, 243.

64. For example, "The Rights of the Colonists and a List of Infringements and Violations of Rights, 1772," drafted by Samuel Adams in Massachusetts reserved the right only to "all christians except Papists." *Documentary History*, 202.

65. Rob Boston, *Why the Religious Right Is Wrong about Separation of Church and State* (Buffalo: Prometheus Books, 1993) 78. In addition, Article 11 of the Treaty of Tripoli, a treaty with Muslim North Africa (1797) stated: "As the Government of the United States is not, in any sense, founded on the Christian religion; as it has in itself no character of enmity against the law, religion or tranquility of Musselmen; and as the states never have entered into any war or act of hostility against any Mohometan nation, it is declared by the parties that no pretext arising from religious opinion shall ever produce an interruption of harmony existing between the two countries."

66. James Madison, "To George Eve," 2 January 1789, *Madison Writings*, vol. 5, 320 n.

67. *Documentary History*, 440.

68. James Madison, "To Thomas Jefferson," 17 October 1788, *Madison Writings*, vol. 5, 272. The United States Constitution granted, or at least implied, broad rights in other respects as well. For example, Hugh Henry Brackenridge, in his "Cursory Remarks" (1788), expressed concerns that the office of the president was not being limited to males only and to white people. Even an "old woman" or a "vile negro" could become the president under the Constitution, he complained. *Documentary History*, 521–522.

69. Richard Henry Lee, *Observations Leading to a Fair Examination of the System of Government*, Letter IV, 12 October 1787, *Letters from the Federal Farmer*, 28.

70. Richard Henry Lee, "To James Madison," 26 November 1784, eds. Robert A. Rutland, et al. *The Papers of James Madison*, 17 vols., vol. 8, (Chicago and London: University of Chicago Press; Charlottesville: University Press of Virginia, 1961–1999), 149.

71. Thomas Jefferson, "Notes on Religion," October 1776, *The Complete Jefferson*, 945 (emphasis in original).

72. Thomas Jefferson, "A Bill for Establishing Religious Freedom," 1779, *The Complete Jefferson*, 947.

73. George Washington, "To the Hebrew Congregation," 18 August 1790, *The Papers of George Washington*, Presidential Series, ed. Dorothy Twohig, et al., 7 vols., vol. 6 (Charlottesville, VA: University Press of Virginia, 1987–2000), 284–285. [Hereafter *Washington Papers*.] See also George Washington, "To Roman Catholics in America," March 1790, *Washington Papers*, vol. 5, 299: "As mankind become more liberal they will be more apt to allow, that all those who conduct themselves as worthy members of the Community are equally entitled to the protection of civil government. I hope ever to see America among the foremost nations of justice and liberality. And I presume that your fellow-citizens will not forget the patriotic part which they took in the accomplishment of their Revolution, and the establishment of their Government: or the important assistance which they received from a nation in which the Roman Catholic faith is professed."

74. Robert Yates, "Letters of Sydney," 1788, *Documentary History*, 524.

75. James Winthrop, "Letter of Agrippa," 1788, *Documentary History*, 517.

76. John Jay, "Address to the People of New York on the Constitution," 1788, *Documentary History*, 563.

77. Thomas Jefferson, "A Bill for Establishing Religious Freedom," 1779, *The Complete Jefferson*, 947.

78. See, for example, Madison's "A Memorial and Remonstrance against Religious Assessments," 1785, *Madison Writings*, vol. 2, 183–191.

79. Levy, among others, has noted the difficulty of arriving at a definition of "establishment." Levy, xxi–xxii.

80. James Madison, "To Thomas Jefferson," 17 October 1788, *Madison Writings*, vol. 5, 271–272.

81. Thomas Jefferson, "A Bill for Establishing Religious Freedom," *The Complete Jefferson*, 947.

82. John Dickenson, "Letters of Fabius," 1788, *Documentary History*, 546.

83. This is readily seen in the following quotations: The *Essex Result*, 1778: "[A] bill of rights, clearly ascertaining and defining the rights of conscience, and that security or person and property, which every member in the State hath a right to expect from the supreme power thereof, ought to be settled and *established*, previous to the ratification of any constitution for the State (*Documentary History*, 344); "Letters of Brutus," 1788: "[T]he common good, therefore, is the end of civil government, and common consent, the foundation on which it is *established*" (*Documentary History*, 506); Jefferson speaks in terms of "*establishing*" religious freedom in his title "A Bill for Establishing Religious Freedom," *The Complete Jefferson*, 946–947; George Washington compared the "means by which most Governments have been *established*" with the establishing of the United States government in his "First Inaugural Address," 30 April 1789 (*Papers of the Presidents* vol. 1, 44), quoted on page [89] herein; Robert Yates's "Letters of Sydney," 1788: "You and all men were created free and authorised to *establish* civil government for the preservation of our rights against civil oppression . . . ." (*Documentary History*, 524, emphasis added).

84. Of course there is much room for theological reflection as to the significance and meaning of this basic theology. For example, John Dunn can be read as holding that Locke's primary influence was Calvin. Wootton, 67. Yet Locke's theological underpinnings can also be read as having a focus that can be compared with Aquinas. Elaborations such as these are better left to others, however, or to a later work because my concern here is not nuances and elaborations, but rather the general framework that emerges from the basic, simple theology itself.

85. For example, John Adams indicated as much when he said:

The general principles, on which the fathers achieved independence, were the only principles in which that beautiful Assembly of young men could unite, and these principles only could be intended by them in their address, or by me in my answer. And what were these general principles? I answer, the general principles of Christianity, in which all those sects were united: and the general principles of English and American Liberty, in which all those young men united, and which had united all parties in America, in majorities sufficient to assert and maintain her Independence. Now I will avow, that I then believed, and now believe, that those general principles of Christianity, are as eternal and immutable as the existence and attributes of God; and that those principles of liberty, are as unalterable as human nature and our terrestrial, mundane system. I could, therefore, safely say, consistently with all my then and present information, that I believed they would never make discoveries in contradiction to these general principles. "To Thomas Jefferson," 28 June 1813, *Adams Works*, vol. 10, 45–46.

86. John Adams, "To Thomas Jefferson," 28 June 1813, *Adams Works*, vol. 10, 46.

87. A persuasive argument can be made that the general principles of America's Sacred Ground, that is, those ensuring human rights, are the general principles of other religions as well, *cf.* Neilia Beth Scoville, *The Liberation of Women: Religious Sources* (Washington, DC: The Religious Consultation on Population, Reproductive Health and Ethics, 1995).

88. Thomas Jefferson, "A Bill for Establishing Religious Freedom," 1779, *The Complete Jefferson*, 946.

89. Of course there is considerable debate about what constitutes "harm." However, my goal here is to reframe the debate so that we are at least discussing such things within the framework established by the founders. The fact that there is something to resolve within the discourse does not undermine the basic framework laid out in this work. That said, the parameters of what constitutes "harm" should focus only on a discussion of harm to the sacred civil rights—that which preserves life, liberty, and property without infringing the same of others.

90. Thomas Jefferson, "Notes on Religion," October 1776, *The Complete Jefferson*, 945.

91. Thomas Jefferson, "Autobiography, January 6–July 21, 1821" and "Notes on the State of Virginia," Q. XVIII, 1782, *The Complete Jefferson*, 1150 and 677.

92. Thomas Jefferson, "Notes on Religion," October 1776, *The Complete Jefferson*, 946.

93. Richard Henry Lee, *Observations Leading to a Fair Examination of the System of Government*, Letter IV, 12 October 1787, *Letters from the Federal Farmer*, 28.

94. Edwin S. Gaustad, *Faith of Our Fathers* (San Francisco: Harper & Row, 1987), 94.

95. See Hardesy, et al. and the other articles in Ruether and McLaughlin, *Women of Spirit*, which illustrate the many ways in which religion has played a role in women's liberation movements.

96. *Essex Result*, 1778, *Documentary History*, 351.

97. Locke, *Letter Concerning Toleration, Political Writings*, 420–421. Thomas Jefferson, "A Bill for Establishing Religious Freedom," 1779, *The Complete Jefferson*, 947; "Notes on Religion," October 1776, *The Complete Jefferson*, 945.

98. James Madison, "Memorial and Remonstrance against Religious Assessments," *Madison Writings*, vol. 2, 184. See Levy, *The Establishment Clause*, 63.

99. Thomas Jefferson, "To a Committee of the Danbury Baptist Association," 1 January 1802, *The Writings of Thomas Jefferson*, Memorial Edition, ed. A. A. Lipscomb and Albert E. Bergh, 20 vols., vol. 16 (Washington, DC, 1903–1904), 281–282.

100. "Letters of Brutus," 1788, *Documentary History*, 506.

CHAPTER 4—TAKING SIDES AND LOOKING LEFT

1. James Davidson Hunter, *Culture Wars: The Struggle to Define America* (New York: BasicBooks, 1991).

2. Alasdair MacIntyre, *After Virtue: A Study in Moral Theory* (Notre Dame, IN: University of Notre Dame Press, 1981).

3. Hunter, 42.

4. Hunter, 320–321.

5. Thomas W. Flynn, *The Trouble with Christmas* (Buffalo: Prometheus, 1993).

6. Thomas W. Flynn, "The Case for Affirmative Secularism," *Free Inquiry*, Spring 1996: 12.

7. Flynn, "Affirmative Secularism," 13.

8. Flynn, "Affirmative Secularism," 14.

9. Flynn, "Affirmative Secularism," 16.

10. Flynn, "Affirmative Secularism," 13–14.

11. Flynn, "Affirmative Secularism," 14, quoting Ronald O. Lindsay, "Neutrality Between Religion and Irreligion: Is It Required? Is It Possible?" *Free Inquiry*, Fall 1990: 19.

12. Flynn, "Affirmative Secularism," 12.

13. Gerard V. Bradley, "Religion and the Court 1995: A Symposium," *First Things* 108, 1995: 24.

14. M. Stanton Evans, *The Theme Is Freedom: Religion, Politics, and the American Tradition* (Washington, DC: Regnery Publishing, 1994).

15. Evans, 8–9.

16. Evans, 11.

17. This later work will be a companion piece for *Rediscovering America's Sacred Ground.* The working title for it is *America's Sacred Ground and the Marketplace.*

18. Evans, 120.

19. Evans, 113.

20. Evans, 114.

21. Evans, 114–115.

22. Evans, 117.

23. Evans, 121.

24. Robert O. Lindsey, 19, quoted at Flynn, "Affirmative Secularism," 14.

25. Flynn, "Affirmative Secularism," 14.

26. Evans, 121.

27. Locke, *Letter Concerning Toleration, Political Writings*, 432.

28. Locke, *Letter Concerning Toleration, Political Writings*, 426.

29. Flynn, "Affirmative Secularism," 14.

30. For example, Flynn, "Affirmative Secularism," 8. Some believe that they find support in Richard Henry Lee's famous quote that the founders were "making a constitution . . . for ages and millions yet unborn." Richard Henry Lee, *Observations Leading to a Fair Examination of the System of Government*, Letter IV, 12 October 1787, *Letters from the Federal Farmer*, 28. However, Lee was not advocating an unanchored Constitution free for reinterpretation by future "ages and millions" with little or no reference to the original intentions of the founders. He was advocating America's Sacred Ground, particularly the "establish[ment of] the free exercise of religion, as a part of the national compact." *Ibid.*

31. John Rawls, "The Idea of Public Reason Revisited," *The University of Chicago Law Review*, vol. 64, no. 3, Summer 1997. [Hereafter *Public Reason*.]

32. Rawls, *Public Reason*, 803.

33. John Rawls, *Political Liberalism* (1993; New York, Chichester, West Sussex: Columbia University Press, 1996), 12–13. [Hereafter, *Political Liberalism*.]

34. Rawls, *Public Reason*, 766.

35. Rawls, *Public Reason*, 770.

36. Rawls, *Political Liberalism*, 3.

37. Rawls, *Public Reason*, 770.

38. Rawls, *Public Reason*, 780.

39. Rawls, *Public Reason*, 766.

40. Rawls, *Public Reason*, 801.

41. Rawls, *Public Reason*, 797, fn. 79 and accompanying text.

42. Rawls, *Political Liberalism*, 12.

43. Rawls, *Public Reason*, 777.

44. Rawls, *Public Reason*, 770.

45. Rawls, *Public Reason*, 799.

46. Rawls, *Political Liberalism*, 239.

47. Rawls, *Political Liberalism*, 233.

48. Rawls, *Public Reason*, 798.

49. Rawls, *Public Reason,* 782 (emphasis added).

50. Rawls, *Public Reason,* 771.

51. Rawls, *Public Reason,* 799.

52. Rawls, *Public Reason,* 782.

53. Rawls, *Public Reason,* 801.

54. Rawls, *Political Liberalism,* 220, fn. 7 and accompanying text.

55. Rawls, *Public Reason,* 786.

56. Rawls, *Public Reason,* 787.

57. Rawls, *Public Reason,* 768 and fn. 15.

58. Rawls, *Public Reason,* 777, 781. To qualify as being a reasonable comprehensive doctrine, those holding to a comprehensive doctrine must be willing to subject their doctrine to public reason. Moreover, they must accept the supremacy of public reason "wholeheartedly." Rawls, *Public Reason,* 781. By this Rawls means that his political conception of democracy must be embraced as being prior to one's comprehensive doctrine. Otherwise, according to Rawls, one is holding one's comprehensive doctrine as a mere *modus vivendi.* In other words, Rawls's political conception is only accepted provisionally until one is able to usurp political power and establish one's comprehensive doctrine as the doctrine for all. However, if one embraces Rawls's political conception as prior and, in fact, incorporates that priority into one's comprehensive doctrine, then that threat to Rawls's political conception of democracy disappears.

59. See, for example, *Marsh v. Chambers,* 463 U.S. 783, 103 S.Ct. 3330, 77 L.Ed.2d 1019 (1983) and *Lynch v. Donnelly Lynch v. Donnelly,* 465 U.S. 668, 104 S.Ct. 1355, 79 L.Ed.2d 604 (1984).

60. See chapter 5, pages 157–158 on accommodation and majoritarian dominance.

61. Rawls, *Public Reason,* 806.

62. Richard Rorty, "The Priority of Democracy to Philosophy," *Objectivity, Relativism, and Truth* (New York: Cambridge University Press, 1991).

CHAPTER 5—LOOKING RIGHT

1. Evans, 18.

2. Evans, 37.

3. Evans, 145–147.

4. As shown in chapter 3, there are certain elements of Christianity that *do* provide the foundations of our freedoms. For example, as Evans points out, the concept of the autonomous individual comes directly out of the theological precepts of Christianity regarding the inherent worth of human beings as creations of God. Evans, 146–147. Moreover, the idea that the autonomous individual is responsible to God personally and,

therefore, God's concern is with individuals and not society as a whole also derives from certain Christian theologies.

5. Evans, 119, 121.

6. Evans, 130.

7. Evans, 121, emphasis omitted.

8. Evans, 121.

9. Evans, 119.

10. Scholars' works that bring to light the role of religion in public life during the founding era imply that because evangelical Christians were significant contributors to the cause of liberty, then evangelicals are contributors to the cause of liberty today. See, for example, Hutson, generally. This is very dangerous thinking, thinking that is reminiscent of earlier times when it was thought that whatever church leaders and kings (by Divine right) do must be right in the eyes of God merely because they are church leaders and kings answerable only to God.

11. Evans, 8.

12. Evans, 18.

13. Evans, 9, emphasis added.

14. Benjamin Franklin, "Toleration in Old and New England," *The London Packet*, 3 June 1772, *Franklin Writings*, 673.

15. Even some of those who attempt to make a more moderate stance make this claim. For example, Stephen L. Carter states that "the fear of the religiously motivated automatons doing in politics what their leaders command is today a delusion." Stephen. L. Carter, *The Culture of Disbelief: How American Law and Politics Trivialize Religious Devotion* (New York, London, Toronto, Sydney, Auckland: Anchor Books, 1993), 120.

16. It is a common claim on the religious right that the founders were only concerned with government interference with religion, not the other way around. For example, Evans and Hutson both contend that the founders were concerned only to limit government interference with religion, not church participation in state governance. But this is contrary to the historical record which clearly shows that both unchecked governmental power and unchecked church power were considered contrary to conscience and, therefore, to America's Sacred Ground.

17. Evans, 31–36.

18. Evans, 36.

19. Evans, 145. Evans makes the connection between these ideas and the origins of the ideas embodied in Locke's social contract theory. Evans, 184, 199. However, in an effort to distinguish Locke from Enlightenment ideology, which he mistakenly assumes is always and inherently antireligion, he concludes that Locke's ideas do not derive from the Enlightenment, but rather from the feudal medieval notions of the limitations on the king and the subjugation of the king to the higher authority of God. Evans, 184. As we have shown, however, Locke's ideas are grounded in a fundamental theology. And that theology

is not based on the idea that the state should be subjected to the higher authority of God as interpreted by church authorities, as Evans contends. It is based on the idea that the state should be subjected to the higher authority of God as understood by such autonomous individuals through individual conscience of God, subject to the Lockean fundamentals that preserve conscience and its expression (as well as the safety and welfare of the people, which in effect is their right to life).

20. Although it is important to note that Thomas Aquinas did recognize the priority of conscience, the determination of what conscience dictates was reserved at that time, for the most part, to the church.

21. It is important to note in this regard that in the founding era some of the states included provisions in their constitutions prohibiting church clergy from serving in any state office.

22. Evans, 31.

23. Evans, 129.

24. Evans, 15, 17.

25. James H. Hutson, *Religion and the Founding of the American Republic* (Washington, DC: Library of Congress, 1998).

26. Hutson, 59–60.

27. See chapter 3, endnote 60, and accompanying text.

28. Hutson, 81.

29. Evans, 97.

30. Evans, 18.

31. Evans, 18.

32. Locke, *Letter Concerning Toleration, Political Writings*, 397. See also chapter 5, page 155, text and footnote.

33. Locke, *Letter Concerning Toleration, Political Writings*, 420–421.

34. Evans, 130.

35. Stephen L. Carter provided his view of the requirements of "civility" in his book *Civility: Manners, Morals, and the Etiquette of Democracy* (New York: HarperPerennial, 1998).

36. Stephen. L. Carter, *The Culture of Disbelief: How American Law and Politics Trivialize Religious Devotion* (New York, London, Toronto, Sydney, Auckland: Anchor Books, 1993). [Hereafter *Disbelief.*]

37. Carter now appears to have become a modified accommodationist. He notes that the accommodationist position provides for religious freedom unless there is a "compelling state interest," and then expresses concern that there are no limits to what the state may find compelling. Stephen L. Carter, *God's Name in Vain: The Wrongs and Rights of Religion in Politics* (New York: BasicBooks, 2000), 162–169. [Hereafter *God's Name.*] However, as we shall see, that is only so if those making decisions about such things fail to rediscover America's Sacred Ground.

38. Carter, *Disbelief*, xx.

39. Carter, *Disbelief*, 145. See also, *God's Name*, 78.

40. Locke, *Letter Concerning Toleration, Political Writings*, 401.

41. Carter, *Disbelief*, 17. Carter's understanding of "religion" entitled to religious freedom has not changed in his later works. See *God's Name*, 174 and note 5.

42. Carter, *Disbelief*, 135.

43. While Carter is right that the two Religion Clauses should be read together, *Disbelief*, 117, he erroneously interprets them as granting freedom to churches, when what was intended was freedom of conscience. See also *God's Name*, 174.

44. Carter, *Disbelief*, 134.

45. Carter, *Disbelief*, 123.

46. Carter, *Disbelief*, 124.

47. "[A]ny definition of religion would seem to violate religious freedom in that it would dictate to religions past and future, what they must be." Jonathan Weiss, "Privilege, Posture and Protection: 'Religion' in the Law." *Yale Law Journal*, 73 (1964): 593, 604, quoted in Carter, *Disbelief*, 18.

48. James Madison, "Speeches in the First Congress, First Session," 8 June 1789, *The Writings of James Madison*, ed. Gaillard Hunt, 9 vols., vol. 5 (New York, London: G. P. Putnam's Sons, 1900–1903), 382. [Hereafter *Madison Writings*.]

49. James Madison, "To Thomas Jefferson," 17 October 1788, *Madison Writings*, vol. 5, 272–273.

50. James Madison, "Federalist Paper No. 10," *The Federalist Papers*, ed. Clinton Rossiter (New York: Mentor, 1999), 49.

51. James Madison, "To Thomas Jefferson," 24 October 1787, *Madison Writings*, vol. 5, 30–31.

52. Locke, *Letter Concerning Toleration, Political Writings*, 406–407.

53. Hutson, 85.

54. Carter, *Disbelief*, 36–37.

55. Carter, *Disbelief*, 105. See also, *God's Name*, 72, 76–77.

56. Carter, *Disbelief*, 85.

57. Carter, *Disbelief*, 154.

58. *God's Name*.

59. Carter, *Disbelief*, 138.

60. Carter, *Disbelief*, 85.

61. Carter, *Disbelief*, 199.

62. Carter, *Disbelief*, 48–49.

63. Carter, *Disbelief*, 111.

64. Carter, *Disbelief*, 134.

65. Carter, 272–273.

66. Carter, *God's Name*, 108.

67. Carter, *Disbelief*, 64–65.

CHAPTER 6—GROUNDING THE DEBATE

1. Matthew 7: 20–21. On this point, see also, Benjamin Franklin, "To Josiah and Abiah Franklin," 13 April 1738, *Benjamin Franklin Writings*, ed. J. A. Leo Lemay (New York: The Library of America, 1987), 426 and "Dialogue Between Two Presbyterians," 10 April 1735, *Franklin Writings*, 256–257.

CONCLUSION—AMERICA'S SACRED GROUND: OUR CIVIC FAITH

1. Alasdair MacIntyre, *After Virtue: A Study in Moral Theory* (Notre Dame, IN: University of Notre Dame Press, 1981), 2.

2. Locke, *A Letter Concerning Toleration, Political Writings*, 415.

3. Jeffrey Stout, *Ethics After Babel* (Boston: Beacon Press, 1988).

4. Stout, *Ethics After Babel*, 242.

5. Locke, *Letter Concerning Toleration, Political Writings*, 421.

6. Elbridge Gerry, *Observations of the New Constitution and the Federal and State Conventions*, 1788, *Pamphlets on the Constitution of the United States*, ed. Paul Leicester Ford (Brooklyn, 1888), 1–2, cited in *Documentary History*, 491–92.

7. Locke, *Letter Concerning Toleration, Political Writings*, 421.

8. Stout, 242.

9. *Essex Result*, 1778, *Documentary History*, 351.

APPENDIX A—A FEW DEFINITIONS

1. Roy Wallis and Steve Bruce, "Secularization: The Orthodox Model," *Religion and Modernization: Sociologists and Historians Debate the Secularization Thesis*, ed. Steve Bruce (Oxford: Clarendon Press, 1992), 11.

2. *Lemon v. Kurtzman*, 403 U.S. 602, 91 S.Ct. 2105, 29 L.Ed. 745 (1971). The continued viability of the "*Lemon* test" is now in question as the Supreme Court has begun to adopt varying rationales for its decisions. For example, the "endorsement/entanglement

test" espoused by Justice O'Connor in *Lynch v. Donnelly*, 465 U.S. 668, 104 S.Ct. 1355, 79 L.Ed.2d 604 (J. O'Connor, concurring, 1984); the "symbolic endorsement test" espoused in *Grand Rapids School District v. Ball*, 473 U.S. 373, 105 S.Ct. 3216, 87 L.Ed.2d 267 (1985); and the "coercion test" adopted by Justice Kennedy in *County of Allegheny v. A.C.L.U.*, 492 U.S. 573, 109 S.Ct. 3086, 106 L.Ed.2d 472 (1989) and *Lee v. Weisman*, 505 U.S. 577, 112, S.Ct. 2649, 120 L.Ed.2d 467 (1992). See Charles Roth, "*Rosenberger v. Rector*: The First Amendment Dog Chases Its Tail," *Journal of College and University Law* 21.4 (1995): 742–750.

3. Wilfred Cantwell Smith, *The Meaning and End of Religion*. (1962; Minneapolis: Fortress Press, 1991).

4. Cantwell Smith, 19.

5. Cantwell Smith, 20–21.

6. Cantwell Smith, 29–37.

7. Cantwell Smith, 37–40.

8. Cantwell Smith, 44–48, 51.

9. Cantwell Smith, 47.

10. Cantwell Smith, 48–49.

11. James Hitchcock, *What Is Secular Humanism: Why Humanism Became Secular and How It Is Changing Our World* (Ann Arbor, MI: Servant Books, 1982), 70, 131.

12. Cantwell Smith, 124.

13. Cantwell Smith, 124; David Lawrence Edwards, *Religion and Change*, rev. ed. (London: Hodder & Stoughton, 1974), 15.

14. Edwards, 15–16.

15. Emile Durkheim, *The Elementary Forms of Religious Life*, trans. Karen E. Fields (New York: Free Press, 1995).

16. *Random House Webster's College Dictionary*, 1991, 575.

17. *Random House Webster's College Dictionary*, 1991, 575.

18. Pauline Marie Rosenau, *Post-Modernism and the Social Sciences: Insights, Inroads, and Intrusions* (Princeton: Princeton University Press, 1992), 81.

19. Rosenau, 6.

20. Rosenau, 82.

21. Stanley Fish, "Condemnation without Absolutes," *New York Times*, 15 October 2001.

22. James Davidson Hunter, *Culture Wars: The Struggle to Define America* (New York: BasicBooks, 1991), 42.

23. See the work of such notables in the sociology of religion as Max Weber, Emile Durkheim, Ernst Troeltsch, and August Comte.

24. For example, see the work of Bryan Wilson, David Martin, and Peter Berger.

25. See, for example, Stephen R. Warner, "Works in Progress toward a New Paradigm for the Sociological Study of Religion in the United States," *American Journal of Sociology* 98.5 (March 1993): 1044–1093; and Roger Finke "An Unsecular America," *Religion and Modernization: Sociologists and Historians Debate the Secularization Thesis*, ed. Steve Bruce (Oxford: Clarendon Press, 1992): 145–169.

26. Olivier Tschannen, *Les Theories de la Secularization* (Geneve: Droz, 1992).

27. For example, Roger Finke, a sociologist, contends that the "secularization model" "has long proposed that as industrialization, urbanization, and rationalization come to dominate a society, religion will recede." Finke, 145. Arguing for a broader, more historical approach to the study of religious change which would allow for decline and growth in religion in modern societies, Callum G. Brown, an historian, identifies the "theory of secularization" as "the assumption of the inevitability of the decline of religion in modern societies." Callum G. Brown, "A Revisionist Approach to Religious Change," *Religion and Modernization: Sociologists and Historians Debate the Secularization Thesis*, ed. Steve Bruce (Oxford: Clarendon Press, 1992): 31. Robin Gill refers to secularization as "church decline." Gill, Robin, "Secularization and Census Data." *Religion and Modernization: Sociologists and Historians Debate the Secularization Thesis*, ed. Steve Bruce (Oxford: Clarendon Press, 1992): 93.

28. M. Stanton Evans, *The Theme Is Freedom: Religion, Politics, and the American Tradition* (Washington, DC: Regnery Publishing, 1994), 23.

Suggested Readings

While some of the works listed below provide further study compatible with the theories in *Rediscovering*, some do not. Rather, they provide the reader with a spectrum of perspectives about John Locke and religion, religion in America, and the role of religion in public life so as to widen the readers' understanding of the debate.

Ahlstrom, Sydney. *A Religious History of the American People*. New Haven: Yale University Press, 1972.

Bailyn, Bernard. *The Ideological Origins of the American Revolution*. Enlarged ed. (orig. publ. 1967), Cambridge and London: The Belknap Press of Harvard University Press, 1992.

Becker, Carl L. *The Declaration of Independence: A Study in the History of Political Ideas*. 1922. New York: Vintage, 1942.

Bellah, Robert N. "Civil Religion in America." *Daedalus* (Winter), 1967.

——— et al. *Habits of the Heart: Individualism and Commitment in American Life*. Berkeley: University of California Press, 1985.

——— et al. *The Good Society*. New York: Alfred A. Knopf, 1991.

———. *The Broken Covenant: American Civil Religion in a Time of Trial*. (orig. publ. 1975), University of Chicago Press, 1992.

Bonomi, Patricia. *Under the Cope of Heaven*. New York: Oxford University Press, 1986.

Boston, Rob. *Why the Religious Right Is Wrong about Separation of Church and State*. Buffalo: Prometheus Books, 1993.

Butler, Jon. *Awash in a Sea of Faith: Christianizing the American People*. Cambridge: Harvard University Press, 1990.

Carter, Stephen L. *The Culture of Disbelief: How American Law and Politics Trivialize Religious Devotion*. New York, London, Toronto, Sydney, Auckland: Anchor Books, 1993.

———. *God's Name in Vain: The Wrongs and Rights of Religion in Politics*. New York: BasicBooks, 2000.

Casanova, Jose. *Public Religions in the Modern World*. Chicago: University of Chicago Press, 1994.

Davis, Derek H. *Religion and the Continental Congress 1774–1789: Contributions to Original Intent*. Oxford, New York: Oxford University Press, 2000.

Demerath, Jay. *Crossing the Gods: World Religions and Worldly Politics*, Piscataway, NJ: Rutgers University Press, 2001.

Dreisbach, Daniel L. *Real Threat and Mere Shadow: Religious Liberty and the First Amendment*. Westchester, IL: Crossways Books, 1987.

Dunn, John. *The Political Thought of John Locke*. Cambridge: Cambridge University Press, 1969.

Dworkin, Ronald. *Life's Dominion*. New York: Alfred A. Knopf, 1993.

Gamwell, Franklin I. *The Meaning of Religious Freedom: Modern Politics and the Democratic Resolution*. Albany, NY: State University of New York Press, 1995.

Gaustad, Edwin S. *Faith of Our Fathers*. San Francisco: Harper & Row, 1987.

Hammond, Phillip E. *With Liberty for All: Freedom of Religion in the United States*. Louisville, KY: Westminster John Knox Press, 1998.

———. *Religion and Personal Autonomy: The Third Disestablishment in America*. Columbia: University of South Carolina Press, 1992.

Handy, Robert. *Undermined Establishment: Church-State Relations in America, 1880–1920*. Princeton, NJ: Princeton University Press, 1991.

Hatch, Nathan O. *The Sacred Cause of Liberty: Republican Thought and the Millennium in Revolutionary New England*. New Haven & London: Yale University Press: 1977.

Heimert, Alan. *Religion and the American Mind*. Cambridge: Harvard University Press, 1966.

Hoffman, Ronald and Peter J. Albert, eds. *Religion in a Revolutionary Age*. Charlottesville: University Press of Virginia, 1994.

Hunter, James Davidson. *Culture Wars: The Struggle to Define America*. New York: BasicBooks, 1991.

Hutson, James H. *Religion and the Founding of the American Republic*. Washington, DC: Library of Congress, 1998.

Huyler, Jerome. *Locke in America: The Moral Philosophy of the Founding Era*. Lawrence: University of Kansas Press, 1995.

Levinson, Sanford. *Constitutional Faith*. Princeton, NJ: Princeton University Press, 1988.

Levy, Leonard W. *The Establishment Clause: Religion and the First Amendment*. New York: Macmillan Publishing Company, 1986.

Locke, John. *Political Essays*. ed. Mark Goldie. Cambridge: Cambridge University Press, 1997.

———. *The Reasonableness of Christianity*, ed. George W. Ewing. (orig. publ. 1965), Washington, DC: Regnery Gateway, 1989.

MacIntyre, Alasdair. *After Virtue: A Study in Moral Theory*. Notre Dame, IN: University of Notre Dame Press, 1981.

Malbin, Michael J. *Religion and Politics: The Intentions of the Authors of the First Amendment*. Washington, DC: American Enterprise Institute, 1978.

Marshall, John. *Resistance, Religion and Responsibility*. Cambridge: Cambridge University Press, 1994.

Murray, John Courtney, S. J. *We Hold These Truths*. New York: Sheed and Ward, 1960.

Neuhaus, Richard John. *The Naked Public Square: Religion and Democracy in America.* Grand Rapids, MI: William B. Eerdmans Publishing, 1984.

Novak, Michael. *On Two Wings: Humble Faith and Common Sense at the American Founding.* San Francisco: Encounter Books, 2001.

Pateman, Carol. *The Sexual Contract.* Stanford, CA: Stanford University Press, 1988.

Rawls, John. "The Idea of Public Reason Revisited," *The University of Chicago Law Review* 64.3 (1997): 765–807.

———. *Political Liberalism.* New York: Columbia University Press, 1993.

Reichley, James A. *The Values Connection.* Lanham: Rowman & Littlefield Publishers, 2001.

Rosenau, Pauline Marie. *Post-Modernism and the Social Sciences: Insights, Inroads, and Intrusions.* Princeton, NJ: Princeton University Press, 1992.

Sandel, Michael J. *Liberalism and the Limits of Justice.* 2d. ed. New York: Cambridge University Press, 1998.

Schwartz, Sally. *A Mixed Multitude.* New York: New York University Press, 1987.

Smith, Steven D. *Foreordained Failure: The Quest for a Constitutional Principle of Religious Freedom.* New York: Oxford University Press, 1995.

Smith, Wilfred Cantwell. *The Meaning and End of Religion.* 1962. Minneapolis, MN: Fortress Press, 1991.

Sullivan, Kathleen. "Religion and Liberal Democracy." *University of Chicago Law Review* 59.3 (1992): 195–223.

Thiemann, Ronald F. *Religion in Public Life: A Dilemma for Democracy.* Washington, DC: Georgetown University Press, 1996.

Vernon, Richard. *Political Morality: A Theory of Liberal Democracy.* London and New York: Continuum, 2001.

Index